Dimensions in Urban History

Dimensions in Urban History

Historical and Social Science
Perspectives on
Middle-Size American Cities

J. Rogers Hollingsworth
and
Ellen Jane Hollingsworth

The University of Wisconsin Press

Published 1979
The University of Wisconsin Press
114 North Murray Street, Madison, Wisconsin 53715

The University of Wisconsin Press, Ltd.
1 Gower Street, London WC1E 6HA, England

First printing

Printed in the United States of America

Library of Congress Cataloging in Publication Data
Hollingsworth, Joseph Rogers, 1932–
      Dimensions in urban history.
          Includes index.
      1. Cities and towns—United States—History.
      2. Cities and towns—Wisconsin—Case studies.
      3. United States—Social conditions—1865–1918.
          4. Urbanization—United States—History.
          5. Sociology, Urban—United States.
      I. Hollingsworth, Ellen Jane, joint author.
                    II. Title.
HT123.H65   301.36′0973   78-65011
              ISBN 0-299-07820-5

To
The University of Wisconsin
Allan G. Bogue
and
Merle Curti

Contents

Acknowledgments

We wish to express our appreciation to the American Council of Learned Societies, the National Endowment for the Humanities, and the University of Wisconsin Graduate Research Committee for financial support for this project. Two scholars who provided much encouragement for us to undertake a somewhat different approach to the study of American history were Allan G. Bogue and Merle Curti. Over the years they have done much to provide a stimulating environment for our work and to make the study of American history an exciting endeavor. As a token of our appreciation, we include them in our dedication of this study.

Many people have shared their time and ideas with us regarding the bridges between social science and history, the problems of studying cities, and methodology. We wish to thank Mike Aiken, Robert Alford, Lee Benson, Robert Berkhofer, Terry Clark, Donald DeBats, Robert Fogel, Jerald Hage, Robert Hanneman, Richard McCormick, Seymour Mandelbaum, Leo Schnore, Stanley Schultz, Burton Weisbrod, and Erik O. Wright. Richard Dusenbery and James B. Smith made valuable contributions to this study, which can be acknowledged only imperfectly. Many Wisconsin students have assisted with data collection and analysis. We are especially grateful to former students Betsy Ginsberg, Jerald Levine, and Jonathan Lurie. To them, to more than two hundred city librarians and clerks throughout the country who helped us, and to the staff of the Wisconsin State Historical Society, we extend particular thanks.

The University of Wisconsin for a number of years has provided the freedom and stimulating environment for us to pursue the study of history and the social sciences. Much of our education has occurred at this university, which has one of the most stimulating interdisciplinary environments anywhere. To the University of Wisconsin, we owe more than we can say.

Dimensions in Urban History

Introduction

THIS STUDY is not a history of one or merely several cities. Rather, it consists of several essays which focus on how social and economic factors have impinged on politics in American cities since 1870. While each essay has a different focus, a central concern of each chapter is with urban politics. By raising different questions, each essay necessitates different research strategies and promotes different perspectives about politics in American urban history. The essays complement one another, but they do have different perspectives.

The analysis proceeds on the assumption that the historical investigation of cities desperately needs to move beyond the study of a single case. We have historical studies of dozens of individual cities, but it is often unclear what they tell us about different types of cities or about a larger society. Certainly urban histories reveal considerable variation in the patterns of city development. But historians of individual cities have seldom been able to move beyond their findings about a single case to a more theoretical form of analysis. Studies which are idiosyncratic in nature, while often insightful and stimulating, are generally not very explicit about the concepts which are being measured or how a single case should be seen in relation to the range of variation among other cities.

In recent years a number of historians have become increasingly concerned with the shortcomings of case studies, but thus far the historical literature has made little advance in providing suggestions for moving to a different type of analysis. We hope that this study can make a modest contribution to a more sociological-historical approach to cities. Even though this study is a venture in the area of comparative historical politics, it is nevertheless fundamentally committed to the concept of case studies. At this stage of our historical scholarship we need systematic conceptual frameworks and typologies to guide our research on individual cities. If we are sensitive in our study of American urban history to a set of typologies, we will, of course, still carry out case studies, but we

3

can then be more explicit about the way in which social processes in a particular city resemble those in other cities. We have undertaken here the task of developing a conceptual framework that will assist in engaging in wide-ranging comparative analysis but at the same time will permit us to focus on the significant dimensions by which the political histories of individual cities vary. This should enhance the possibilities of reaching our ultimate goal of abstracting from cities the properties which they have in common and of moving to a more theoretical level of analysis. In other words, there should be no contradiction between a historical case study approach and the effort to develop generalizations which transcend particular cities.

As we attempt to move beyond the historical study of the single city, we should be mindful that in the social sciences there are two basic approaches to social phenomena, either of which may be useful to historical investigators. And this study attempts to utilize both. Without going into great detail, the two modes of analysis may be labeled the *comparative variable analysis* and the *historical specification approach*.[1] The first strategy assumes that we must find some way of constructing operational indicators of theoretically important concepts such as social class, political power, centralization, participation, community power, community autonomy, and so on and that the necessary steps to construct and validate social theory are possible only if one has decided upon consistent concepts which have utility across space and time. Hence, this mode of analysis assumes that one can measure complex concepts across cultures and over time. Comparative variable analysis emphasizes the structural and cultural dimensions of societies, while minimizing situational and contextual considerations. This strategy allows the analyst to study numerous cases simultaneously, sometimes using statistical techniques for analysis. It permits the historian to work not only with a large number of cases but also with numerous variables which may be rigorously manipulated in a complex fashion, and it allows the analyst to develop and test generalizations which might otherwise be impossible. In the process there is the danger of losing certain information. While asking new questions, the analyst makes deliberate choices not to pursue those unrelated to the comparative variable paradigm. And the researcher who confines his analysis to this type of strategy risks encountering certain blind spots.

The other strategy, historical specification, assumes that one must have a rich understanding of the context within which phenomena occur. This mode of analysis also assumes that the role of specific actors and

---

1. Robert Alford helped to clarify these two types of analyses.

interest groups, as well as the interaction of structures can only be understood within a specific historical context. With this strategy, the analyst must focus on one or preferably no more than a few cases simultaneously so that the contextual complexity can be comprehended. Being more process oriented, this type of analysis is likely to be less statistically based than the first research strategy. The analyst who employs it both uses social theory in order to carry out the analysis of a particular case and relies on the particular case in developing general statements. While the study of a small number of cases permits the researcher to collect comparable data in each community, it is nevertheless difficult to sort out rigorously and systematically the complex interaction of a large number of variables.

This study attempts to demonstrate not only some of the strengths and weaknesses of each of these methods for historical investigation but also how they complement one another. While both strategies are useful in historical research, neither is unilaterally superior.

Employing the comparative variable approach, chapter 1 presents a conceptual framework with which to study the evolution of political change in American cities since 1870. The chapter focuses on the dimensions by which the political world varies from one city to another, as well as the social and economic dimensions which shape urban political systems. By focusing on the dimensions along which cities evolve, it attempts to demonstrate the way in which changes in dimensions move in a predictable way. After specifying the predictability with which changes in the social, economic, and political dimensions of cities occur, we conclude the chapter with a number of ideal types of American cities in the period following 1870. In other words, the chapter confronts the problem of specifying the circumstances under which certain types of urban configurations occur. The generalizations are essentially tendency statements (if x then probably y).

The construction of the ideal types is based on our examination of numerous studies of American cities as well as on our empirical work. The ideal types, however, are mental constructs which transcend space and time. While they do not correspond completely to any specific city, they nevertheless are useful guides for understanding specific American cities at particular points in time.

The social and political processes specified in these ideal types are less satisfactory for understanding large cities—those with populations over 250,000 persons—than as guides for research on smaller cities. Very large cities have a political process different from that of the smaller city because of their higher population density and because of the unique functions which they play in a hierarchy of cities. Most of the types dis-

cussed in chapter 1 have existed in all periods since 1870, though one or two types (for example, upper class suburb) are twentieth-century phenomena.

Whereas chapter 1 relates to all but the very largest American cities since 1870, chapters 2–4 focus on American cities during the late nineteenth century, cities with populations between 10,000 and 25,000 persons in 1900. Chapter 2 is an effort to apply the framework from the first chapter to the study of three Wisconsin cities during the late nineteenth century, and is therefore more consistent with the historical specification approach. In chapter 2 we might have chosen different cities, a different time period, or cities of a different size for our analysis. Had we done so, we would still have raised the same questions which are inherent in chapter 1. In other words, the discussion in the first chapter is open ended and is applicable to numerous time periods and to cities of different sizes. In contrast, the discussion in chapter 2 is only a "snapshot" of a small segment in time and of a few cities. For this reason, the second chapter can only deal with part of the processes presented in the first. Chapter 2 brings the discussion in chapter 1 "down to earth," and is only a partial representation of that chapter.

The discussion in chapter 2 attempts to demonstrate how economic and social changes in three Wisconsin cities influenced changes in their political structure and policy outcomes. The purpose of the discussion of economic and social structural change is not to explain the economic development of these cities so much as it is to illuminate the way in which changes in the economic structure affected the political process and political outcomes.

Whereas the second chapter focuses on the way in which changes in the economic and social structure interact with the political system *over time* in a *few* cities, the third chapter is concerned more with the way that social, economic, and political structural variables interact to shape public policy in a large number of cities and is in the tradition of comparative variable analysis. Because the concern of chapter 3 is with a large number of cities, a very different research strategy is required, even though a number of questions raised in chapters 2 and 3 are similar.

The concluding chapter is an effort to draw from the earlier chapters the conceptual dimensions most useful for classifying cities, to suggest indicators for such concepts, and to classify all the cities of the late nineteenth century which are treated in the second and third chapters. The basic aim of the chapter is to investigate which of these cities resembled one another in important dimensions, and, on a larger scale, to develop a classification grid to give guidance for and comprehension of case studies. Like chapters 1 and 3, it is in the tradition of comparative variable analysis.

These chapters represent only the first set of steps in a very complicated process of moving urban political history to a more theoretical
level of analysis. Because the concern here is with American cities at a
time when society was moving through the industrialization process, it
is unclear to what extent the structures and processes suitable for their
analysis are appropriate for cities for earlier points in time and for other
places. We are hopeful, however, that these chapters will enhance the
understanding of the political changes in American cities during a period
when the nation was moving through several stages in the industrialization process.

1

Types of American Cities

TYPOLOGICAL COMPONENTS

TO ADVANCE our understanding of American urban history, we very much need answers to the following questions: What are the basic underlying dimensions by which cities differ from one another? If we can identify these dimensions, do they have predictable relationships? How should we proceed in classifying cities according to some of their underlying characteristics?

For historians and social scientists these are not new questions. Even though scholars have in recent years constructed numerous models for the study of many contemporary American cities, there have been very few efforts to analyze changes in the structures of large numbers of cities over extended periods of time. In other words, social scientists have focused on cities in a society already highly industrialized, with relatively high levels of professionalization and bureaucratization, and in which federal and state governments exert considerable influence. In contrast, the concern here is with specifying certain social, economic, and political processes which numerous American cities have encountered in their development over much of the last century. Focusing on most American cities smaller than 250,000 during the period since 1870, this chapter is primarily concerned with specifying the dimensions by which the political world varies from one city to another, as well as the social and economic dimensions which shape the political characteristics of cities. While doing this, we wish to move the historical study of cities to a more theoretical level of analysis.

Excepting economics and psychology, however, the social sciences have not been very successful in developing bodies of theory, and they are not likely to be very successful for some while to come. Theories

specify the relations among concepts in law-like propositions without regard to space and time, and by definition are *ahistorical*. In our research on American cities, we wish to work with concepts which ultimately have the potential of carrying us to the level of theory construction, but, being historians, we wish at the same time to incorporate elements of space and time in our analysis. The strategy here is not to engage in theory construction but to construct ideal types of political systems in small and middle-sized American communities during the last century. The typological scheme employed not only incorporates elements of time and space but also is evolutionary in nature, as there is an effort to develop types of American cities from the latter part of the nineteenth century to the present and to identify the direction in which urban change has been moving. This strategy represents a compromise between the construction of social theory abstracted from time and space and the description of particular communities at specific times and places.

Ideal types are nothing new, but perhaps we associate them with historical scholarship largely as a result of the writings of Max Weber. According to Weber, an ideal type is the synthesis of a great many diffuse, more or less concrete phenomena which are arranged into a unified analytical construct: "In its conceptual purity, this mental construct [the ideal type] cannot be found empirically anywhere in reality . . . . Historical research faces the task of determining in each individual case, the extent to which the ideal construct approximates to or diverges from reality."[1]

Though every city is unique, our goal is to abstract from a large number of cities certain properties which they share in common. To comprehend diverse kinds of cities, it is necessary to ignore the uniqueness and the enormous complexity of cities. Typologies, by their very nature, simplify reality. And in this sense they do not depict reality in all of its concrete manifestations. Of necessity, ideal types are distortions of reality, though they are invaluable for simplifying and ordering data in terms which are comparable and for sensitizing us to the properties of social phenomena.

While our typologies are constructed from an extensive historical study of many cities, the types, in turn, are designed to assist our understanding of particular cities, especially our effort to compare changes

1. Max Weber, *The Methodology of the Social Sciences*, trans. Edward A. Shils and Henry A. Finch (Glencoe, Ill.: Free Press, 1949), p. 90. For the use of ideal types in historical analysis, see also the discussion in Don Martindale, "Sociological Theory and the Ideal Type," in *Symposium on Sociological Theory*, ed. Llewellyn Gross (Evanston, Ill.: Row, Peterson and Co., 1959); and Guenther Roth, "Sociological Typology and Historical Explanation," in *Scholarship and Partnership: Essays on Max Weber*, ed. Reinhard Bendix and Guenther Roth (Berkeley: University of California Press, 1971).

in individual or large numbers of cities over time. Ideal types do not
have the formal properties of either hypotheses or theories, but they are
useful for formulating explicit hypotheses about social change. They are
valuable devices which assist us in grasping causal relations and in moving eventually to a level of theory construction.

To advance in the direction of our goal, we suggest a set of typologies of urban units based on analyzing the interrelationships among
certain types of components: *the structural, cultural, situational, and
environmental characteristics of cities.*[2] Very much concerned with understanding the public policy process, we are also hopeful that our typologies will illuminate the way in which social, economic, and political
variables get translated into public policy. Moreover, we will attempt
to construct typologies that specify the relationship among these various
components. Because the typologies are deliberately cast at a rather high
level of generality and abstraction, we must ultimately have greater
specification and systematic analysis of the interaction of these components if we are to move historical analysis to the level of theory construction—and some of this is offered in the next chapter.

By structural factors we mean those characteristics of cities which
are relatively unchanging on a day-to-day basis. For example, the economic structure of a city includes not only the type of activity in which
business firms are engaged but also their size, whether the city has few or
many firms, and the extent to which the firms are integrated into a
national economy.

Political structure includes the type of government (mayor-council,
town meeting, etc.), partisan make-up of the city (whether nonpartisan,
bipartisan, one party, etc.), the nature of elections (whether at large
or by ward, whether low or high level of participation, whether highly
competitive), the level of political bureaucratization and professionalization, the nature of political recruitment (from what strata of society
political elites are chosen, whether there is frequent turnover among
political elites, etc.), and the level of centralization (whether power is
highly concentrated or diffused).

Other societal structures include the stratification system, by which
we mean the way that social status is distributed. In the American context, useful indicators of status are income, wealth, occupation, ethnicity,
and religion. While stratification measures social relations vertically,

2. For an extended discussion of these terms, see Robert R. Alford, "The Comparative
Study of Urban Politics," in *Urban Research and Policy Planning*, ed. Leo F. Schnore and
Henry Fagin (Beverly Hills, Calif.: Sage Publications, 1967), pp. 263-302. Also see Erik
Allardt, *Structural, Institutional, and Cultural Explanations*, Publication no. 89 (Helsinki:
Institute of Sociology, University of Helsinki, n.d.), for a useful discussion of these terms.

we also want to measure social structural relations horizontally and are therefore interested in comparing communities in terms of their occupational complexity as well as their religious and ethnic heterogeneity. And finally, the age, size, and degree of community autonomy are other structural variables of importance for community analysis.

Structural factors provide the context in which situations or day-to-day events take place, the things which usually catch the eye of the narrative historian. Defining the limits in which situations occur, structures create the situation in which it would be difficult for actors to behave differently. On the other hand, situational factors include such things as the ability of individual leaders, the type of political strategies and alliances employed to cope with specific issues, the occurrence of disasters, and the sequence and timing with which issues arise. And while much of this chapter emphasizes the influence of structural factors in shaping outcomes, situational factors (for example, fires, floods, assassinations, and so on), as every historian knows, are also of importance in shaping policy outcomes.

The distinction between structural and situational factors is sometimes fuzzy. This occurs for the obvious reason that structural factors vary in their permanence. For example, the population of a city may be stable over time, change quickly, and then again become relatively stable. Thus, a variable that is usually a structural characteristic may become a situational factor at another time.

Decisions at any one point in time are influenced by the accumulated experience of the entire community (political culture), the particular situational context within which an issue arises, as well as the social, economic, and political structures of the city. And the way in which issues are confronted at any particular point in time may influence the manner in which similar events are met in the future. In other words, historical events establish predispositions and attitudes which later influence subsequent events. In discussing political culture, Max Weber made this point years ago, using the analogy of the loaded dice: once the dice come up with a certain number, they tend to come up with the same number again and again.[3] Thus, the historical experiences of cities provide norms which guide future conduct, which are important in defining options for both elites and the electorate (see figure 1).

All political activity is embedded in a political culture which gives order and meaning to participants in the political process. Political culture consists of the values, beliefs, and attitudes which provide the underlying assumptions, norms, and rules for political activity. In other words,

3. Weber, *Methodology of the Social Sciences*, pp. 182-85.

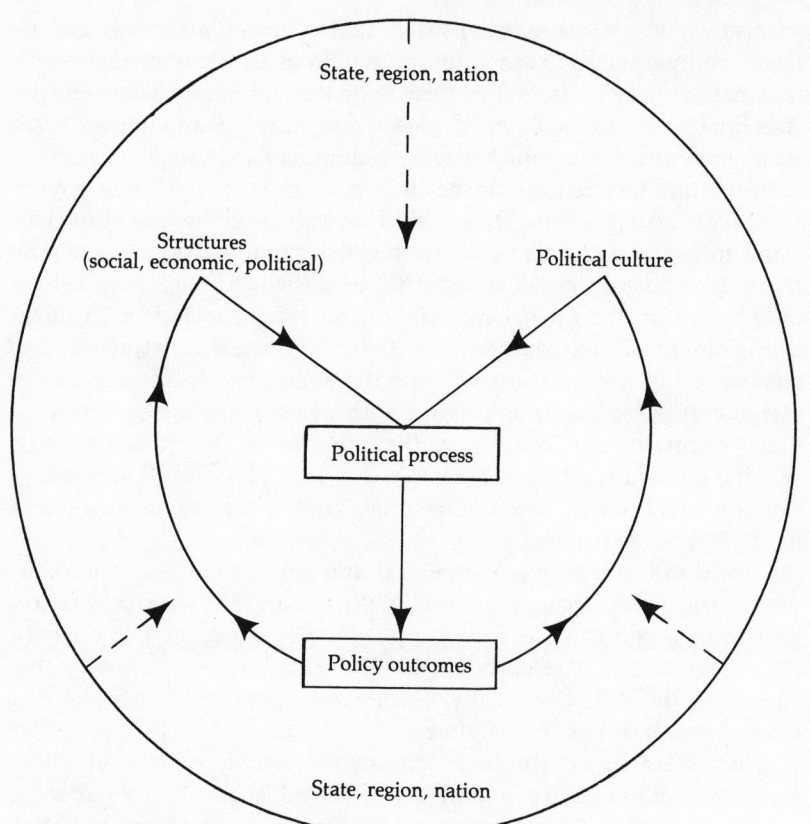

Figure 1. Diagram of a local political system

political culture governs the style of political behavior; it involves the subjective realm of politics.

As Sidney Verba has suggested, political culture "refers not to what is happening in the world of politics, but what people believe about those happenings . . . . Political culture regulates who talks to whom and who influences whom. It also regulates what is said in political contacts and the effects of these contacts. And it influences the ways in which formal institutions operate as well."[4] Because it is obviously not enough to assert that political culture is important in shaping outcomes, we must attempt to establish in what ways and under what circumstances political culture is important. But our ultimate goal is to specify the way in which

4. Lucien W. Pye and Sidney Verba, eds., *Political Culture and Political Development* (Princeton, N.J.: Princeton University Press, 1965), pp. 516-17. The essays by Pye and Verba in this volume are useful introductions to the subject of political culture.

social and economic structures become intertwined with political structures, political culture, and situational factors, for it is the variation in the interaction of structural, cultural, and situational factors which is responsible for the diverse urban configurations which exist. And it is the interaction of the structures and culture of a city which provides the dynamics of historical change.

While figure 1 describes in a most general way the nature of these relationships, we attempt, by constructing typologies below, to analyze this interaction in greater detail. Even though we incorporate some elements of time in our ideal types, some of the types tend to transcend time. That is, some types of cities may have existed at any point in time since 1870, while others (elite suburbs, for example) are relatively recent communities and hardly existed in the late nineteenth century.

STRUCTURAL CHARACTERISTICS OF COMMUNITIES

In developing typologies of cities it is useful to measure their structural characteristics along several dimensions, but there are three which we consider to be of major importance: vertical differentiation, horizontal differentiation, and community autonomy. As we measure the vertical differentiation of a community, we are primarily concerned with stratification hierarchies, the number of and the distance between individuals at various levels of the stratification system. All communities, either explicitly or implicitly, classify their members into categories above or below one another, and it is this process which determines who gets deference and who gives it. The critical problem here is the shape of the stratification system, the size of the top, middle, and bottom of the system —whether the stratification system has a pyramidal, cone, or diamond shape. A community has a high level of vertical differentiation if the stratification system has a pyramidal or cone shape, while the more diamond-shaped the system, the lower its level of vertical differentiation.

An increase in the level of horizontal differentiation means that there is an emergence of new roles to perform more distinct functions within a community. Increased horizontal differentiation implies a higher level of specialization or division of labor. Horizontal differentiation increases as new functions occur in a society, as new structures arise. A high level of horizontal differentiation is associated with communities having large numbers of institutions, a considerable amount of institutional autonomy, and a high degree of internal diversity within institutions.

By community autonomy we refer to the degree to which community decisions are made by residents of the local community. Of course, no community in an industrial society is ever completely autonomous, but

the autonomy of the economic and political structures of communities
is one of the most important variables on which communities should be
compared. By law, American communities may undertake only those
political functions granted them by state governments, but the ratio of
governmental revenues raised for local purposes to all governmental
expenditures at the local level (an index to local political autonomy)
varies considerably from community to community. In other words, a
community which raises all of the money which it spends has more political autonomy than one which receives all of its revenues from the state
or national government. Economic autonomy refers to the proportion
of a community's goods and services consumed at the local level, and,
of course, this also varies across communities.[5]

The three dimensions discussed above are very useful in moving us
toward a classification of American cities since 1870 into various types:[6]

1. In one type of community (*autocratic*), there is high vertical differentiation or considerable inequality in the distribution of status,
power, income, and wealth. The cities have a small upper or elite group
and a large lower or working strata, especially a large unskilled labor

5. For a very interesting use of the concept community autonomy in historical writing,
see Michael Zuckerman, *Peaceable Kingdoms: New England Towns in the Eighteenth
Century* (New York: Alfred A. Knopf, 1970). A good discussion of political autonomy is
Duane W. Hill, "Some Aspects of the Problem of Local Autonomy of Cities and Towns in
Iowa" (Ph.D. diss., University of Iowa, 1953). The idea of economic autonomy is developed
in Douglass C. North, *The Economic Growth of the United States, 1790-1860* (Englewood
Cliffs, N.J.: Prentice-Hall, 1961), pp. 1-14, and "Location Theory and Regional Economic
Growth," *Journal of Political Economy* 63 (June 1955): 243-58; and Wilbur R. Thompson,
A Preface to Urban Economics (Baltimore, Md.: The Johns Hopkins University Press,
1965), pp. 15-16.

6. In developing the types which follow, we have been very much aided by the following
literature: Daniel Elazar, *Cities of the Prairie: The Metropolitan Frontier and American
Politics* (New York: Basic Books, 1970); Michael Aiken, "The Distribution of Community
Power: Structural Bases and Social Consequences," in *The Structure of Community Power*,
ed. Michael Aiken and Paul Mott (New York: Random House, 1970), pp. 487-525; Terry N.
Clark, ed., *Community Structure and Decision Making: Comparative Analyses* (San
Francisco: Chandler, 1968), and "Community in the National System: Federalism, Localism,
and Decentralization," in *Comparative Community Politics*, ed. Clark (Beverly Hills,
Calif.: Sage Publications, 1973); David Rogers, "Community Political Systems: A Framework and Hypotheses for Comparative Studies," in *Current Trends in Comparative Community Studies*, ed. Bert E. Swanson (Kansas City, Mo.: Community Studies, 1962),
pp. 31-48; Claire W. Gilbert, *Community Power Structure* (Gainesville, Fla.: University
of Florida Press, 1972); Irving P. Leif and Terry Nichols Clark, "Community Power and
Decision-Making: A Trend Report and Bibliography," *Current Sociology*, 20 (1972):
5-138; and Peter H. Rossi, "Power and Community Structure," *Midwest Journal of Political
Science* 4 (November 1960): 390-401.

population. In other words, the social structure is pyramidal in nature, and the status system is rigid, in that there is very little mobility from one stratum to another. There are marked differences in the life-styles of the people in the various strata, with very little effective communication among the strata. Moreover, there is a tendency for this type of social structure to be associated with an *autocratic* political system, that is, one which is governed by someone who essentially monopolizes political power—a phenomenon known in the American vernacular as "boss rule." This type of community historically was quite small and had a social process fundamentally different from the larger cities, which had political bosses and about which Moisei Ostrogorski and others have brilliantly written over the years.[7] Of course, "bossism" in small communities of this type was often characterized as paternalism and is usually described as such in the historical literature.[8]

In contrast to such large cities as Chicago, Boston, and Philadelphia, which have had "political bosses," these rather small communities have a low level of horizontal differentiation—that is, the political, economic, and social systems have a low level of complexity. In the economic sector this means that the occupational structure is quite simple, while in the political sector there are very few formal political roles. Because the political system has a low level of complexity, the political elites tend to hold their positions on a part-time basis. There is considerable status congruence in these communities, in that those who rank high in one sector of society generally rank high in all sectors. For example, the economic elites and political elites are generally one and the same. And in communities where political and economic elites overlap, official decisions generally reflect the private interests of public officials.

The ethnic diversity in American cities was often an important consideration in explaining the lack of solidarity among lower income groups and the high vertical differentiation in cities of this type. In the South, for example, a virtual caste system existed for many decades following the Civil War, with the division of labor very much along racial lines. Moreover, there was a horizontal color bar with very little, if any,

---

7. A population which is unskilled, ethnically diverse, and poorly educated has traits that are frequently associated with "machine rule" or "boss rule." Most of our historical literature on "boss rule" in American cities, however, focuses on very large cities. For example, see James C. Scott, "Corruption, Machine Politics, and Political Change," in *The Politics of Nation and State Building*, ed. J. Rogers Hollingsworth (Boston: Little, Brown, 1971). The concern here, however, is with autocratic rule in smaller cities.

8. For example, see Randolph Longenbach, "An Epic in Urban Design," *Harvard Bulletin* 1 (April 15, 1968): 18-28, in which the control of a community is described as "corporate paternalism."

intercaste mobility. In addition, the lower caste (blacks) were denied most legal rights.[9] In contrast, many communities outside the South had parallel ethnic structures, co-existing side by side but often with considerable disdain for one another. As Lee Benson, Clyde Griffen, Stephan Thernstrom, and numerous other historians have demonstrated with various types of communities, differences between particular ethnic groups were often more important than those between social classes. Associations within immigrant groups cut across socioeconomic lines, whereas class solidarity in multiethnic communities has traditionally been quite weak.[10]

9. John Dollard, *Caste and Class in a Southern Town* (Garden City, N.Y.: Doubleday Anchor Books, 1957); Allison Davis, Burleigh Gardner, and Mary Gardner, *Deep South* (Chicago: The University of Chicago Press, 1941); Mozell C. Hill and Bevode C. McCall, "Social Stratification in 'Georgia Town,' " *American Sociological Review* 6 (December 1950): 721-29; Ethel S. Arnett, *Greensboro, North Carolina: The County Seat of Guilford* (Chapel Hill: The University of North Carolina Press, 1955); Rupert B. Vance and Nicholas J. Demerath, eds., *The Urban South* (Chapel Hill: The University of North Carolina Press, 1954); Samuel M. Kipp III, "Urban Growth and Social Change in the South, 1870-1920: Greensboro, North Carolina as a Case Study" (Ph.D. diss., Princeton University, 1974); Bradbury Seasholes, "Negro Political Participation in Two North Carolina Cities" (Ph.D. diss., University of North Carolina, 1962); and Robert E. Perdue, "The Negro in Savannah, 1865-1900" (Ph.D. diss., University of Georgia, 1971). For the place of blacks in the social structure of a northern middle-sized city, see Robert Warner, *New Haven Negroes—A Social History* (New Haven, Conn.: Yale University Press, 1940).

10. This view of American history is sometimes labeled an ethnocultural interpretation. The most influential and one of the earliest statements of this view is Lee Benson, *The Concept of Jacksonian Democracy* (Princeton, N.J.: Princeton University Press, 1961). For statements by other scholars of this view as it regards different types of American cities, see Stephan Thernstrom, "Urbanization, Migration, and Social Mobility in Late Nineteenth Century America," in *Towards a New Past: Dissenting Essays in American History*, ed. Barton J. Bernstein (New York: Random House, Vintage Books, 1969), pp. 158-75; Clyde Griffen, "Workers Divided: The Effect of Craft and Ethnic Differences in Pough-keepsie, New York, 1850-1880," in *Nineteenth Century Cities*, ed. Stephan Thernstrom and Richard Sennett (New Haven, Conn.: Yale University Press, 1969), pp. 49-97; Donald B. Cole, *Immigrant City* (Chapel Hill: The University of North Carolina Press, 1963); Richard Kolbe, "Culture, Political Parties and Voting Behavior: Schuylkill County," *Polity* 8 (Winter 1975): 241-68; Tamara K. Hareven, "The Laborers of Manchester, New Hampshire," *Labor History* 16 (Spring 1975): 249-65; Robert H. Zieger, "Workers and Scholars: Recent Trends in American Labor Historiography," *Labor History* 13 (Spring 1972): 245-66; Paul Faler, "Working Class Historiography," *Radical America* 3 (March-April 1969): 56-68; Gordon William Kirk, "The Promise of American Life: Social Mobility in a Nineteenth Century Immigrant Community, Holland, Michigan, 1847-1894" (Ph.D. diss., Michigan State University, 1970); Charles C. Buell, "The Workers of Worcester: Social Mobility and Ethnicity in a New England City, 1850-1880" (Ph.D. diss., New York University, 1974); John E. Bodnar, "Socialization and Adaptation: Immigrant Families in Scranton, 1880-1890," *Pennsylvahia History* 43 (April 1976): 147-162, and "Immigration and Modernization: The Case of Slavic Peasants in Industrial America," *Journal of Social History* 10 (Fall 1976):

Historically, autocratic type communities have had a simple economic base, and it has been the nature of the economic base which has placed constraints on opportunities for individual upward mobility and on the degree of horizontal differentiation in these communities. Some were one-industry towns, and frequently they were company towns, with an economic base generally dependent on lumber, mining, or textiles. Usually, there was very little specialization within the labor force, meaning that most wage earners performed similar tasks. The number of these communities was larger when the society was at a relatively low level of industrialization and had a very labor intensive economy. Most of the citizens were poor, had a low level of education, and were virtually dependent for their well-being on the economic elites of the community. Cities approximating this type in the late nineteenth century were mining towns in Pennsylvania, lumber towns in Wisconsin, and textile towns in the South, and they were usually independent cities, rarely suburbs. Examples are Irontown, Pennsylvania; Greenville, South Carolina; and Marinette, Wisconsin.[11]

These communities often had even higher in-out migration rates than most American cities, with many workers thinking of themselves as temporary employees. The high migration rates were another consider-

---

44-71; Richard Joseph Hopkins, "Patterns of Persistence and Occupational Mobility in a Southern City: Atlanta, 1870-1920" (Ph.D. diss., Emory University, 1972); Philip T. Silvia, Jr., "The Spindle City: Labor, Politics, and Religion in Fall River, Massachusetts, 1870-1905" (Ph.D. diss., Fordham University, 1973); William A. Reader, "Yankees, Immigrants, and Social Climbers: A Study of Social Mobility in Greenfield, Massachusetts, 1850-1970" (Ph.D. diss., University of Massachusetts, 1973). For a discussion of the absence of labor consciousness in Warren, Pennsylvania, see Michael P. Weber, "Patterns of Progress: Social Mobility in a Pennsylvania Oil Town, 1870-1910" (Ph.D. diss., Carnegie-Mellon University, 1972).

11. James B. Smith, "Lumbertowns in the Cutover: A Comparative Study of the Stage Hypothesis of Urban Growth" (Ph.D. diss., University of Wisconsin, 1973); Dale Arthur Peterson, "Lumbering on the Chippewa: The Eau Claire Area, 1845-1885" (Ph.D. diss., University of Minnesota, 1970); Carl Krog, "Marinette: Biography of a Nineteenth Century Lumbering Town, 1850-1910" (Ph.D. diss., University of Wisconsin, 1971); Rowland Berthoff, "The Social Order of the Anthracite Region, 1825-1902," *Pennsylvania Magazine of History and Biography* 89 (July 1965): 261-91; Victor R. Greene, "A Study in Slavs, Strikes, and Unions: The Anthracite Strike of 1897," *Pennsylvania History* 31 (April 1964): 119-215; James Glasgow, *Muskegon, Michigan: The Evolution of a Lake Port* (Chicago: The University of Chicago Press, 1939); Gustavus G. Williamson, "Cotton Manufacturing in South Carolina, 1865-1892" (Ph.D. diss., John Hopkins University, 1954); Melton McLaurin, *Paternalism and Protest: Southern Cotton Mill Workers and Organized Labor* (Westport, Conn.: Greenwood Press, 1971); Liston Pope, *Millhands and Preachers: A Study of Gastonia* (New Haven, Conn.: Yale University Press, 1942); and Lois MacDonald, *Southern Millhands: A Study of Social and Economic Forces in Certain Textile Mill Villages* (New York: A.L. Hillman, 1928).

ation which prevented most workers from becoming very integrated into the community's political system. Daniel Rodgers has estimated that the annual turnover among workers in the nation's factories during the early part of the twentieth century was in excess of 100 percent. In the southern textile industry—for which we have survey data—the turnover rate was 176 percent in 1907.[12] New arrivals in a community or people planning to depart generally tended to be less involved in community affairs than those who resided permanently in the community.[13] Of course, most low income people had neither the time for much involvement in politics nor an understanding of the way the political process operated. But even if they had the time and understanding, the "paternalistic" political and economic elites usually had adequate control measures to prevent their own influence from diminishing.[14] A somewhat extreme example of this phenomenon occurred in a number of southern communities during the late nineteenth and early twentieth centuries as rigid use of instruments of social control kept the levels of political mobilization (especially among blacks) at very low levels.[15]

Because these were communities with most workers employed in the same industry and performing similar tasks, however, sometimes workers' grievances easily found reinforcement from their fellow workers. As a result, some autocratic communities—especially those with extensive mining and lumbering activities—did experience periodic eruptions, motivated by both political and economic grievances. These disruptions

12. We are especially indebted to Daniel T. Rodgers for these insights. See his "Tradition, Modernity, and the American Industrial Worker: Reflection and Critique" *Journal of Interdisciplinary History* 4 (1977): 655-82. See also U.S. Commission on Industrial Relations, *Final Report and Testimony*, 64th Cong., 1st sess., 1916, 4: 3507, 3510; and Daniel T. Rodgers, *The Work Ethic in Industrial America 1850-1920* (Chicago: The University of Chicago Press, 1978), pp. 163-65.

13. For useful literature on high geographical migration during the late nineteenth century, see Thernstrom, "Urbanization, Migration, and Social Mobility"; Paul B. Worthman, "Working Class Mobility in Birmingham, Alabama, 1880-1914," in *Anonymous Americans: Explorations in Nineteenth Century Social History*, ed. Tamara K. Hareven (Englewood Cliffs, N.J.: Prentice-Hall, 1971), pp. 172-213; Richard J. Hopkins, "Occupational and Geographic Mobility in Atlanta, 1870-1896," *Journal of Southern History* 24 (May 1968): 200-213; Daniel T. Rodgers, "The Work Ethic in Industrial America, 1865-1917" (Ph.D. diss., Yale University, 1973).

14. Stuart D. Brandes, *American Welfare Capitalism, 1880-1940* (Chicago: The University of Chicago Press, 1976), is an excellent source for the paternalistic practices which existed in a number of American communities; James B. Allen's *The Company Town in the American West* (Norman: University of Oklahoma Press, 1966), should also be consulted.

15. See J. Morgan Kousser, *The Shaping of Southern Politics: Suffrage Restriction and the Establishment of the One-Party South, 1880-1890* (New Haven, Conn.: Yale University Press, 1974).

were usually of a short duration, however, for those in the lower levels of the social strata had little political experience and had few organizations with which they could maximize economic and political power. In those few communities in which labor unions developed, however, the political process frequently assumed a slightly different complexion, especially if the union boundaries transcended the local community. In this situation, the workers began to counter the economic and political power of the homogeneous elite structure, thus bringing into existence a political process which was less autocratic and somewhat more fluid.[16]

Autocratic communities, however, had few institutions which effectively channeled lines of cleavage. For example, political parties for mobilizing demands at the local political level rarely existed, and when they did they played very little role in shaping public policy. Because these communities had low levels of per capita income, wealth, and education, the political process involved low levels of professionalization and bureaucratization, political activity was generally informal, and the functions of government were quite limited.

These communities were generally small, and as they were part of a larger society which had a low level of economic development, they had a relatively high level of *political* autonomy. Because most were economically dependent on exporting goods elsewhere—especially if they were lumber, mining, or textile towns—they usually did not enjoy very much *economic* autonomy. As the larger society underwent economic development, this type of community acquired greater internal complexity. Or to phrase the matter differently, the community acquired greater horizontal differentiation as the larger society underwent economic development, which in turn decreased the community's vertical differentiation and increased the number of its ties with the outside world, thus diminishing its community autonomy.

2. As we move along the continuum on each of these variables, we find, as implied above, *oligarchic* cities, with lower levels of vertical differentiation, higher levels of horizontal differentiation, and somewhat less political autonomy. In this type of community, the social structure is somewhat cone-shaped, in that there is a small upper stratum and a sizable lower stratum, but unlike the community with the pyramidal

16. Herbert Gutman, *Work, Culture and Society* (New York: Alfred A. Knopf, 1976), "The Worker's Search for Power: Labor in the Gilded Age," in *The Gilded Age: A Reappraisal*, ed. H. Wayne Morgan (Syracuse: Syracuse University Press, 1963), pp. 38-68, "Social and Economic Structure and Depression: American Labor in 1873 and 1874" (Ph.D. diss., University of Wisconsin, 1959); Hareven, "The Laborers of Manchester, New Hampshire," pp. 249-65; and Melvyn Dubofsky, "The Origins of Western Working Class Radicalism, 1890-1905," *Labor History* 6 (Spring 1966): 131-55.

social structure, this one has a larger and more complex middle stratum and is thus somewhat less elite dominated. Moreover, the economic and political structures are more complex, and the communities are somewhat larger. In addition, the levels of per capita income and education are somewhat higher, reflecting that the economic base is more complicated than the pyramidal community. Here, the economy is a bit mixed, with manufacturing and commercial activities usually being the key elements. And this type of city is more integrated into a national or regional economy and has less economic autonomy.

An example of this somewhat more complex community was the Newburyport, Massachusetts, of 1850, which Stephan Thernstrom has described:

> Approximately one quarter of the employed males of the city were semi-skilled workers, while almost 40 percent were skilled laborers. The diversity of skilled trades was striking—thirty-nine varieties of artisans could be counted on the local census schedules for 1850. It is misleading to classify mid-century Newburyport as a "mill town;" its occupational structure was not heavily weighted toward unskilled and semiskilled callings. The community had a highly diversified craft economy, with almost two-thirds of its labor force in the top two occupational categories and less than a tenth at the very bottom.[17]

The power structure of such a community is slightly more fragmented than that with a pyramidal social structure, the political activity has a somewhat higher level of bureaucratization and professionalization, and the political process is slightly less informal. *Oligarchy* is the type of political system generally associated with these phenomena. There are two kinds of oligarchy, however, the single element and the multiple element. In the single-element oligarchy those who exercise major control over the community's economic resources also dominate the city's social and political activities. These are generally businessmen who are either from a single firm, from several firms in a single industry, or from several industries. The more complex the economic structure, the larger the number of different kinds of business activities represented in the oligarchy.

The community's economic and social structures generally provide the opportunity for the economic dominants to have frequent contact and communication with one another, thus enhancing the prospects for political consensus on the issues confronting the community. The economic elites usually view themselves as men full of responsibility and *noblesse oblige* toward their community. And while the economic dom-

17. Stephan Thernstrom, *Poverty and Progress: Social Mobility in a Nineteenth Century City* (Cambridge, Mass.: Harvard University Press, 1964), p. 95.

inants reserve to themselves the important decisions of the community, they generally have enough contacts with the local citizenry through churches and other organizations so that there is a sufficient flow of communication across the numerous strata of society to legitimate the decisions of the business oligarchy. In general, the oligarchs are the archetypes of the patricians described in Robert Dahl's *Who Governs?* or of the Ball family in the Lynds' *Middletown*.[18]

Business leaders who are most active in an oligarchic system generally control firms which are locally owned. Business elites involved in absentee-owned firms play a less important role in the day-to-day affairs of city government than local entrepreneurs. Thus the political process of Waltham, Massachusetts, was somewhat more open and fluid and less oligarchic during the late nineteenth century because the largest firms were absentee-owned. On the other hand, economic dominants representing absentee-owned firms generally tend to become heavily involved in a local oligarchy when their enterprises are relatively immobile, as in such extractive industries as oil, mining, and lumbering. Extractive industries cannot easily move elsewhere unless their resources are depleted, and the management of such firms tend to become more involved in local politics as a means of protecting their vested interests than the management of absentee-owned firms which have much more mobility. In other words, the more immobile an absentee-owned firm, the greater its involvement in local politics.[19]

18. Robert Dahl, *Who Governs? Democracy and Power in an American City* (New Haven, Conn.: Yale University Press, 1961), chap. 4; and Robert Lynd and Helen Lynd, *Middletown* (New York: Harcourt, Brace, 1929). Also see Carrolyle M. Frank, "Politics in Middletown: A Reconsideration of Municipal Government and Community Power in Muncie, Indiana, 1925-1935" (Ph.D. diss., Ball State University, 1974). For other examples of oligarchic communities, see Elazar, *Cities of the Prairie*; William H. Ridgway, "A Social Analysis of Maryland Community Elites, 1827-1836: A Study of the Distribution of Power in Baltimore City, Frederick County, and Talbot County" (Ph.D. diss., University of Pennsylvania, 1973); Carl V. Harris, *Political Power In Birmingham, 1871-1921* (Knoxville, Tenn.: University of Tennessee Press, 1977); Durward Long, "The Making of Modern Tampa: A City of the New South, 1885-1911," *Florida Historical Quarterly* 59 (April 1971): 333-45; and Paul Isaac, "Municipal Reform in Beaumont, Texas, 1902-1909," *Southwestern Historical Quarterly* 78 (April 1975): 409-30; Kipp, "Urban Growth and Social Change in the South, 1870-1920."

19. Howard M. Gitelman, *Workingmen of Waltham: Mobility in American Urban Industrial Development, 1850-1890* (Baltimore, Md.: The Johns Hopkins University Press, 1974). For further literature on the role of absentee ownership in local affairs, see R.O. Schulze, "The Bifurcation of Power in a Satellite City," in *Community Political Systems*, ed. Morris Janowitz (New York: The Free Press, 1961), pp. 19-80; M.N. Goldstein, "Absentee Ownership and Monolithic Power Structures: Two Questions for Community Studies," in *Current Trends in Comparative Community Studies*, ed. B.E. Swanson (Kansas

The multiple-element oligarchy, as the term implies, is much less monolithic than the single-element oligarchy, consisting of elites from business, as well as from labor unions, universities, and so on. While a multiple-element oligarchy may be found in an independent city, industrial suburbs often have this type of structure.[20] An oligarchy made up of *three* groups is obviously a bit more responsive to community demands than a dual- or single-element oligarchy. Moreover, those communities having multiple-element oligarchies have a much higher level of horizontal differentiation and a somewhat more fragmented power structure than those with the single-element oligarchy. But regardless of type, an oligarchy derives its distinctive character from the fact that in each instance it consists of a closed group of people who dominate the institutional and organizational life of the community.

Though a small group of elites dominate the political life of the oligarchic community, it does have a higher level of voter participation than in the autocratic community. Furthermore, voluntary organizations are somewhat numerous and established in the social life of this type of community, and for this reason they can be relatively important in facilitating political participation.

Occasionally, the elites poorly articulate the values of the community, and ethnic, class, ideological, and other disputes erupt. Citizen participation, however, even though higher than in autocratic communities, is moderately low in cities of this type—though it does tend to increase with population and economic growth, economic and social diversity, and a rise in the level of education. Political parties are relatively common in these communities—especially in the more eastern part of the country. In general, oligarchic systems maintain their legitimacy partly through political parties, though these communities have political systems in which there are few expectations from government.

The level of political participation is influenced by the amount of social diversity within the community. While black-white cleavages in the American South represent an exception, the sharper the ethnic cleavages in communities, the better organized and the more competitive the local party structure and the higher the level of political participation. And where there is ethnic diversity, the successful elites are those who are sensitive to the ethnic symbolic meaning of their actions and words.

City, Mo.: Community Studies, 1962), pp. 49-59; Daniel Jensen Prosser, "Coal Towns in Egypt: Portrait of an Illinois Mining Region, 1890-1930" (Ph.D diss., Northwestern University, 1973).

20. Gilbert, *Community Power Structure*, p. 50; and Graham R. Taylor, *Satellite Cities: A Study of Industrial Suburbs* (New York: Appleton, 1915).

In other words, the power structure in oligarchic communities was neither static nor always dominated by a powerful industrial elite, as Herbert Gutman's stimulating work has demonstrated. During crises, such as strikes or economic depressions, a few of the key variables causing modifications within the power of an oligarchic structure were the city's ethnic diversity, the strength of political parties and labor unions, and the legitimacy and status of the industrial elite. At moments of crises there could, indeed, be in oligarchic communities sharp cleavages between industrial elites on the one hand, and the rest of the community on the other. Alan Dawley has demonstrated how labor disputes in Lynn, Massachusetts, in 1860, 1878, and again in 1890 dented local oligarchic structures. But these eruptions were only temporary. And as David Montgomery has pointed out, it is difficult to find a labor reform party which was able to win more than a single election before the very end of the nineteenth century.[21]

3. With the next type of city (*polyarchic*), we move to the opposite end of the continua: there is low vertical differentiation, high horizontal differentiation, and low political autonomy. The community's social structure is rather diamond-shaped, having even a larger and more complex middle stratum, a small upper stratum, and a small lower stratum. Having somewhat high levels of income, wealth, and education, the community has economic, social, and political structures with relatively high levels of complexity.

While the term *diamond-shaped social structure* is not uncommon, certain qualifications about our use of the concept are in order. We believe the middle stratum in American cities has expanded during the last century, but we certainly do not mean to imply that the United States has become an egalitarian society. In the United States—like most highly industrial non-Socialist societies—the richest tenth of the population generally receives as much money income as the entire bottom half of the population.

Despite considerable change in the middle stratum, cities with diamond-shaped social structures are highly stratified. And while there is considerable occupational mobility in middle-sized communities with diamond-shaped social structures, much of the mobility is lateral and

21. Herbert G. Gutman, "Class, Status, and Community Power in Nineteenth-Century American Industrial Cities—Patterson, New Jersey: A Case Study," in *The Age of Industrialism in America*, ed. Frederic C. Jaher (New York: The Free Press, 1968), pp. 263-87. Also consult Gutman's bibliography, ibid., note 26, p. 287, and his *Work, Culture and Society*; Alan Dawley, *Class and Community: The Industrial Revolution in Lynn* (Cambridge, Mass.: Harvard University Press, 1976); David Montgomery, "Gutman's Nineteenth Century America," *Labor History* 19 (Summer 1978): 416-29.

not vertical. In this respect it is important to differentiate between an upper-middle stratum and a lower-middle stratum. Because the service sector of the occupational structure has expanded over time, some observers have erroneously interpreted this to mean that there is a homogenizing of the middle class. In fact, income for service workers as a whole tends to be lower than for blue collar workers. Analysis of recent occupational and income distribution by city size suggests that the middle stratum has expanded relative to the lower and upper levels to a greater extent in middle-sized cities than in the nation's largest cities.[22]

The changes in the occupational structure for the entire United States between 1900 and 1970 are reflected in table 1.1. The most important shift in occupations has been in the increase in size of the professional, technical, managerial, clerical workers, more broadly categorized as white collar workers. And it is on this basis that we argue that the middle stratum has expanded in size for the nation as a whole.

A diamond-shaped social structure is generally associated with a *polyarchic* type of political system. In this kind of polity, political power is diffused or decentralized. There are diverse and competing centers of power, with no group able to dominate the political life of the community. Because the community's social and economic structures are so differentiated, each area of the community has a different set of elites, and having resources in one area of the community does not mean having power in other sectors. And the more complex the social and economic system becomes, the more complex is the status system. People have different ranks in occupational prestige, education, income, and ethnic status—which means that individuals have different amounts of resources and influence in various issue areas.

These more complex structures are reflected in the fact that there are many more power centers and many more public policies occurring as a result of constantly shifting coalitions among citizens and interest groups. Unlike the autocratic system, political elites in the polyarchic system cannot coerce or order but must bargain through constantly changing coalitions. As issues change, coalitions change, but generally groups are activated politically only by those issues which they perceive as having a high level of saliency.

The increased level of complexity of the community means that the range of political problems and the scope of political activities also increase substantially. When the range and scope of problems are limited,

22. Joseph Bensman and Arthur J. Vidich, *The New American Society* (Chicago: Quadrangle Books, 1971); Richard Parker, *The Myth of the Middle Class* (New York: Harper & Row, 1972).

Table 1.1. Percentage of the Labor Force in Major Occupation Groups[a]

Occupation groups	1900	1910	1920	1930	1940	1950	1960	1970
White collar workers	17.6	21.3	24.9	29.4	31.1	36.6	42.0	46.7
Manual workers (except farm and mine workers)	35.8	38.2	40.2	39.6	39.8	41.1	37.5	36.3
Service workers	9.0	9.6	7.8	9.8	11.7	10.5	12.6	12.4
Farm and mine workers	37.5	30.9	27.0	21.2	17.4	11.8	7.9	4.6

Sources: Victor Fuchs and Irving F. Leveson, *The Service Economy* (New York: National Bureau of Economic Research, 1968); U.S. Department of Commerce, Bureau of the Census, *Historical Statistics of the United States* (Washington, D.C.: U.S. Government Printing Office, 1975); Daniel Bell, *The Coming of Post Industrial Society* (New York: Basic Books, 1973).

[a] Percentages may not add to 100 because of rounding.

as in many autocratic, and even oligarchic, communities, those who hold political office usually do so on a part-time basis. But as the complexity of problems and scope of government increase, the number of full-time political roles becomes larger. Political roles become increasingly professionalized and bureaucratized, meaning that those who serve as polticial elites are not the same as those who serve as economic elites. When political and economic elites become increasingly differentiated, there are more formal channels of influence, more explicit rules governing the operations of various aspects of the political system, and greater reliance on the formal procedures of government. As cities grow, attain higher levels of per capita income, and acquire greater internal complexity, the level of participation also increases over that which exists in the autocratic and oligarchic systems. Voluntary associations increase in number, many of which play an important role in shaping political outcomes. There is a limit to the rise in political participation, however, as increases in the levels of bureaucratization tend ultimately to discourage many citizens from participating in politics, for the increase in the level of administrative decision making removes many issues from the open political arena.

Smaller cities are less differentiated horizontally than larger cities, however, and as a result there are somewhat fewer demands for, and a different order of, outputs emerging in such cities. As cities grow in size, so does the horizontal differentiation,[23] resulting in a greater demand for more elaborate hospitals, museums, libraries, and transportation facilities. This occurs, in part, because growth causes the city to coordinate and supply many functions for smaller surrounding areas.

The polyarchic city also has a more complex "stage system" of issue development.[24] In all cities, issues are initiated, discussed or debated, resolved, implemented, and eventually evaluated. In the autocratic and oligarchic cities, the participants in the decision-making cycle tend to be the same people, while in the polyarchic city, each stage in the cycle is more likely to involve a different set of participants.[25]

23. For a discussion of the relationship between size and social processes, see Bruce Mayhew, "System Size and Ruling Elites," *American Sociological Review* 38 (August 1973): 468-75.

24. For an analysis of polyarchic type communities, see Dahl, *Who Governs?*; Robert R. Alford, *Bureaucracy and Participation: Political Culture in Four Wisconsin Cities* (Chicago: Rand McNally, 1969); Elazar, *Cities of the Prairie*. For a historical case study of a polyarchic type community, see Ridgway, "Social Analysis of Maryland Community Elites."

25. For a summary and analysis of the literature on American political participation, see J. Rogers Hollingsworth, "Problems in the Study of Popular Voting Behavior," in

The higher the level of economic development of the country or region, the larger the number of cities with polyarchic structures and political processes. And as these cities become more bureaucratized and professionalized, norms and reference groups transcending the community increasingly govern the style of local bureaucrats and professionals. There are significant differences in the way that bureaucracies operate, however. They vary according to the level of professionalization, length of time that they have existed, level of centralization, and the degree to which they are subject to review by other agencies and elected officials. For example, public schools are generally subject to greater public control and are more centralized than public hospitals and clinics.

Some bureaucracies are part of state or national organizations and are supervised under very rigid rules, while others operate under loose guidelines. And, of course, some bureaucracies are under the strict control of a mayor's office, city council, or city manager, while others have considerable independence.

In general, the more horizontal differentiation in the community, the more fragmented the political system and the more difficult it is to mobilize community power. If there are effective integrative mechanisms (for example, political parties) which coordinate the differentiated mechanisms, however, it is possible for the community to mobilize more of its resouces. There are some regional variations in the political process and structures of polyarchic middle-sized cities, however. Within the political system, for example, professionals and bureaucrats have less independence in eastern than in western cities. Moreover, eastern cities tend to have partisan elections and a mayor-council form of government, are older, have a larger percentage of their population of foreign-born parentage, have fewer nonpartisan elections, are less likely to have a city-manager type government, are likely to have higher levels of voter participation, and tend to have political parties which are more highly institutionalized. Because western cities have more nonpartisan elections and are more likely to have a city-manager form of government, professionals and bureaucrats are somewhat more immune to the electoral process. As study after study has demonstrated, partisan elections tend to provide greater popular access to decision makers. As party structures become weaker in all parts of the country, however, professionals and bureaucrats are able to assume greater independence in the political process at all levels of government. As bureaucratic structures become

American Political Behavior: Historical Essays and Readings, ed. Lee Benson et al. (New York: Harper & Row, 1974), pp. 1-25.

more immune to electoral influences, there is an increase in the political power of those groups which are highly organized and which have very intense political interests. For it is the highly organized groups that are effectively able to penetrate government bureaucracies, while the poor and other unorganized have little influence in shaping bureaucratic decisions.

With increases in economic development, economic dominants tend to be less concerned with managing local affairs. There is a bifurcation in the local power structure, with those who are politically more influential no longer being those who wield the most economic power. This trend is especially marked with economic dominants employed by absentee-owned corporations, as these elites devote most of their attention to a world that transcends the local community. Even though political participation increases as economic development increases, issues involving the economic well-being of communities are not very susceptible to local political decisions. Agencies and organizations responsive to dominant economic interests become institutionalized beyond popular control.[26]

As the community becomes integrated into a larger society, socio-economic-political problems become less local and more regional and national in scope. Community autonomy diminishes, not only as the economic dominants become the local representatives of absentee-owned enterprises but also as labor unions, political parties, and trade associations are integrated into regional and nationwide organizations which intrude in community affairs. Cities which in recent years would be categorized as polyarchic are Madison, Wisconsin, East Lansing, Michigan, and New Haven, Connecticut.

26. Robert R. Alford and Eugene C. Lee, "Voting Turnout in American Cities," *American Political Science Review* 62 (September 1968): 796-813; Robert R. Alford and Harry Scoble, "Political and Socio-economic Characteristics of American Cities," in *The Municipal Yearbook, 1965,* ed. Orin F. Nolting and David S. Arnold (Chicago: International City Managers' Association, 1965); C. Vernon Gray, "Political and Social Structures as Determinants of Voter Participation: A Comparative Study of American Cities" (Ph.D. diss., University of Massachusetts, 1971); Alford, *Bureaucracy and Participation;* Frank M. Steward, *A Half Century of Municipal Reform* (Berkeley: University of California Press, 1950); Eugene Lee, *The Politics of Non-partisanship* (Berkeley: University of California Press, 1960); and Daniel N. Gordon, "The Social Bases of Municipal Government: A Comparative Study of the Forms of Government and Elections in American Cities" (Ph.D. diss., University of Wisconsin, 1967). For the role of the poor and nonpoor in urban politics, see Robert R. Alford and Roger Friedland, "Political Participation and Public Policy," *Annual Review of Sociology* 1 (1975): 429-79; and Roger Friedland, Frances Fox Piven, and Robert R. Alford, "Political Conflict, Urban Structure, and the Fiscal Crisis," in *Sage Yearbook in Politics and Public Policy,* ed. Douglas Ashford (Beverly Hills: Sage Publications, 1977).

CHANGES IN STRUCTURES

Once the industrializing process is well underway, the community's economic base is the most important determinant of its social and political structure as well as its political process. The economic structures of cities set limits within which their social and political structures may vary. But even though the economic structures place limits on the type of social and political structures which may emerge within a city, the economic structures do not in any deterministic or mechanistic fashion dictate the type of other structures which emerge within communities. Thus, a lumber or coal mining economy is unlikely to have a polyarchic political structure or a very large middle class.[27]

Table 1.2 suggests some of the changes which have taken place among American middle-size communities since 1870. For example, the pyramidal-autocratic community frequently undergoes a change in its economic base. As long as the community has an economic base which is labor intensive, that is, generally dependent on such industries as mining, lumbering, or textiles, there is a tendency for pyramidal-autocratic structures to persist. Ultimately, the economy of these communities may stagnate, causing the community to decline in population, and in this respect a number of lumber towns of the late nineteenth century in upper Michigan and Wisconsin or western mining communities immediately come to mind.[28]

If the economic base of the pyramidal-autocratic community expands, it may generate the oligarchic community, which usually has a substantial manufacturing and commercial base. And less commonly, the economic base of the pyramidal-autocratic community may shift directly to the kind of economic base found in the polyarchic community without first acquiring the economic base of an oligarchic community. Another alternative is for the economic base of the pyramidal-autocratic community to shift to the kind of economy associated with the oligarchic community and then to the economy which gives rise to the polyarchic

27. Also consult Schulze, "Bifurcation of Power in a Satellite City," pp. 19-80, and "The Role of Economic Dominants in Community Power Structure," *American Sociological Review* 23 (February 1958): 3-9; M.N. Goldstein, "Absentee Ownership and Monolithic Power Structures: Two Questions for Community Studies," in *Current Trends in Comparative Community Studies*, ed. Swanson, pp. 49-59; Paul E. Mott, "The Role of the Absentee-Owned Corporation in the Changing Community," in *The Structure of Community Power*, ed Aiken and Mott, pp. 170-79. For views similar to those expressed here, see Erik O. Wright, *Class, Crisis, and the State* (London: New Left Books, 1978).

28. Harvey S. Perloff et al., *Regions, Resources, and Economic Growth* (Lincoln: University of Nebraska Press, 1967), pp. 109-90. For a very interesting study of the growth and decline of these cities, see Smith, "Lumbertowns in the Cutover."

Table 1.2. Types of Cities[a]

	SMALL UPPER STRATA		LARGE UPPER STRATA	
	MIDDLE STRATA		MIDDLE STRATA	
	Large	Small	Large	Small

LARGE LOWER STRATA	(A)
	Oligarchic type
	Attleboro, Mass.
	Cohoes, N.Y.
	Eau Claire, Wis.
	Green Bay, Wis.
	Janesville, Wis.
	Naugatuck, Conn.
	S. Bethlehem, Pa.
	
	1. Moderate level of vertical differentiation
	2. Moderate level of horizontal differentiation
	3. Moderate level of political autonomy
	4. Cone-shaped social structure
	5. Single- or multiple-element oligarchy
	6. Mixed political culture
	7. Trading, commerce, manufacturing city
		(B)
		Autocratic type
		Irontown, Pa.
		Marinette, Wis.
		Shenandoah, Pa.
		Spartanburg, S.C.
		Wilkinsburg, Pa.
		
		1. High vertical differentiation
		2. Low horizontal differentiation
		3. High political autonomy
		4. Pyramidal social structure
		5. Autocratic government
		6. Traditional political culture
		7. Mining, lumber, textile towns
		8. Low expenditures per capita
		9. Unskilled and cheap labor
		10. High minority/ethnic
		11. Economic base
		  a. textiles
		  b. mining
		  c. lumber
		
		Directions of change
			(C)
			
			No cases
				(D)
				
				No cases

	(E) *Polyarchic type*	(F) No cases	(G) *Upper middle class suburb*	(H) *Elite suburb*

Table 1.2 (continued)

| | SMALL UPPER STRATA | | LARGE UPPER STRATA | |
| | MIDDLE STRATA | | MIDDLE STRATA | |
	Large	Small	Large	Small

SMALL LOWER STRATA	(E)
	Polyarchic type
	Ann Arbor, Mich.*
	East Lansing, Mich.*
	New Haven, Conn.*
	Madison, Wis.*
	
	1. Low vertical differentiation
	2. High horizontal differentiation
	3. Low political autonomy
	4. Diamond-shaped social structure
	5. Polyarchic political system
	6. Legal-rational political culture
	7. Economic base
	  a. Education center
	  b. Adminstrative center
	  c. Suburb
	  d. Commercial, service center
	8. Blacks and other minority groups enjoy more social mobility and equality
	9. Direction in which nation is moving
		(F)
		
		No cases
			(G)
			Upper middle class suburb
			Brookline, Mass.
			Evanston, Ill.
			
			1. Low vertical differentiation
			2. High horizontal differentiation
			3. Low political autonomy
			4. Inverted cone social structure
			5. Polyarchic political system
			6. Legal-rational political culture
			7. Often resort or suburb
			8. High expenditures per capita
				(H)
				Elite suburb
				Grosse Point, Mich.*
				Kenilworth, Ill.*
				Lake Forest, Ill.*
				
				1. Low vertical differentiation
				2. High horizontal differentiation
				3. Low political autonomy
				4. Inverted pyramidal social structure
				5. Polyarchic political system
				6. Legal-rational political culture
				7. Exists because of proximity to large city
				8. High expenditures per capita

^aThese types are developed in fuller detail in the pages that follow.

*Cities with asterisks are grouped according to 1970 characteristics; those without asterisks are grouped according to 1900 characteristics.

community. Unlike those of the other two city types, the polyarchic community's economic base is generally heavily dependent on service industries. Indeed, a sizable percentage of its population is usually engaged in administrative-type tasks. Accordingly, a number of state capitals, county seats, university towns, and suburbs fall within this category. And the industrial sector is more footloose—that is, based on industries which have a broad number of loactional alternatives available to them.

In an earlier period some small cities—for reasons different from those elaborated here—had something resembling a diamond-shaped social structure. For example, frontier towns in the process of evolving often had a homogeneous social structure. And Michael Frisch and others have described a similar situation in a number of New England communities prior to the arrival of numerous immigrants and the development of a complicated industrial economic base.[29]

Meantime, there are two other types of communities which may have polyarchic-type political systems: those with either an inverted-cone (upper middle class suburbs) or inverted-pyramid (upper class suburbs) social structure. These types of communities are suburbs of very large cities and generally derive their existence from that fact. (See table 1.2, cells G and H, where upper middle class and elite suburb communities are described.) The most distinctive characterititics of these cities is that each has a large upper stratum—usually consisting of some of the wealthiest families active in the nearby city. The two types of cities differ from each other in that one has a sizable upper middle stratum and the other does not, though each has a small lower stratum. Suburbs, of course, tend to rank quite low on scales of political and economic autonomy, for they have semiautonomous Balkanized jurisdictions for many functions and are dependent on neighboring communities for services.

Cities with a pyramidal, cone, or diamond-shaped structure are not likely to be transformed into cities with an upper middle class or upper

29. Michael B. Frisch, "The Community Elite and the Emergence of Urban Politics: Springfield, Massachusetts, 1840-1880," in Nineteenth-Century Cities, ed. Thernstrom and Sennett, pp. 277-96, and Town Into City: Springfield, Massachusetts and the Meaning of Community, 1840-1880 (Cambridge, Mass.: Harvard University Press, 1972); Zuckerman, Peaceable Kingdoms; Robert R. Dykstra, The Cattle Towns (New York: Atheneum, 1970), pp. 371-78; Stanley Elkins and Eric McKitrick, "A Meaning for Turner's Frontier," Political Science Quarterly 69 (1954): 321-53; Stephen Robert Davis, "From Plowshares to Spindles: Dedham, Massachusetts, 1790-1840" (Ph.D. diss., University of Wisconsin, 1973); Ralph Emerson Mann II, "The Social and Political Structure of Two California Mining Towns, 1850-1870" (Ph.D. diss., Stanford University, 1970).

class social structure. Nor is an upper middle class suburb likely to be transformed into an elite suburb, though an elite suburb could be transformed into an upper middle class suburb as large numbers of upper middle stratum families move into a fashionable suburb, thus changing its character.

As table 1.2 suggests, the changes in the structure of American cities are moving many of them in the direction of the polyarchic community (cell E). With higher levels of industrialization, a society has a smaller percentage of its cities of the pyramidal and oligarchic types and more communities with pluralistic structures. Forces external rather than internal to local communities have been primarily responsible for moving structures in the diamond-shaped polyarchic direction, meaning that communities lose autonomy as they become polyarchic.

Indeed, one of the most important changes to take place has been in the decline of political autonomy. Of course, local communities have never been completely autonomous. Technically, local governments derive their legal authority from state governments, and their economies have always been conditioned by larger economic units. Over the past eighty years, however, American communities have slowly lost more and more of their independence.

As the level of industrialization of American society has increased, there has developed a greater division of labor and differentiation of interests and associations within local communities. And as the internal structures of cities have become more differentiated, their parts have become increasingly linked with state and national systems beyond their boundaries. Not only has America become a nation made up of large-scale organizations as a result of higher levels of industrialization, but decisions, policies, programs, and norms involving local communities are increasingly shaped in offices of complex organizations which transcend local communities.

Naturally there is variation in this kind of phenomenon, as some communities are more subject to external forces than others, and when communities lose their autonomy, the explanations may vary considerably. A city dependent on decisions made by an automobile headquarters in Detroit or by the Pentagon has lost autonomy for reasons quite different from those affecting a city which becomes a dormitory suburb. Suburbs sometimes attempt to minimize the cost of their system maintenance activities (highways, utility services, airports, water, sewage, etc.) by sharing these activities with surrounding communities. The cost-sharing is often achieved by the establishment of areawide governing

authorities which may be more efficient and economical than the providing of these services on a community by community basis. But one of
the consequences is a decline in local autonomy.[30]

As the parts of local communities become tied to an external world,
solidarity within local units may weaken. Many citizens have much
stronger ties to specialized organizations which transcend their communities
than to local groups and institutions. Professionals have strong affiliations
with state and national professional associations, workers are organized
into nationwide labor unions, and giant corporations dominate much of
local industry. Some of these trends have been analyzed in Arthur J.
Vidich and Joseph Bensman's excellent study, *Small Town in Mass Society*,
in which they describe the process by which experts and specialists in
outside organizations shape such traditional local affairs as schools,
highways, public health, and fire and police protection.[31]

Elsewhere, Roland Warren has described the process by which local
community units have become increasingly oriented toward extra-
community systems:

> various parts of the community—its educational system, its recreation, its
> economic units, its governmental functions, its religious units, its health
> and welfare agencies, and its voluntary associations—have become in-
> creasingly oriented toward district, state, regional, or national offices and
> less and less oriented toward each other. . . . as local community units
> have become more closely tied in with state and national systems, much of
> the decision-making prerogatives concerning the structure and function of
> these units has been transferred to the headquarters or district offices of
> the systems themselves, thus leaving a narrower and narrower scope of
> functions over which local units, responsible to the local community, ex-
> ercise autonomous power.[32]

30. These generalizations are supported by the findings of Oliver P. Williams et al.,
Suburban Differences and Metropolitan Policies (Philadelphia: University of Pennsylvania
Press, 1965); and Robert C. Wood, *1400 Governments* (Garden City, N.Y.: Doubleday,
1964). Also see John Kasarda, "The Impact of Suburban Population Growth on Central
City Service Functions," *American Journal of Sociology* 77 (May 1972): 1111-24; Amos H.
Hawley, "Metropolitan Population and Municipal Expenditures in Central Cities," in *Cities
and Society*, ed. Paul K. Hatt and Albert J. Reiss (New York: The Free Press, 1957);
William Neenan, "The Suburban—Central City Exploitation Thesis: One City's Tale,"
National Tax Journal 23 (June 1970): 117-39. For a historical discussion of the impact of a
city's being a suburb on its governmental expenditure level, see J. Rogers Hollingsworth
and Ellen Jane Hollingsworth, "Expenditures in American Cities," in *The Dimensions of
Quantitative Research in History*, ed. William O. Aydellotte, Allan G. Bogue, and Robert
W. Fogel (Princeton, N.J.: Princeton University Press, 1972), pp. 347-89.

31. Arthur J. Vidich and Joseph Bensman, *Small Town in Mass Society* (New York:
Doubleday, Anchor, 1960).

32. Roland L. Warren, *The Community in America* (Chicago: Rand McNally, 1963),
p. 5. For a historical analysis of the impact of the federal bureaucracy on a community,
see Frank, "Politics in Middletown."

Some of these changes have often occurred in the following manner: families which historically have been powerful become less active in community affairs as succeeding generations lack the dynamism of their ancestors; meanwhile, outside firms purchase local industries and subsequently provide a managerial-professional class with weak attachments to the local community.[33]

Even though nationwide corporations have become increasingly important in shaping the nation's economy, the managerial elite of most absentee-owned corporations, as suggested above, wield much less political influence in local politics than the economic dominants of the nineteenth century who owned and operated local enterprises. The managers of absentee-owned firms derive their status and power in a corporate world which transcends the local community, with the result that they are involved in local affairs only on those issues which clearly involve their firm's economic interest, with little time for other local issues.

Of course, it is extremely difficult to measure influence in local politics. To evaluate the local political role of elites in absentee-owned firms, it is imperative to specify the kind and timing of decisions on which one is focusing. For example, an absentee-owned firm when first moving to a community may play a very important role in shaping policies involving taxation, zoning, water supply, waste disposal, transportation routes, and police and fire protection. The role of the absentee-owned firm in making these initial decisions could influence the subsequent historical dynamics of a community, though an examination of the political process at some subsequent point in time may convey the impression that the absentee-owned firm is uninvolved in local decisions. Once the basic parameters of policies involving these issues are determined, they are quite difficult to reverse. Moreover, the elites of absentee-owned firms do get involved in key decisions of a regional nature which impact on local communities. As the internal political structure of communities has become somewhat more open and democratic, the resolving of major issues has moved to higher levels of government or to agencies beyond the reach of the local electorate.[34]

If representatives of absentee capital become less directly involved in

33. For an extensive bibliography on this process, see the varous essays in Michael Aiken and Paul Mott, ed., *The Structure of Community Power* (New York: Random House, 1970), as well as their bibliography on pp. 527-38. For some of these processes which involved a Massachusetts shoe manufacturing town, see William R. Cole, Jr., "Brockton, Massachusetts: A History of the Decline of a Shoe Manufacturing City, 1900-1933" (Ph.D. diss., Boston University, 1968).

34. This type of process is discussed in Mott, "Role of the Absentee-Owned Corporation in the Changing Community," pp. 170-79, an essay which focuses on Ypsilanti, Michigan; and Alford and Friedland, "Political Participation and Public Policy."

local politics, a power vacuum often develops in the local polity, thus bringing about fundamental changes in the interaction among various components of the local social structure. In the same period in which absentee economic dominants have become less involved in local affairs, labor unions not only have increased their membership but also have increased their influence in local politics. Labor unions have become especially important in balancing the influence of other powerful groups, as our studies of Lansing, Michigan, Lorain, Ohio, and other cities demonstrate.[35]

Increased industrialization not only leads to more structural differentiation, increased complexity, and greater heterogeneity in the community social structure, but also to a more pluralistic political structure. Partly as a result of this pluralism, lower income groups are able to wield greater influence in local politics. Communal ties, which formerly restrained such groups, become weaker. Workingclass people clearly exercise greater influence over those decisions of a purely local nature than was the case a century ago. And as state and national bureaucracies set guidelines for local government, increased opportunities for lower income groups to wield local political power have appeared in many communities. For example, blacks in southern cities have increased their political influence, protected by the federal courts and bureaucracies, though at the expense of the political autonomy of southern cities.

Of course, there is variation in the influence which lower income groups exert in local affairs, and differences in the political structures of cities help to explain this variation. For example, Samuel P. Hays has demonstrated with research on several cities that increasing the size of city councils and providing ward-based elections usually enhance representation for lower income groups by providing them with their own spokesmen. If such spokesmen become influential in legislative bodies with budgetary, investigatory, and various supervisory powers over the urban bureaucracy, the influence of the lower income group increases. This view can, however, easily be overstated. It is important to observe that

35. James R. Hudson, "Power with Low Prestige: A Study of Labor Unions in a Dependent Community" (Ph.D. diss., University of Michigan, 1966); Warner Bloomberg, Jr., "The Power Structure of Our Industrial Community" (Ph.D. diss., University of Chicago, 1961); James B. McKee, "Status and Power in the Industrial Community: A Comment on Drucker's Thesis," *American Journal of Sociology* 108 (January 1953): 364-70; Charles R. Walker, *Steeltown* (New York: Harper, 1950); William H. Form, "Organized Labor's Place in Community Power Structure," *Industrial and Labor Relations Review* 12 (1959): 526-39; James B. McKee, "Organized Labor and Community Decision-Making" (Ph.D. diss., University of Wisconsin, 1953).

groups may exercise influence over some types of issues, but not over others. Decentralizing and fragmenting urban structures have increased the power of lower income groups over symbolic goods (for example, patronage jobs). This has usually intensified ethnic rivalries and minimized the potential for class alignments. As a result, urban fragmentation and decentralization have minimized the influence of lower income groups over issues involving collective goods (that is, goods such as public parks, clean air, and fluoridation that everyone can share). Robert R. Alford and Roger Friedland have concluded that the decentralization of cities has encouraged low income groups to participate at a level of government where the political and economic power of those interests that control resources critical to the solution of such problems is not located. In other words, the structure of the urban political system encourages low income groups to participate at those points where effective policy making does not take place. This is, in certain respects, what Murray Edelman means by symbolic politics.[36]

Industrialization has fundamentally altered both the internal and external relations of American communities. Internally, communities have become more socially heterogeneous, more competitive politically, more egalitarian as to social structure, and more pluralistic. In the process, however, communities have tended to lose their political autonomy. Decisions made hundreds or even thousands of miles away may determine whether the economy of a community will die, stagnate, or flourish.

As one scans the history of American communities over the last century, it appears that those with the greatest autonomy generally had more centralized and monolithic social and political power structures. And those communities which have become more pluralistic in their power structures have become less autonomous, less capable of controlling their destiny.[37]

Even though the number of functions performed exclusively by American cities has declined over time, we must not assume that the society's political system has become entirely centralized. Political problems have

36. Alford and Friedland, "Political Participation and Public Policy." Also consult Terry N. Clark, "Community Power," *Annual Review of Sociology* 1 (1975): 271-95, for a discussion of the literature supporting these views. Also see Samuel P. Hays, "The Social Analysis of American Political History, 1880-1920," *Political Science Quarterly* 80 (September 1965): 373-94; Murray Edelman, *The Symbolic Uses of Politics* (Urbana: University of Illinois Press, 1964), and *Politics as Symbolic Action: Mass Arousal and Quiescence* (*Chicago: Markham, 1971*).

37. Support for these views is provided in Aiken and Mott, eds., *The Structure of Community Power.*

steadily increased in complexity and scope, with the result that functions and powers are shared by local, state, and national levels of government. All levels increasingly share in most policy areas. The formulation, implementation, funding, and evaluation of policies have become increasingly defined by interdependence between local and higher levels of government. Power has become increasingly diffused at all levels of the political system. As Donald Haider reminds us, "government levels have become . . . mutually interdependent and inseparable in decisional sphere and sharing of powers."[38] More and more, however, revenues are raised and policies are formulated at the central level, and the local level implements them. As this trend continues, the structure and well-being of cities are beyond the control of their inhabitants.

POLITICAL CULTURE COMPONENTS

Despite the preceding efforts to outline prevailing patterns of relationships among economic, social, and political structures of cities, it is important to keep in mind that there is no direct one-to-one relationship between changes in the social and economic structures and changes in the political structures of cities. Even as we analyze tendencies for certain kinds of socioeconomic structures to be associated with specific types of political structures, we recognize that situational and cultural factors also influence the relationships between socioeconomic structures and political structures.

A situational factor is unpredictable, the result of a random or accidental act which influences an event or set of events. Cultural factors refer to the norms which provide legitimacy, justification, and meaning to acts. As Robert Alford has reminded us, cultural traits represent "the historical cumulation of community experiences" which provide the norms by which individuals act.[39] Cultural factors may transform the economic, political, and social structures of a community, though cultural factors in turn are influenced by the socioeconomic as well as political structures of a community.

Political culture refers to individuals' political orientations and attitudes toward the political system and its parts, toward the role of individuals in the political system. Political culture is an enduring pattern of interaction among status groups. It reflects norms as well as orientations and attitudes and refers to the psychological dimension of politics, to how governments ought to be conducted and what governments should try

38. Donald Haider, "The Political Economy of Decentralization," *American Behavioral Scientist* 15 (September-October 1971): 113.

39. Alford, "Comparative Study of Urban Politics," p. 268.

to do.[40] And cultural differences across communities help to account for variations in governmental structure, rhetorical styles, administrative practices, and functions of government. Every historian knows that the political culture of southern communities differed from that in New England at the turn of the century, but so far we have not been very successful in systematically analyzing the two types of political cultures.

It is useful to think of political culture as a continuum (see table 1.3). At one extreme is a *traditional political culture* and at the other end is a *legal-rational political culture*. Elements of both of these types are to be found in most every American community, though some communities have essentially a traditional political culture and others have a legal-rational culture. For example, the traditional political culture is more likely to be dominant in a community which has a pyramidal social structure and an autocratic political system. Significantly, the traits of a traditional political culture are more widespread in communities which have a low per capita income and wealth, as well as a relatively uneducated citizenry. Historically, this type of culture was more common in the American South than in any other part of the country, and prior to the arrival of the Irish and of immigrants from southern and eastern Europe it was quite uncommon in New England.[41]

While there are exceptions—for example, the Irish—those who share the characteristics of the traditional political culture not only feel a low obligation to participate in the political process but also believe that they have little ability to influence or manipulate the political system. In other words, there is little concern with the upward flow of policy, and there is much more concern with the way policy affects individuals—or the downward flow of power.

Among those who share the traditional political culture, there is considerable cynicism toward the political system. There is the belief that decisions are made on the basis of particularistic and ascriptive criteria. The political system is highly personalized, with friends and relatives perceived as shaping decisions. In cities with a traditional culture, political elites are indeed recruited very much as a result of ethnic, racial, religious,

40. Donald Devine, *The Political Culture of the United States* (Boston: Little, Brown, 1972), p. 15. Two studies which analyze political culture in American history from a perspective very different from the one here are Robert Kelly, "Ideology and Political Culture from Jefferson to Nixon," *American Historical Review* 82 (June 1977): 531-62; and Ronald P. Formisano, "Deferential-Participant Politics: The Early Republic's Political Culture, 1789-1840," *American Political Science Review* 68 (1974): 473-87.

41. Terry N. Clark, "Catholics, Coalitions, and Policy Outputs," in *Urban Problems and Public Policy*, ed. Robert Lineberry and Louis H. Masotti (Lexington, Mass.: D.C. Heath, 1975), pp. 65-78, and "The Irish Ethic and the Spirit of Patronage," *Ethnicity* 2 (1975): 305-59.

Table 1.3. Central Dimensions of Political Culture

	Traditional	Legal-Rational
Conception of participation	Low obligation to participate Low expectations from government	High obligation to participate High expectations from government
Conception of recruitment patterns	Ascriptive, particularistic criteria important	Achievement and universal-istic criteria important
Conception of political process	Decisions very much influ-enced by particularistic, ascriptive criteria Highly personalized approach to political issues Politics is dirty and sordid	Rational, pragmatic con-siderations influence reactions to policy Bureaucratic and profes-sional norms employed in policy making Politics is purposive for improving society, is public service centered around conception of public good
Conception of public policy	Role of government should be limited Government primarily involved in caretaker and traditional type functions	Government to promote well-being of society Government is highly innovative, very much concerned with amenity-type policies
Level of eco-nomic develop-ment of city	Relatively low level of economic development, usually found in preindustrial or early industrializing stage	Relatively high level of economic development, usually found in highly urbanized society and service-oriented economy
Type of social structure of city	Culture shaped by those who are poorly educated, who generally have very low level of skills, and who are low in the stratification system	Culture generally shaped by those who are well educated, who have high levels of skills, and who are in the middle or higher strata of the stratification system

or family considerations. And participation is heightened when it is viewed as a means of advancing the interests of particularistic ethnic and religious groups.

Those sharing the traditional culture clearly view politics in particu-laristic terms. Indeed, many who participate in politics frequently do so primarily to promote private interests and their own advancement. There

is very little effort to professionalize or bureaucratize the political process in order to increase the level of governmental efficiency, for this would interfere with the use of personal influence. In general, there is a low commitment to or expectation of honesty in government.

Even though politics is perceived in particularistic terms, there is a widely held view that the role of government should be limited. There is very little expectation that government should undertake policies which are designed to benefit the public interest. Rather, it is believed that the public interest benefits only as the unintended consequence of actions by a selfish group of political elites. As a result of these attitudes, the function of government is perceived primarily as that of caretaker, of simply providing the traditional and minimum level of services for the community.

The various components of a legal-rational political culture are at the opposite end of the continuum on each of these variables. Significantly, the legal-rational political culture is generally most widely found in cities with a diamond-shaped social structure and a polyarchical political system. (See the five types of cities at the end of this chapter.) Among those who share the legal-rational culture, there is a strongly held view that it is their duty to participate in politics. They also have a high sense of efficacy—that is, the belief that they can influence the political system.

Moreover, there is a high expectation that people will be recruited to political positions on the basis of demonstrated achievement and competence. And while recruitment on the basis of ascriptive criteria occurs to some extent in any political system, there nevertheless is a belief that people should not be recruited on the basis of religion, race, ethnicity, and family considerations.

Concerned very much with considerations of efficiency and economy in government, legal rationalists advocate systematic and detailed planning in the solving of community problems. There is a willingness, if not outright demand, for government to be involved in solving community problems. There is also the expectation that government should be innovative, especially in the areas involving health and welfare, police, and education. Because larger cities often are more involved in planning than smaller cities, legal-rational considerations—especially in ethnically homogeneous cities—tend to increase as the size of cities rises.

Related to the emphasis on planning is a willingness to have professionals involved in the making of community decisions—especially in areas involving public health, education, and safety. While informal agreements are necessary in any political system, there is considerable willingness to use litigation, the police, the courts, and other public agencies to reach formal agreements in the solving of community conflicts. This leads to higher levels of bureaucratization which in turn lead to higher

levels of professionalization, greater emphasis on efficiency, and more formal communication.

In a legal-rational political culture, strains and contradictions emerge as the result of the interaction of heightened levels of participation on the one hand, and increases in the levels of professionalization and bureaucratization on the other. In a highly developed society the population becomes increasingly politicized and demands for equality and social rights continue to rise: the rights of women, school children, the poor, and racial and ethnic minority groups. Demands for more and more public services are made. To cope with demands the scale of governmental activities increases, political roles become more differentiated, and the size and complexity of private and public bureaucracies increases. In the process the norms of bureaucratization slowly begin to prevail throughout the political system.

As a society's as well as a community's level of economic development increases, populations become more politicized at the same time that expectations increase for high levels of professionalization and bureaucratization. But the emphasis on egalitarianism and on individual participation in shaping community decisions frequently clashes with the demands for professional services and bureaucratization. Because bureaucratization tends to insulate elites from outside forces, there is a tendency for bureaucratic activity to become shrouded with a great deal of secrecy. Within bureaucracies, professionals tend to be more concerned with the opinions of their colleagues in other communities, and even other countries, than with the attitudes of their clients. Moreover, the norms of professionalization require that decisions be made according to professional standards— which may run contrary to popular opinions. When citizens demand a voice in managing community affairs and at the same time insist on having a highly professional and bureaucratized government, the tensions between popular participation and bureaucratization become exposed. Professionalization of administrators and a kind of populism clash, as the desire for participation reacts to "technocratic" decision making.[42]

Because all cities have some elements of the traditional as well as the legal-rational political culture, any statements about the types of structures associated with specific political cultures are by necessity *tendency* state-

---

42. These trends in the industrialization process are discussed elsewhere in J. Rogers Hollingsworth, "Political Change in Industrializing Societies," in *Emerging Theoretical Models in Social and Political History*, ed. Allan G. Bogue (Beverly Hills, Calif.: Sage Publications, 1974), pp. 97-121, "Social Development in the North Atlantic Community," in *Problems in Political Development*, ed. Kemal Karpat (Ankara: Hacettepe University Press, forthcoming), and *The Politics of Nation and State Building: The American Experience* (Boston: Little, Brown, 1971), pp. 251-77.

ments. As indicated above, communities with a pyramidal social structure and autocratic political system *tend* to have a traditional political culture, while cities with sizable middle and upper classes and a polyarchic political system *tend* to have a legal-rational political culture. But neither the traditional nor legal-rational political culture is dominant in cities with a cone-shaped social structure and oligarchic political system. In these cities there are various mixes of both types of political cultures. Cities with mixed political cultures tend to be ethnically heterogeneous, with one group (for example, the Irish) ranking high on indicators of a traditional political culture and other groups (for example, the Scandinavians) ranking high on the legal-rational dimension. Moreover, each ethnic group, like each city, is a mixture of the traditional as well as the legal-rational political culture. In his illuminating work on Slavic immigrant groups John Bodnar has demonstrated that the traditional culture was slowly integrated with the new culture, the result being a blend of the traditional and "the modern."[43]

As the economic base of a community with a pyramidal social structure shifts from extractive to manufacturing or tertiary activity, political culture shifts as well. Obviously there is a circular process involving the relationship between structural and cultural variables. While the political culture of a community influences political structures, the new structures in turn bring about new attitudes in the community. As the middle stratum of communities expands, the population becomes more politicized and the support for higher levels of professionalization and bureaucratization increases. Thus, the pattern of American historical change is one in which a higher percentage of cities becomes the polyarchic type (cell E in table 1.2).

Some communities that have diamond-shaped social structures still have oligarchic political systems, for political cultural traits tend to persist once having come into existence. Socioeconomic structures may alter political structures only after a time lag. In other words, styles of leadership and political decisions shaped in the past often establish a set of procedures and processes which are difficult to alter—although changes in social and economic structures eventually do bring about within the community new kinds of political structures, perspectives, rhetoric, and goals.

PUBLIC POLICY

While structural, cultural, and situational factors act upon one another,

43. For an excellent discussion of the political culture of Scandinavians in the United States, see Elazar, *Cities of the Prairie*. On the Irish, see Clark, "Irish Ethic and the Spirit of Patronage." Also see Bodnar, "Immigration and Modernization."

their interaction shapes policy outcomes. One may devote much attention to analyzing communities in terms of their structural and cultural characteristics, but ultimately the study of politics is incomplete unless we enhance our understanding of the policy dimension, unless we concentrate on what political systems do. We must now attempt to understand how the interaction of structural, cultural, and situational factors shape public policy. To what extent do cities with different kinds of structural and cultural traits vary in terms of who benefits, what type of policies are implemented, and what kind of issues are seldom raised? In other words, what kind of policy configuration exists with reference to variation in the structural and cultural traits of communities?

Public policy is one of those commonplace terms that we often do not know how to define but seem to know what it means when we encounter it. Perhaps most definitions of public policy are in basic agreement and differences are essentially semantic. For our purposes, however, we accept Robert Salisbury's definition: "public policy consists of authoritative or sanctioned decisions by governmental actors. It refers to the 'substance' of what government does and is to be distinguished from the processes by which decisions are made. Policy here means the outcomes or outputs of governmental processes."[44]

To discuss policies over time and to compare policies in one city with another poses difficult problems, foremost of which is the choice of policy categories to be used. There are two appealing ways of classifying public policy. First, one may use such traditional categories as police and fire, highways, parks and recreation, education, justice, health, etc. And this is, indeed, what we propose in chapter 3 and to a limited extent here. Second, one might use more abstract or more generalizable concepts. As both approaches are quite legitimate, we employ each, beginning first with the latter approach.

With that strategy we analyze local government policies within the following four categories: (1) promoting economic growth and the generation of wealth; (2) maintaining caretaker or traditional services; (3) providing amenities; and (4) promoting community morality and order (that is, social control policies).[45]

44. Robert Salisbury, "The Analysis of Public Policy: A Search for Theories and Roles," in Political Science and Public Policy, ed. Austin Ranney (Chicago: Markham, 1968), p. 152.

45. For other attempts to categorize public policy, see Theodore Lowi, "American Business, Public Policy, Case Studies, and Political Science," World Politics 16 (July 1964): 677-715; and Lewis A. Froman, Jr., "An Analysis of Public Policies in Cities," Journal of Politics 29 (February 1967): 94-108. The categorization to which this study is most indebted is Oliver P. Williams and Charles Adrian, Four Cities (Philadelphia: University of Pennsylvania Press, 1963), pp. 23-26, 272.

Policies promoting economic growth are designed to increase the wealth and size of a community. The American tradition of local activity in promoting community growth is a long one, involving, for example, such nineteenth-century activities as dealing with land development and the attraction of railroads and industry. In the twentieth century, cities have attempted to promote economic development by implementing tax policies designed to attract business firms to the community and by maintaining high-quality local services, governmental efficiency, and a reputation for fair play to all citizens. These policies generally call for a fairly high level of local expenditures, with the result that support often comes from higher income groups. As James O'Connor and others have pointed out when discussing these types of policies, urban governments generate an infrastructure and provide subsidies which allow for the accumulation of wealth.[46]

A local government which is concerned primarily with the maintenance of traditional services obviously perceives itself in very conservative terms. Certainly these governments are not very innovative and are reluctant to undertake services which go beyond the maintenance and/or support of minimal levels of schools, streets, sidewalks, police, and so on. Governments which perceive themselves in these terms are usually in cities which justify tax increases in order to carry out the traditional functions of government. The major concern of such a government, however, is maintaining low taxes. Cities which have governments of this type generally have a high percentage of adults who are homeowners with quite modest incomes, who feel that they are living beyond their means, who cannot afford high taxes, and who usually do not perceive the need for innovative

46. Useful literature on the economic development and "booster" spirit in American cities consists of Daniel J. Boorstin, *The Americans: The National Experience* (New York: Random House, 1965), pt. 3; Frank Freidel, "Boosters, Intellectuals, and the American City," in *The Historian and the City*, ed. Oscar Handlin and John Burchard (Cambridge, Mass.: M.I.T. Press, 1966), pp. 115-20; Bayard Still, "Patterns of Mid-Nineteenth Century Urbanization in the Middle West," *Mississippi Valley Historical Review* 28 (September 1941): 187-206; Harlan Hahn, "The Lost History of Boomtown: Some Interpretations of Hamlin Garland," *Annals of Iowa*, 3rd ser., 37 (Spring 1965): 606, 609-10; Justin Fuller, "Boom Towns and Blast Furnaces: Town Promotion in Alabama, 1885-1893," *Alabama Review* 29 (January 1976): 37-48; Doris Ann Phelan, "Boosterism in St. Louis" (Ph.D. diss., St. Louis University, 1970); Golda M. Crawford, "Railroads of Kansas: A Study of Local Aid, 1859-1930" (Ph.D. diss., Syracuse University, 1963). Also consult the extensive bibliographic citations in Carter Goodrich, *Government Promotion of Canals and Railroads in the United States* (New York: Columbia University Press, 1960). On the role of state and local government in promoting economic development, see Harry H. Scheiber, "Federalism and the American Economic Order, 1789-1910," *Law and Society Review* 10 (Fall 1975): 57-118. An important study on the role of government in the accumulation of wealth process is James O'Connor, *The Fiscal Crisis of the State* (New York: St. Martin's Press, 1972).

policies. While cities such as these will from time to time hire outside experts (that is, professional city managers), government is generally controlled by "locals"—Main Street merchants, local attorneys, and professional politicians.

The caretaker government is concerned primarily with those items which are considered necessities for the community, whereas some governments are primarily concerned with pursuing amenities or comforts for the community. The amenity-oriented government emphasizes beauty, quiet, and safety. Population growth is often viewed as objectionable, for growth may not be synonymous with restfulness and beauty. The amenity policies generally call for higher expenditures and high quality services, while support for such policies generally comes from higher income groups.

All governments make some effort to enforce certain components of the moral code of its citizenry. The kind of morality and the intensity with which moral codes are defined in public policy are obviously shaped by a number of variables—with the level of income, wealth, and education of the citizenry and the ethnocultural character of the community among the most important ones. The maintenance of prohibition, the passage and enforcement of blue laws, and the enforcement of gambling laws are examples of issues which fall within this policy area.

Policy for promoting community morality and order (that is, social control) may also be defined more broadly, as all policies preventing social disruption in either the short or long run. Thus, welfare for the indigent may be considered a form of social control policy. Or education policy, which presumably socializes youth into structures and predominant cultures, may be considered social control.

Morality-oriented law in communities in a highly industrialized society differs greatly from that in a society with a low level of economic development. In the former, law becomes more technical and complex, causing litigation to become more costly and courts to be busier. In less complex societies most everyone is familiar with the law—especially as it relates to morality—for there is very little about law which is technical or complicated. In this society the outcomes of violations are much more predictable, and there is much more enforcement of morality involving sex, blasphemy, and the like. But the more highly industrialized the society, the less concerned is the legal system with enforcements of profanity and religious statutes. As the needs of the society change, so do the kind of demands which are placed on the political system. Lawrence Friedman reminds us that law reflects the agenda of controversy—the things that are in actual dispute. As the society industrializes, there is a necessary change in the kinds of disputes confronting the society. This results in communities'

pursuing different moral policies over time, with less emphasis on religion-centered morality as secularization increases. The communities most concerned with morality policies are those with the lowest levels of economic development, or those in which a group in a heterogeneous population uses morality policies as a form of political control over other population segments.[47]

An effort to classify specific policies poses some problems, however. First, no scheme can predict with accuracy whether a specific city will initiate, adopt, and implement specific policies, though we can understand the general limits or parameters on governmental policies. Second, every policy cannot easily be categorized. Indeed, the classification of certain policies is by necessity arbitrary. An amenity policy, by making a community attractive, may be supporting economic growth. Moreover, the extent to which a policy is an amenity is culturally defined. The paving of streets or the building of a high school might have been considered an amenity in 1870, whereas in 1960 such policies might have been considered traditional or caretaker in nature. Third, policies are determined not only by the preferences of how citizens wish to live but also by the needs of a community. Thus, a new city with preferences for a caretaker city policy may have needs for certain amenities in the short run—though over time its policy configuration tends more toward the caretaker. Thus, age and rate of growth influence policy choices. Even so, we believe that these four policy categories are useful in helping us to understand the local policy process and the kinds of policies which are related to certain kinds of community structures. Communities usually support all four kinds of policies simultaneously, though in varying degree. Indeed, most cities have a complex profile, though some of them can be classed as supporting certain types of policies more frequently than others.

For example, cities with a traditional political culture, a pyramidal social structure, and an autocratic political system generally emphasize the caretaker function of government and devote very few resources to economic growth or to amenities. Economic development policies for these communities tend to increase the level of wages, something which is anathema to the elites which tend to dominate this sort of community.

47. Lawrence M. Friedman, "Notes Towards a History of American Justice," *Buffalo Law Review* 24 (1975): 111-34, "Explorations in Criminal Justice" (paper presented before the Yale University Law Faculty, New Haven, Conn., February 26, 1976), and "San Benito, 1890: Legal Snapshot of a County," *Stanford Law Review* 27 (February 1975): 687-701. For a discussion of law as an instrument of social control in an ethnically diverse community, see Reader, "Yankees, Immigrants, and Social Climbers." Also see Paul Boyer, *Urban Masses and Moral Order in America, 1890-1970* (Cambridge, Mass.: Harvard University Press, 1978).

And the per capita income of the community is too low and the population too transient to be very concerned with amenities.

Cities with a mixed political culture, a cone-shaped social structure, and an oligarchical political system also place considerable emphasis on caretaker functions. Some of these communities support policies designed to promote economic development, though amenities are generally minimized. Having mixed political cultures, these communities often have acrimonious political debates, particularly over policies involving social control. Not only are disputes involving corruption and dishonesty frequent, but these communities tend to have sharp cleavages involving race and ethnic relations.

Cities with considerable resources tend to place more emphasis on amenity-type policies. Generally, these are cities which have either a diamond-shaped, inverted cone, or inverted pyramidal social structure and have a polyarchic political structure and a legal-rational political culture. This sort of city, on a per capita expenditure basis, invests considerable resources on amenities, as well as on maintaining the standard caretaker functions.

Thus far we have emphasized the relationship between the policy orientation of cities and their cultural and structural dimensions. The problem of comprehending variation in urban policies is more complicated than this, however, since variations in urban configuration are also very much influenced by city age, size, and regional location. We observe this when we consider another dimension or continuum of political activity: the scope or pervasiveness of government, the extent to which cities assume few or many functions of government. Unfortunately, there is little literature which has systematically focused on the variation in the scope of governmental activities at the urban level.[48]

We might think of a continuum with cities at one end having responsibility for few functions of government, and those at the other end having responsibility for most functions. In the American setting there are at least ten functions of government which all communities may share: police, fire, highways, welfare, courts, hospitals, education, sewers, preventive health (sanitation, water purification, food inspection, etc.), and parks and recreation.

Nearly every city provides police, fire, and highway functions, but there is considerable variation in the extent to which they provide the

48. A useful place to begin is with the literature to which this section is indebted: Roland J. Liebert, *Disintegration and Political Action: The Changing Functions of City Governments in America* (New York: Academic Press, 1976), and "The Functional Scope of City Governments in America: An Interorganizational Analysis of Causes and Consequences for Political Action" (Ph.D. diss., University of Wisconsin, 1973).

other functions. Moreover, a city could be amenity-oriented—that is, it could provide excellent schools, parks, and recreational facilities—but be relatively uninvolved in welfare, the judicial process, hospital care, and preventive health activities because governments at other levels assume responsibility for those functions. In other words, an amenity-oriented city could have a very limited scope of functions. Similarly, a city could be "caretaker-oriented" but be involved in each function, though spending a bare minimum in each category.

The age and region of cities best explain the variation in the scope of their activities. For example, the oldest cities of the country—those extending from Maine to New York City—have provided more functions than cities elsewhere, with cities in the Middle Atlantic and eastern border states close behind. In cities of the South and West, however, the scope of government diminishes. The explanation for this phenomenon is largely a historical one. For example, seventeenth- and eighteenth-century cities were granted extensive powers to deal with the full range of governmental functions. And while the functions of cities did not vary substantially until the twentieth century, the time at which a city was established brought certain institutional arrangements and practices into existence that have tended to persist to the present and that explain much of the variation in the functional scope of city governments.

As Michael Zuckerman has pointed out, colonial New England towns were little kingdoms which had almost exclusive jurisdiction over most of the governmental functions performed within them. New England counties were and have continued to be relatively inactive. Because the counties have been relatively unimportant in New England's history, the functions of government in even small New England cities have been similar to those in larger cities such as Boston, Providence, or New Haven.[49]

In the South in the eighteenth and nineteenth centuries, however, there were few cities. And, of course, it was out of the question for plantations to have the functions of government carried out by cities in the East. As a result, power was consolidated in the county and state govern-

---

49. Andrew E. Nuquist, *Town Government in Vermont* (Burlington: University of Vermont Press, 1964); Frank A. Updyke, "County Government in New England," *Annals of the American Academy of Political and Social Science* 47 (May 1913): 26-38; Zuckerman, *Peaceable Kingdoms;* Liebert, "Functional Scope of City Governments in America," pp. 6, 20, 46; E.S. Griffith, *History of American City Government: The Colonial-Period* (New York: Oxford University Press, 1938); Jon C. Teaford, "The Municipal Revolution in America: Origins of Modern Urban Government, 1650-1825" (Ph.D. diss., University of Wisconsin, 1973); James A. Merino, "A Great City and Its Suburbs: Attempts to Integrate Metropolitan Boston, 1865-1920" (Ph.D. diss., University of Texas, 1968).

ments of the South—a pattern which has persisted to the present. And in the trans-Mississippi West, state and county governments usually developed in advance of city governments, with the result that western cities never developed a tradition of the extensive scope of government which has persisted in New England.[50]

In recent years relatively new cities, regardless of region, have tended to emerge with rather few functions, reflecting the twentieth-century belief that city government should have specialized roles rather than the more diffuse functional mandates provided in seventeenth- and eighteenth-century cities. Moreover, in the process of "modernization," the nation has become more committed to the notion that higher governmental authorities should be involved in the functions which older cities have assumed as their prerogative. As Roland J. Liebert reminds us, "newer cities have assumed a narrower scope of functions than older cities, and have somewhat less political autonomy." Thus, suburban cities in the East provide fewer functions than older central cities of the same region and have less economic and political autonomy than older cities. But there are more complex reasons why suburban cities—regardless of region—have a narrow scope of government. Many suburbs are merely small parts of a large metropolis, and in many respects suburbs depend on central cities for hospitals, museums, zoos, and other facilities. But even though city size is positively related to the functional scope of cities, scholarship demonstrates that it is the age and region of a city—the maintenance of inherited traditions—which best predict the scope of a city government.[51]

While the economic and social structures help to explain whether a city is amenity- or caretaker-oriented, they are not very predictive as to whether a city has a broad or narrow scope of functions. As figure 2 demonstrates, political structural and process variables are strongly associated with broad functions. Cities with broad functional scope tend not only to be older and more eastern but also to have a political system which is more innovative, to have higher levels of voter participation, and to have a mayor-council form of government. Cities with a narrow scope of functions tend to be newer, to be less innovative, to have lower levels of voter

50. Kirk H. Porter, *County and Township Government in the United States* (New York: Macmillan, 1922); and Liebert, "Functional Scope of City Governments in America," pp. 53-56.

51. Liebert, "Functional Scope of City Government in America," and *Disintegration and Political Action*. See also A.H. Hawley, "Metropolitan Population and Municipal Government Expenditures in Central Cities," in *Cities and Society*, ed. P.K. Hatt and A.J. Reiss, Jr. (New York: The Free Press, 1957), pp. 773-82; Kasarda, "Impact of Suburban Population Growth on Central City Service Functions" and Phillip Earl Vincent, "Public Expenditure Benefit Spillovers and the Central City Exploitation Thesis" (Ph.D. diss., Stanford University, 1968).

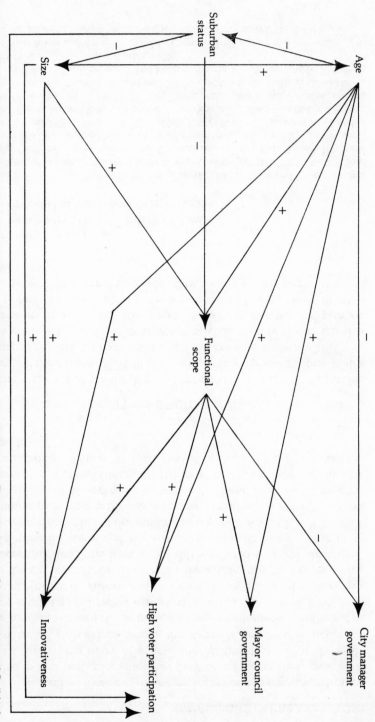

Figure 2. Relationship among variables.   For further commentary on these relationships, see Roland J. Liebert, *Disintegration and Political Action: The Changing Functions of City Governments in America* (New York: Academic Press, 1976), and "The Functional Scope of City Governments in America" (Ph.D. diss., University of Wisconsin, 1973).

participation, and to have city-manager forms of government. While it is possible to find particular cities that may deviate from these generalizations, a considerable body of scholarship demonstrates that there are strong statistical correlations among the variables presented in figure 2.[52] The precise causal connections between these phenomena and the scope of policy must await detailed historical investigation—though Michael Aiken and Robert R. Alford have offered theoretical explanations for some of these relationships. They make the assumption that cities with a broad scope of functions have more differentiated political structures. And the more differentiated the structures and the process, the more interaction and communication among key actors. And it is this increase of communication among diverse actors and institutions which increases the probability of innovations in particular issue arenas.[53] Similarly, the broader the scope of functions, the more points of access to elites by organized groups, which in turn stimulate higher levels of political participation.

TYPES OF CITIES

At this stage in our scholarship it is not possible to provide a complete typology of the structural, cultural, and policy considerations which have shaped the full configuration of all American cities since 1870. Instead, one must choose those characteristics which tend to cluster together from variables assessing age, size, region, structures, culture, and policies. And it is these characteristics from which the following types of cities emerge, types which tend to apply only to cities with populations of 250,000 or less.

A. *Autocratic community*
    (1) high level of vertical differentiation
    (2) low level of horizontal differentiation

52. Leo F. Schnore and Robert R. Alford, "Forms of Government and Socio-economic Characteristics of Suburbs," *Administrative Science Quarterly* 8 (June 1963): 1-17; Alford and Scoble, "Political and Socio-economic Characteristics of American Cities"; Raymond E. Wolfinger and John Osgood Field, "Political Ethos and the Structure of City Government," *American Political Science Review* 60 (June 1966): 308-26; Robert L. Lineberry and Edmund P. Fowler, "Reformism and Public Policies in American Cities," *American Political Science Review* 61 (September 1967): 701-16; Liebert, *Disintegration and Political Action*, and Bill John Henderson, "An Analysis of Economic Policies in American Cities: A Comparative Study of the Effect of Socio-Economic and Political System Variables on Public Policies in Cities" (Ph.D. diss., University of Kansas, 1972).

53. Michael Aiken and Robert R. Alford, "Community Structure and Innovation: The Case of Urban Renewal," *American Sociological Review* 35 (August 1970): 650-65.

   (3) high political autonomy
   (4) power monopolized by autocratic elite
   (5) rigid stratification system
   (6) traditional political culture
   (7) public policy oriented toward social control and caretaker characteristics with few amenities
   (8) narrow scope of policy functions
   (9) low level of political participation
  (10) low levels of professionalization and bureaucratization
  (11) relatively small community
  (12) level of economic autonomy varies
  (13) economy dominated by few firms
  (14) nonsuburban status

Examples of late-nineteenth-century cities:
   Irontown, Pennsylvania
   Marinette, Wisconsin
   Shenandoah, Pennsylvania
   Spartanburg, South Carolina
   Wilkinsburg, Pennsylvania

B. *Oligarchic community*
   (1) moderate level of vertical differentiation
   (2) moderate level of horizontal differentiation
   (3) high to moderate level of political autonomy
   (4) commercial or manufacturing economic base
   (5) level of economic autonomy varies
   (6) power dominated by one or more oligarchic groups
   (7) public policy oriented toward social control, caretaker, and/or economic development
   (8) scope of policy functions unpredictable
   (9) citizen participation in decision making restricted
  (10) city manager or nonpartisan elections unlikely
  (11) generally larger than autocratic communities
  (12) a mixture of traditional and legal-rational political culture
  (13) moderate to low level of professionalization and bureaucratization in city government
  (14) generally nonsuburban status, though occasionally community is industrial suburb

Examples of late-nineteenth-century cities:
   Attleboro, Massachusetts
   Cohoes, New York

Eau Claire, Wisconsin
Green Bay, Wisconsin
Janesville, Wisconsin
Naugatuck, Connecticut
South Bethlehem, Pennsylvania

C. *Polyarchic community*
   (1) low level of vertical differentiation
   (2) high level of horizontal differentiation
   (3) low level of political autonomy
   (4) fluid stratification system
   (5) commerce and/or service economic base, with administrative
       and professional activities increasing
   (6) legal-rational political culture
   (7) increasingly amenity-oriented public policy
   (8) in eastern part of country tendency to have mayor-council govern-
       ment, partisan elections, high levels of participation, broad
       functional scope of policies, older cities; in West tendency runs
       in opposite direction on each of these characteristics
   (9) suburban status variable
   (10) population wealthier, better educated, and less ethnically con-
        scious than in autocratic or oligarchic communities
   (11) high levels of professionalization and bureaucratization
   (12) the proportion of cities in this type increases as the society
        industrializes, per capita income increases, and the level of
        education rises

Examples of contemporary cities:
   Ann Arbor, Michigan
   East Lansing, Michigan
   Madison, Wisconsin
   New Haven, Connecticut

D. *Elite suburb*
   (1) low level of vertical differentiation
   (2) high level of horizontal differentiation
   (3) moderate level of political autonomy
   (4) legal-rational political culture
   (5) amenity-oriented public policy
   (6) relatively new city
   (7) narrow functional scope of policies
   (8) small population

    (9) tendency to have city manager and nonpartisan election
  (10) high level of professionalization and bureaucratization
  (11) political process quite open
  (12) dormitory community for large central city

Examples of contemporary cities:
    Grosse Point, Michigan
    Kenilworth, Illinois
    Lake Forest, Illinois

E. *Upper middle class suburb*
   (1) low level of vertical differentiation
   (2) high level of horizontal differentiation
   (3) low level of political autonomy
   (4) commercial base as well as dormitory for large central city
   (5) legal-rational political culture
   (6) amenity-oriented public policy
   (7) relatively new city but older than upper class suburb (above)
   (8) narrow functional scope of policies
   (9) tendency to have city manager and nonpartisan elections
  (10) high level of professionalization and bureaucratization

Examples of late-nineteenth-century cities:
    Brookline, Massachusetts
    Evanston, Illinois

As implied above, these ideal types, while they are extracted from primary and secondary historical sources, are mental constructs which do not exist in reality. They are conceptual tools for descriptive purposes and for making historical comparisons. All American communities will deviate, in some respects, from these predicted types, but the constructed type does serve as a basis for the comparison of individual cities. The types serve as statements about the behavior of cities, sensitizing devices to assist us in understanding deviations from expected behavior. Ideal types isolate behavior which is considered to be theoretically significant without specifying the frequency of that behavior. In this sense ideal types represent attempts to advance historical investigation beyond sheer description to a more theoretical level of analysis.

Ideal types, of course, are not precise statements of fact that can easily be directly validated or invalidated. By combining empirical observations with our ideal types, we enrich our potential for developing useful hypotheses about urban change. In the final analysis, we must, of course, subject our hypotheses to empirical verification. There is a circular process whereby

our historical research permits us to develop ideal types from which we generate hypotheses which in turn direct additional historical research, eventually permitting us to redefine our ideal types. It is the constant interplay of historical ideal types and historical specificity that will broaden our understanding of the subtle and complex patterns of social change.

2

Empirical Case Studies:
Eau Claire, Janesville, and Green Bay

INTRODUCTION

WHILE CHAPTER 1 delineated the types of cities based on comparative variable perspectives, this chapter will introduce considerations of time, space, and context to illuminate and refine these types of cities. Specifically, the focus is on three Wisconsin cities (Eau Claire, Janesville, and and Green Bay) during the last third of the nineteenth century. This chapter basically relies upon the historical specificity approach, a strategy different from but complementary to comparative variable analysis. Ideally, it is through historical specificity that comparative variable analysis is shaped and tested, and through comparative variable analysis that historically specific investigations gain greater order and focus.

This chapter, then, has several purposes: to provide a more concrete representation of the abstractions of chapter 1, to show how the dimensions set forth in that chapter can help in comprehending historical situations, and to show the limits in analytical models that may inhere due to cultural lags and external forces. There is no effort to test all the models from chapter 1, which would require a much larger universe of cities, and greater specification of variables, as well as data from many points in time.

This chapter is also intended to indicate some of the limits of the oligarchical type of city set forth above, to show some of the varieties of urban behavior that fit under the oligarchical model, to point out the mixtures of autocratic, oligarchic, and polyarchic characteristics that may develop in a single city, and to illustrate the complexity and variety of historical situations as we try to comprehend them.

These three cities can shed light on only a modest portion of the conceptual scheme from the preceding chapter. Study of the cities is limited

to about thirty years, which is usually not long enough for a community to move from one major type of city to a different major type. All of these cities were in the Midwest, and thus may exemplify stages and processes that would have unfolded somewhat differently in another region. The pages which follow show how the oligarchical city was represented in late-nineteenth-century reality. There may be other guises, too, for oligarchic cities. And the materials which follow make no claim toward the substantiation of the autocratic or polyarchic city. Other studies must do that. We seek in this chapter to indicate how the dimensions of oligarchic cities can be illustrated, and how those dimensions interacted. As we discuss these three cities, our major concern is with political dimensions.

One cannot relate the types of cities, or the concepts, in chapter 1 to space and time without considerable exploration of historical context, but, as we consider historical context, we need to bear in mind that urban units are constantly interacting with a larger world. Events at county, state, national, and even international levels impinge on local institutions and events, and the way in which communities could and did respond was shaped by their historical patterns and structures. Long-term subtle effects from the outside world were inescapable for middle-sized and other cities, and cities adjusted to them depending on the variety and strength of local institutions. There was a kind of inevitability in the interplay between external force and internal adjustment, at least in the long run. But in the short run, events had different local manifestations due to variations in historical context.[1]

As we turn to oligarchical cities we will be concerned in each case study with structural variables, political culture, and public policy, in that order. Given the shaping of culture and policy by structures, we will

---

1. For general information on Wisconsin during the late nineteenth century, see Robert C. Nesbit, *Wisconsin: A History* (Madison: The University of Wisconsin Press, 1973); Frederick Merk, *Economic History of Wisconsin during the Civil War Decade* (Madison: The University of Wisconsin Press, 1916); Eric Lampard, *The Rise of the Dairy Industry in Wisconsin: A Study in Agricultural Change, 1820-1920* (Madison: The State Historical Society of Wisconsin, 1963); David P. Thelen, *The New Citizenship: Origins of Progressivism in Wisconsin, 1885-1900* (Columbia: University of Missouri Press, 1972); Charles N. Glaab and Lawrence H. Larsen, *Factories in the Valley: Neenah-Menasha, 1870-1911* (Madison: The State Historical Society of Wisconsin, 1969); Robert F. Fries, *Empire in Pine: The Story of Lumbering in Wisconsin, 1830-1900* (Madison: The State Historical Society of Wisconsin, 1951). In our judgment the best single book on Wisconsin during this period is James Willard Hurst's *Law and Economic Growth: The Legal History of the Lumber Industry in Wisconsin, 1836-1915* (Cambridge, Mass.: Harvard University Press, 1964). Indeed, this relatively unknown book is one of the most important books yet written on nineteenth-century American history.

devote more attention to structures, the main measures of which are horizontal differentiation, vertical differentiation, and autonomy (political and economic).

EAU CLAIRE

Structural Dimensions

Economic Structure

The late nineteenth century was a time of great change in the complexity of structures of Eau Claire, be they economic, social, or political. New units were coming into existence on all fronts—not only new units in name, but new types of organizations and groups came into being. Although these increases in horizontal differentiation—in the number and types of local institutions, to state it differently—were most visible in the economic sector, they were also manifest in social and governmental aspects of city life.

Between 1870 and 1900 Eau Claire was transformed from three small villages with a population of less than 2500 to a city of over 20,000 in 1885, when it called itself the "second city of Wisconsin," and later to a moderately diversified city mixing industry and commerce. It moved, thus, from primary, extractive activity toward secondary manufacturing as its economic base. At its 1880s peak it was a lumber boom town, one of several dozen in the Midwest in the late nineteenth century. It was lumber that wholly set the tone of the city; when one spoke of economic structure or economic elites, one was talking of the lumber industry. Even in comparison to most other boom lumber cities, however, Eau Claire handled very large amounts of lumber. In its peak year, 1883, Eau Claire processed 253 million board feet. Among all lumber cities, this was a great volume, though not so much as was recorded at Muskegon or Bay City, Michigan, or for the twin cities of Marinette, Wisconsin and Menominee, Michigan.[2]

Eau Claire was at that stage in its economic development when the goal was to obtain as much lumber with as little effort and with as little

---

2. For additional information on Eau Claire and its economy, see Dale A. Peterson, "Lumbering on the Chippewa: The Eau Claire Area, 1845-1885" (Ph.D. diss., University of Minnesota, 1970); Duane D. Fischer, "The John S. Owen Enterprises" (Ph.D. diss., University of Wisconsin, 1964); Charles E. Twining, "Lumbering and the Chippewa River" (M.A. thesis, University of Wisconsin, 1963); James B. Smith, "The Movements for Diversified Industry in Eau Claire, Wisconsin, 1879-1907: Boosterism and Urban Development Strategy in a Declining Lumber Town" (M.A. thesis, University of Wisconsin, 1967); Charles Twining, *Downriver: Orrin H. Ingram and the Empire Lumber Company* (Madison: The State Historical Society of Wisconsin, 1975).

time as possible. At the individual level, the emphasis was on getting rich. There was little concern about the lumber industry's destruction of the environment. Few wondered what would happen to Eau Claire when lumber was exhausted, though the more successful the local industry, the sooner the day when Eau Claire's economic base would be eroded. Caught up in the ideology of laissez-faire market activity, residents believed that short-term maximization of the productive capacity of the community would promote the well-being of the citizenry in the long run.

Eau Claire was a town known throughout the Midwest for its lumber. At the confluence of the Chippewa and Eau Claire rivers, the city had excellent facilities for the holding and sorting of logs from the Chippewa pinery in bow-shaped Half Moon Lake. The damming of the Chippewa River in the late 1870s created a huge reservoir for logs and enabled a sizable lumber industry to emerge. Even such superior facilities, however, did not guarantee Eau Claire prosperity when logs were abundant. Local lumber interests had to struggle to protect themselves from competitors as well as the uncertainties of supply and markets. Protection required relatively unified action by lumber owners and firms, but even with relatively strong cooperation of lumber firm owners firms were unstable. Mergers and closures were common, and the dozen firms of the boom years of the eighties decreased eventually to four by the end of the century.

Certain interests in other cities favored driving logs past Eau Claire and taking them to saw mills at Mississippi River railheads. To enhance their investments, Eau Claire lumbermen wanted logs sawed locally and sent down river in cribs or moved by train from Eau Claire. They were interested in keeping the Chippewa south to the Mississippi River navigable by large lumber rafts, a point of no merit to the driving interests elsewhere that wanted to bypass the city. The latter wanted to improve log holding facilities south of Eau Claire, and they were willing to lower the water level of the Chippewa in order to improve the holding area known as Beef Slough. Lumbermen of Eau Claire fought such efforts as best they could, using both city and state government, but in 1879 over half of the logs on the Chippewa bypassed Eau Claire.[3] In the early 1880s the Eau Claire interests and the Mississippi men, headed by lumber baron Frederick Weyerhauser, came to an agreement, forming the Chippewa Logging Company, which owned five of every seven logs on the Chippewa. Under the agreed terms, "The Pool" controlled virtually all the organizations buying, handling, and sawing logs on the river, with Weyerhauser interests receiving 65 percent of "Pool" profits. Once "The Pool" was formed, only the Eau Claire mills participating in it had much prospect of survival.

3. Peterson, "Lumbering on the Chippewa."

The formation of "The Pool" helped Eau Claire to maintain its prominent position in "Chippewa logging," which otherwise would have more and more bypassed the city as the log-driving interests prevailed. Moreover, its activities demonstrated that a few men could dominate the economy of the area. Significantly, "The Pool" strengthened both the lumber industry and the oligarchical structure of Eau Claire.

A good lumbering year depended on many things: a cold, long winter, so the logs could be cut in the forest and moved over the packed snow easily to river banks; spring rains in April that moved the logs south— though not too much rain, for floods would sweep away river booms for catching logs and perhaps drive logs past mills. If the river was too low, the logs would not move, as in the winter of 1877-78.

Aside from competition with Mississippi log-driving interests, Eau Claire lumber firms also suffered from the uncertainties of climate, river level, and log jams, all of which kept log deliveries uncertain and irregular. During the years of greatest lumber activity the industry was never controlled or dominated by one firm or person. The lumber companies worked together on a variety of problems, from bonding for waterway improvements to lobbying for changes in railroad rates, and other powerful economic leaders or groups did not exist locally. The forces making for production and market instability did, of course, favor the companies that were economically strongest, and had some reserves upon which to draw.

Estimates are that some 7,000 men worked in the Chippewa pinery at its peak in the 1880s. With only 20,000 residents in Eau Claire at the time, it seems that virtually all workingmen were in the lumber industry—meaning that the economy of Eau Claire fluctuated seasonally. In the spring a large percentage of woodsmen left the forest and went to Eau Claire, some finding employment but most failing to do so. During the summer months some were involved in rafting logs downriver, a skilled and reasonably well-paid job. Others took jobs in the mills and thus had year-round employment. Unfortunately, no unemployment data are available, but the newspapers suggest that in any season of the year there were large numbers of unemployed men in Eau Claire. In the winter many mill workers were unemployed, unless they worked in the forests. The surplus of workers meant that wages were low and the problems of organizing workers into unions were difficult—another factor that facilitated an oligarchical structure.

In the 1870s and early 1880s Eau Claire lumber traveled west, but after the Michigan forests were depleted, Chippewa lumber was also needed in the East. With exports going to distant points, Eau Claire mill owners, in concert with the city's political elites, were engaged in a cease-

less battle with the railroads over rates. Most Eau Claire lumber moved by water because of the discriminatory railroad rates applied to lumber sent from Eau Claire. Not until 1891 did a decision favorable to Eau Claire emerge from the Interstate Commerce Commission concerning railroad rates, and by then the lumber industry was in serious decline.

Although a few mill owners were not residents of Eau Claire, and others resided there but had very substantial investments elsewhere, most of the mill owners were residents of Eau Claire. Their economic interests transcended their mills, sometimes by necessity, sometimes by choice. Mill owners sometimes associated themselves with manufactures which either facilitated the conversion of logs to lumber (for example, machine tool shops) or used lumber for finished products. The making of staves for barrels, the manufacture of boxes, the production of furniture, or of wagons and carriages, were all attractive investments for lumber men with extra capital. The roots of a somewhat diversified economy thus lay in spillover from the lumber industry. In the early 1880s the development of the Chippewa Valley required capital from other regions, but by the end of the decade the area was capital-exporting. The scale of lumber production in Eau Claire encouraged entrepreneurs to invest in wood-using industries, and thus they reinvested in city enterprises over the years. Later, when the primary product base of the economy collapsed, there were some ongoing nonlumber companies with manufacturing capabilities.

Lumber and the mills set the tone of Eau Claire life for most of the late nineteenth century. Eau Claire's population boomed with Chippewa lumber and contracted when the bounty of the forests was depleted. Having doubled in population between 1880 and 1885, Eau Claire lost 20 percent of its population between 1885 and 1890. Even so, Eau Claire's economy proved equal to the need to reorient itself, and by 1900 a relatively diversified commercial and industrial city had emerged. The success with which Eau Claire made this transition was due to several things: railway connections to distant points, the availability of prime manufacturing sites as centrally located sawmills closed, the reasonably fertile farm lands in the area, the availability of some skilled workers, and considerable local capital for reinvestment.[4]

The city's social and economic institutions were relatively well developed before the supply of trees were exhausted. What had been a frontier town in 1870 had become by 1890 a relatively settled city, with increasing horizontal differentiation in economic structures. When the lumber boom slowed, the city had enough capital, economic diversity, and dedicated

4. Fischer, "John S. Owen Enterprises," esp. pp. 406-7.

citizens to survive. As the economy shifted to a more diversified economic base, economic elites became more concerned with how they might contribute to the well-being of the community's future, whereas as long as the elites' economic interests had been tied to the cutting and processing of lumber, they were relatively unconcerned with building a community. A few other cities with reasonably long boom periods, where the boom slowed before it stopped, had much the same ability to adjust to the conditions which befell the lumber industry. Muskegon and Bay City, Michigan, are cases in point. On the other hand, Marinette, Wisconsin, and Menominee, Michigan, were twin lumber cities which went into a sharp and permanent decline once the surrounding forests were depleted. At the time of their peak lumber production, they milled substantially more lumber than Eau Claire in her peak years. But there were fewer good lumber years in Marinette-Menominee, and while mill owners lived in the communities, they had more of a tendency to invest their capital elsewhere. As a result, few feeder industries were spawned in the half-generation of lumber profit. Although mill owners were aloof to even minimal city needs, the end of the boom was not the end of the twin lumber cities—that is, not quite. But the economy did not adjust to the decline of lumber, and one-third of the population left in five years. Highly elite dominated, Marinette was more typical of what we think of as a boom town with an extractive base, and most boom towns eventually declined. Eau Claire, however, shifted to a more diversified economy with a multiple-element oligarchy and was thus able to survive.[5]

Eau Claire did experience a decline from a population of 21,668 in 1885 to a population of 17,415 in 1890. About a tenth of the population was in manufacturing in 1885, 1890, and 1900, but the nature of the manufacturing sector began to change substantially in the late 1880s. As was usually the case as saw milling declined, wood products of various types remained important to the economy. A few saw mills did continue to operate, even into the twentieth century. After 1890, however, Eau Claire became increasingly a trade center, prospering modestly with the development of west central Wisconsin. There were more types of non-wood industries, including footloose industries, and a more balanced secondary sector emerged, along with the beginning of a service sector.

5. Carl Edward Krog, "Marinette: Biography of a Nineteenth Century Lumbering Town, 1850-1910" (Ph.D. diss., University of Wisconsin, 1971); Fischer, "John S. Owen Enterprises"; and Smith, "Movements for Diversified Industry in Eau Claire, Wisconsin." For an interesting anaylsis of another city which survived the decline of lumber, see Richard D. Kurzhals, "Initial Advantage and Technological Change in Industrial Location: The Furniture Industry of Grand Rapids, Michigan" (Ph.D. diss., Michigan State University, 1973).

Table 2.1 demonstrates that the capitalization of timber-using firms in Eau Claire declined from 73 percent of all business sector capitalization in 1880 to 56 percent in 1900. And much of this 56 percent consisted of box, sash, and door factories instead of simply logging. Meantime, the capitalization of firms engaged in wholesale trade as well as in secondary manufacturing substantially increased during those two decades.

The adjustment process which Eau Claire underwent, away from primary products toward a more complex, diversified economy, was a process experienced wherever lumber dependency was pronounced. In a larger sense this effort to shift away from lumber dependency is a part of the process familiar in most mining and extractive areas, as the resource base fails and alternatives must be found.

The lumber industry, very much shaped by the business of markets elsewhere, along with the transportation changes approved by the ICC and the competition from other lumbering areas, permitted Eau Claire very little economic autonomy. Nor did the subsequent wood products

Table 2.1. Eau Claire: Capitalization of Firms, 1880–1900

	1880	1890	1900
Primary sector			
Timber-using	73.2%	57.4%	55.6%
Farm-product-processing	.1	1.0	.4
Secondary manufacturing			
Wood-using	1.2	4.2	3.4
Sawmill machinery	—	3.9	4.7
Other metal-using	—	2.6	—
Other	.1	.8	3.5
Wholesale trades	.1	1.7	7.6
Retail trade, service	25.3	28.4	24.8
Total	100.0%	100.0%	100.0%
Total capitalization	$3,147,000	$5,098,000	$5,576,000

Source: These data were compiled by using the Mercantile Agency's *Reference Books* for the appropriate years tabulating the nature of economic activity and capitalization of each firm. Firms were placed in categories according to guidelines developed by scholars working with economic growth patterns. The total capitalization for each of a dozen and a half economic sectors, as well as the number of firms therein, was collected, but the tables reported herein contain only more general types of economic activity. The classification technique was developed by James Bruce Smith, and it has been applied in his study of lumber towns in the cutover. See his "Lumbertowns in the Cutover: A Comparative Study of the Stage Hypothesis of Urban Growth" (Ph.D. diss., University of Wisconsin, 1973).

The Mercantile Agency was a division of R.G. Dun and Company, from which the Dun and Bradstreet Corporation descended. The records compiled by the Mercantile Agency and later by Dun and Bradstreet have enormous potential for the study of the American economy, but hitherto the sources have received limited use.

and diversified manufacturing phases. Later, Eau Claire was continuously involved in a national goods and services network, although in a different manner. The recognition that Eau Claire was tied into a national economic system in which it could exercise little influence was common to the city's elites throughout the late nineteenth and early twentieth centuries.

Social Structure

Substantial changes in Eau Claire were not, of course, confined to economic structures. As Eau Claire assumed a more settled aspect, as the influence of woodsmen declined, as the tide of immigration slowed, more and more social institutions emerged, and the social fabric altered in texture.

The most important changes were the increase in organizations (which served to integrate residents into the community and its subgroups) and the decrease in the percentage of the population that held jobs as unskilled laborers. Both of these changes gave rise to a greater sense of shared community, even in a city in which native-born persons were a minority.

Churches, with auxiliaries and friendship clubs, were established in larger numbers; social, patriotic, and benevolent organizations formed. In short, during the late nineteenth century after the boom days many organizations through which people might identify and speak had their beginnings. Still, many of these organizations were weak and small, or of uncertain duration. It is unclear what fraction of the population was involved in church or secular organizations. Extensive newspaper analysis, however, indicates that social elites belonged to many organizations and that there was considerable overlapping of memberships. Over time more ethnic organizations emerged, providing more opportunity for non-elite participation. But a careful reading of the Eau Claire newspapers suggests that most of the nonelite participation in voluntary organizations was related to ethnic ties.

While horizontal differentiation in economic and social structures was increasing in Eau Claire's social structure during the late nineteenth century, vertical differentiation was decreasing. Eau Claire's social structure had initially been a direct reflection of her dependence on lumber: the lumber industry required large numbers of men with low level skills. True, some aspects of log driving (scaling, for example) required expertise, but for most lumbermen, skill requirements were low. Though work conditions were hard and wages low, the possibility of *any* work was enough to attract large numbers of workingmen—particularly immigrants—to Eau Claire. Some came with families, or sent for them. Many lived alone, residing in boarding houses during the half of the year that they were not in the forests.

In this situation, two separate communities emerged by the early

1880s. On the one hand, there was a large, preponderantly male working class community, many of whom were without work much of the year, and on the other there was the much smaller commercial proprietor-professional community which lived somewhat apart from the workers. With this kind of life-style segregation, there was a certain amount of hostility between the two communities, although various factors mitigated sharp cleavages between them. For example, mill owners lived in Eau Claire and were highly visible to their employees. Such intermingling promoted company loyalties among some workers and made them somewhat willing to "trust the boss"—though there was variation from firm to firm.

The most important factor in minimizing friction between the two communities was the ethnic diversity of the lumber employees. To many observers Eau Claire was predominantly a foreign community from 1870 on, with over 70 percent of the population either born abroad or descended from foreign parents. And this ethnic diversity did much to minimize the development of class consciousness among workers.

As Lee Benson reminds us, the more ethnically diverse the community, the less the social class cohesion and social class conflict. And while there was more conflict in Eau Claire than in Green Bay and Janesville during the late nineteenth century, the ethnocultural diversity in Eau Claire was sufficient to keep class conflict to a minimum. And it is for this reason that Eau Claire does not lend credibility to the argument of Clark Kerr and Abraham Siegel that if employees live and work in a setting which multiplies their contacts with one another while reducing their access to other social groups and strata (for example, mining and lumber), there will be high class cohesion and social conflict.

Norwegians were the most numerous of the foreign groups—with Canadian, German, and Irish elements also large. Whereas Norwegians were solidly Lutheran, Germans were both Catholic and Protestant. Though Eau Claire supported several Catholic churches throughout the period, the general tone of community rhetoric—especially among the elites after the decline of the lumber industry—was of righteous Protestant wrath. One aspect of this fervor was temperance activity, relatively unceasing for about fifteen years. Another aspect of the tensions in the community, exacerbated by the pyramidal social structure, was the existence, in the 1890s, of chapters of the American Protective Association (see table 2.2).[6]

6. *Eau Claire Sunday Leader*, March 25, 1894; *Eau Claire Weekly Free Press*, June 7, 1894. For theoretical perspectives on class conflict, see Lee Benson, "Group Cohesion and Social

Table 2.2. Ethnic Characteristics of Heads of Families in Eau Claire: 1870, 1880, 1905

	1870	1880	1905
Foreign-born			
Canadian	12.8%	16.0%	8.5%
Irish	9.5	5.8	2.1
German	8.9	11.0	11.9
Norwegian	17.6	17.8	23.1
Other	8.5	7.6	7.0
Total	57.3	58.2	52.6
Native-born total	42.7	41.8	47.4
Grand total	100.0%	100.0%	100.0%
N =	1698	3408	3830

Source: Data were compiled from federal census manuscripts for 1870 and 1880, and from tabulated State of Wisconsin census materials for 1905. These materials are on deposit at the Wisconsin State Historical Society, Madison, Wisconsin.

Until the lumber industry fell on hard times, almost half the jobs in Eau Claire required only unskilled manual work, and these jobs were held disproportionately by Norwegians and Germans. Tabulated census data for 1870 reveals 77 percent of the labor force in low status positions (47 percent unskilled), with approximately 23 percent of the labor force in professional, managerial, or clerical work. Native-born Americans were overrepresented in higher status occupations. In 1880 the percentage of unskilled workers had increased to 60 percent. By 1905, however, the lumber industry had declined, and only 28 percent of the work force was in unskilled jobs. Thus, the shape of Eau Claire's social pyramid was changing during the latter part of the nineteenth century as vertical differentiation declined markedly (see table 2.3).[7]

Political Structure

Over time, political structures in Eau Claire altered from being fairly

---

and Ideological Conflict," in *Emerging Theoretical Models in Social and Political History,* ed. Allan G. Bogue (Beverly Hills, Calif.: Sage Publications, 1973), 123-49; Clark Kerr and Abraham Siegel, "The Interindustry Propensity to Strike," in *Industrial Conflict,* ed. Arthur Kornhauser et al. (New York: McGraw-Hill, 1954); James R. Lincoln, "Community Structure and Industrial Conflict," *American Sociological Review* 63 (April 1978): 199-220.

7. The U.S. Census manuscripts, Wisconsin State Census Reports, and unpublished tabulated census materials on population in Eau Claire during the late nineteenth and early twentieth centuries were useful for making these generalizations. These materials are available at the Wisconsin State Historical Society in Madison.

Table 2.3. Occupations of Heads of Families in Eau Claire: 1870, 1880, 1905ᵃ

	1870	1880	1905
Professionals	2.5%	2.4%	4.6%
Proprietors, managers, and officials	16.0	12.2	17.2
Clerks	4.4	4.3	11.0
Skilled and semi-skilled laborers	30.1	20.9	38.8
Unskilled laborers	47.0	60.2	28.4
Total	100.0%	100.0%	100.0%
N =	1634	3386	3464

Source: These data were compiled from federal census manuscripts for 1870 and 1880, and from tabulated State of Wisconsin materials for 1905. These materials are on deposit at the Wisconsin State Historical Society, Madison, Wisconsin.

ᵃPersons whose occupations were not listed in census manuscripts are omitted from this table. The number was 36 in 1870, 109 in 1880.

informal and unaccountable to a somewhat more complicated, slightly more responsive set of arrangements. Early city fervor about fusion politics moderated during the last third of the century, but political structures in Eau Claire remained relatively open.

In the political system, horizontal differentiation increased as the economic system became more diversified and complex: public employment expanded as more and more people were needed to provide specialized services in connection with schools, fire, police, streets, etc. By the end of the century, citywide there was more citizen expectation of services by the city, and some willingness to compensate those who undertook municipal services.

In the early 1870s Eau Claire had a relatively simple political structure. It had a mayor-council form of government—as it did throughout the late nineteenth century—with the mayor having rather modest powers aside from the authority to make appointments. The aldermen were elected from wards for two-year terms, the mayor for only a year. City government was, for most of the period, characterized by little long-range planning or systematization of procedures. For example, Eau Claire lacked routinized reporting from the city treasurer or any other city office. There were constant transfers of money among city, county, and state levels of government, and with poor bookkeeping, fiscal confusion was constant. Not until 1895 were regularity of accounting and more professionalism in money management arranged, as fiscal responsibilities were more carefully specified.

Similarly, in education, Eau Claire did not have a coordinated school

system until 1889. Prior to that time the school systems from each of the three small villages that joined to make up Eau Claire in 1872 continued to exist. Faced with state law requirements, Eau Claire finally initiated a unified school district, which meant the establishment of a more specialized bureaucracy in the public domain. After unification of the school districts, there was more attention to school affairs by city government and citizens, although the voice with which the schools spoke for themselves was neither loud nor clear. The authorities of the unified school district were still very much subject to council authority, and were not clearly recognized as separate in responsibility. And when a separate structure emerged, it was a rather simple one.

Within the city government, there were persons charged with police, fire, and health duties. Of these, the fire department drew the greatest resources and support. If new equipment were needed to keep the city from burning down, the city council would buy it. If the fire department needed more people, they would, within reason, be hired. The fire department, though small by modern standards, was recognized as having separate responsibilities and skills.

Although a Board of Health existed, it was generally inactive. Police were much more subject to questioning and control by municipal authorities than firemen or the health authorities. In that police were caught in the uneasy business of enforcing morality and standards only modestly shared by many citizens, their performance was limited. Partly as a consequence, police were not recognized as having legitimate or discrete responsibilities, duties, and skills. Some citizens saw police as shirkers; others saw them as busybodies, even sources of harassment. Given the lack of consensus about police roles, there was little possibility that a highly distinctive police bureaucracy could emerge during the boom days of Eau Claire. More established community elements were distrustful of saloons and brothels, but willing to tolerate them so long as they were not too obvious in the downtown, or too available to youth. There might be crusades for temperance, or short-lived antivice campaigns, but the basic attitude of Eau Claire elites was one of casual acceptance. With the shift to a more diversified economy, however, and the increase in city population stability and rootedness, there was more recognition of the police department as a separate, professionalized group.

In regard to most public activities, Eau Claire in the 1870s had very little involvement by state or outside authorities in local decisions. The city obviously held its charter from the state and had to have recourse to the state legislature for charter change. But overall, state and other authorities had little effect on city decisions or parties. As time passed, and the state elaborated its review procedures and strengthened its fledgling bureau-

cracies, its ability to affect city governments changed. State legislation determined the options in and the frequency of liquor license elections and some of the conditions about municipal elections and bonding limits, to mention some of the ways in which the influence of the state was felt. State inspectors' comments about high schools, factories, and prison facilities acted as a pressure for both private and public action.

In the late nineteenth century the state was more of a threat than a resource. There were very modest state funds available for education, especially education of the deaf and blind, but for the most part the state was making demands without paying bills. It did not behoove a city to be reprimanded for the inadequacy of its high school, or for lacking a pesthouse, and thus the reports of state inspectors were seriously considered as debates about bonding and spending raged. Local politicos did not, however, worry much about the intervention of state government. Requirements set outside the community were modest, even though they were more evident as the nineteenth century drew to a close.[8] The real problem was not how often a local community might hold a liquor license fee election, but how the citizens would vote.

Though both the Republican and Democratic parties were active throughout this period in Eau Claire, they were often outflanked by fusion or mass parties. Reform waves—calls for fiscal conservatism coupled with more rectitude and vice control—were common in Eau Claire, and most often resulted in some type of fusion organization. Sometimes the two regular parties, especially the Democrats, acquiesced by not providing separate nominating slates. Candidates from a fusion ticket in one election might run on a regular party ticket the next year, as fusion politics did not endure from one election to the next. Fusion or mass parties provided a certain instability in politics. Though they seemed to provide structural options for political expression, their transient nature did little to impose a sense of responsibility on the major, continuing parties.

Two other national parties—basically working-class parties—were represented in Eau Claire during this period: the Populists and the Social Democrats. Both carried on more activity at the county level than at the local, but the very fact of their existence made for more lively local debates and rhetoric of intense political cleavage. Even though party activity was quite intense during the late nineteenth century, parties were not as highly institutionalized and differentiated in local politics as on the state

8. Thelen, *The New Citizenship;* Herbert P. Secher, "The Law and Practice of Municipal Home Rule in Wisconsin Under the Constitutional Home Rule Amendment of 1926" (M.A. Thesis, University of Wisconsin, 1949), chap. 1; Merle Curti et al., *The Making of An American Community* (Stanford, Calif.: Stanford University Press, 1959), chap. 10.

level or as in many other cities of comparable size, especially eastern cities. At times the labor influence in politics resulted in a separate political party, and at other times laborers were elected as aldermen. Most of the time, however, labor did not represent a separate political force in Eau Claire, but its occasional efforts and successes introduced an element of challenge on the political scene. In Eau Claire, political elites changed their partisan identification in local politics more frequently than on the state and national levels. Moreover, there was considerable split-ticket voting on the local level, and the average percentage of votes received by each party varied enormously from election to election. In contrast, there was little splitting of tickets, and the percentage received by each party remained relatively stable in state and national elections.

Another vigorous source of complexity as well as political turmoil was prohibition politics, which took the form of separate party activities for about twenty years. Prohibition frequently became the rallying cry of those who held themselves to be the respectable folk, unlike the "uncouth and drunken woodsmen." Though the Prohibition party never carried the mayoralty race, it came very close, and by the size of its vote, helped to defeat several Republican candidates. Just as labor politics was to a considerable extent a protest against mill-owner domination of the city, prohibition politics was a protest against "the roughness" of a lumber town and was very active throughout the late nineteenth century.

The frequency of fusion parties and of ticket splitting obviously suggests that partisan identification in local politics was not strong in Eau Claire. However, an analysis of partisan politics at the ward level during the 1880s and 1890s suggests that insofar as partisan identification did exist, Scandinavians, native-born Americans of native-born parents, and German Protestants were usually Republicans, while German and Irish Catholics tended to be Democrats.[9]

Political Culture

Eau Claire evolved from a traditional to a mixed political culture during the 1870-1900 period. Serenity and balance in politics did not characterize Eau Claire, although they increased. Though there was less

9. The intensity of Eau Claire prohibition sentiment is discussed in *Eau Claire Free Press*, February 24, 1880, March 31, 1881, August 31, September 2, 1882, January 16, April 17, 1884, July 8, August 24, September 7, 1885, March 20, September 13, 1886, July 13, 1889, February 11, 1892; and *Eau Claire Weekly Free Press*, March 29, 1894. The discussion about voting behavior and the political activities of political elites in these three cities is based on a careful reading and detailed analyses of voting data as presented in the newspapers of Eau Claire, Janesville, and Green Bay between 1870 and 1900.

turmoil and turnover than one might expect to find in a boom lumber town with such a large immigrant population, there was considerable heat in the political arena.

A business oligarchy dominated Eau Claire during most of the late nineteenth century, an oligarchy composed to a considerable extent of members of lumber families or businesses. The immobility of the Eau Claire lumber industry apparently required the continued interest of lumber men in local politics. So long as their investments were fixed, they were unwilling for local policies to be determined by other people with less stake in the development of the region or people who might not be sympathetic to a lumber products-based economy. As their investments were difficult to liquidate, they also were anxious to broaden Eau Claire's economic base when they perceived the eventual decline of the lumber boom. Their local investments might ultimately continue to yield handsome profits if a lumber-products base could continue to flourish and compete in national markets. And Eau Claire was their hometown, even if a few of them chose to make investments elsewhere.[10] Among the oligarchs, it mattered little whether elected officials were owners of lumber mills or were owners of industries related directly to lumber, for in a city in which lumber interests were so paramount, bank officers or utility company owners were quite conscious of the need for protection of lumber interests. The control of the business oligarchy did not go unchallenged or unchanged. Labor, prohibition, and fusion political efforts, the major currents in Eau Claire, kept the political arena lively. Even so, the business elites and their supporters remained able to dominate the tone and substance of local politics. The one-sidedness of the economic base—providing most workingmen with a strong bond in common—did allow for the emergence of a group counter to the lumber oligarchy, a labor challenge.

Despite occasional challenges, the business and professional elites dominated the politics of Eau Claire. In the 1880s, however, John Bailey mounted a serious challenge to the business oligarchy of Eau Claire when he became mayor. Convinced that the interests of log and lumber owners were being protected at the expense of other Eau Claire citizens, he waged a campaign against the oligarchy. Through his campaign to drive the lumber barons from politics he was able for several years to maintain a large following by carrying on a sort of populist revolt against the "lumber interests."

Businessmen had become involved in Eau Claire politics as soon as the three villages joined together in the early 1870s, and they did not

10. See Fischer, "John S. Owen Enterprises," for a discussion of Eau Claire elites and their investment practices.

release their hold for thirty years. They became heavily involved initially because the success of the lumber industry required the building of the Dells dam to improve the logholding facilities of Eau Claire. And to build the dam required considerable public funding—over $90,000 in bonded debt. Too, the lumber industry planned to capitalize on railroad shipment of lumber, and thus lumber barons were active in city policies that sponsored rail construction.[11]

Usually Eau Claire mayors served only one term and were not sought for renomination. Mayors were seldom flattered by the press and public, although they were not vilified to the extent that aldermen were. It is, then, no surprise that few people wanted to be mayor. A regular feature of the annual political conventions was that the candidate chosen for mayor would refuse the nomination, an event particularly likely if a mass or fusion ticket were already in the field. Still, relatively prominent men accepted the nomination and even, on occasion, sought it.

The major issues in the political arena were fiscal stability and vice control, including temperance. Complaints about high taxes and fiscal management were both commonplace and inevitable, given the social structure and political culture. Candidates for office made ever more emphatic calls for fiscal prudence.

There were good reasons for the domination of fiscal issues and morality in Eau Claire politics. In terms of finances, Eau Claire's rapid population change and resulting heavy indebtedness made for a real crisis, while the fiscal shortages were exacerbated by the lack of routinization in accounting and reporting. As for morality, the issues arose in part because of the fear in the year-round community of the loggers during the six months when they were not in the woods. So fearful were some citizens of loggers that there was even talk of holding municipal elections in February before loggers returned to town. Evidently, it was acceptable to nonloggers that there be some vice. After all, saloon license income was important to the city as a source of funds for streets and sidewalks. It was not acceptable, however, that saloons and brothels should exist throughout the city and that their operation should affect people who were not woodsmen. If saloons were open to children, had no curtains on the windows, or were open Sundays, many citizens became outraged, and those promising "reform" could always build a following.

Within the council there were often sharp differences of opinion, and one year there was a six-month period during which no business was done because of disagreement between mayor and council about powers of appointment. The tone of the council meetings were often acrimonious,

11. For a discussion of the Dells Dam issue, see Peterson, "Lumbering on the Chippewa."

with attacks sometimes based on questions of reasonable importance and sometimes based on what seemed idle whim.

There was a fairly constant newspaper criticism not only of what the City Council did, but of its demeanor. The same skepticism extended to the police, in that attacks were quite personal, sometimes implying that police and criminals were both quite unsavory. The police were believed to have a working arrangement with gamblers and prostitutes, so that regular fines took the place of embarrassing raids or arrests.[12]

Eau Claire politics and government seesawed constantly between reform and rowdiness. As most people had a low opinion of many of those in office, they were readily mobilized by mass movement for reform. In general, the tone of Eau Claire politics, as reflected by the press, resembled a tendency more toward a traditional political culture than toward a legal rational political culture. The scope of government was narrow, with the political process being highly personalized.

Specific evidence on the intensity of cleavages is often lacking, but the fact that mill owners were elected as mayors throughout the period—often with large numbers of workers voting—suggests some tolerance by workers for employers. On the other hand, some doubt is cast on this tolerance and trust by the following: (1) labor challenger candidates were frequently nominated for public office; (2) work disruptions were frequent;[13] and (3) economic elites expressed considerable anger from time to time over strikes and labor activities. Eau Claire's "settled elements" viewed as even more troublesome problems with liquor and vice control, containing such "menaces" as best they could with petitions to keep the young from "entertainments," with calls for fewer, or differently situated brothels, and with demands for enforcement of saloon ordinances, Sunday closing laws, and so on.[14]

Public Policy

The most striking characteristic of Eau Claire's policies was the City

12. *Eau Claire Weekly Leader*, October 29, 1893; *Eau Claire Sunday Leader*, May 1, 1888; *Eau Claire News*, April 20, 1890; *Eau Claire Weekly Leader*, October 29, 1893; *Eau Claire Sunday Leader*, June 8, 1895.

13. For information on one strike in which the state militia was called, see *Eau Claire Free Press*, July 18-July 28, 1881. For other evidence of serious labor-management cleavages, see ibid., May 13, July 21, 1885.

14. For data on the variation in the number of arrests and problems which police encountered in dealing with laws to regulate "vice," see *Eau Claire Free Press*, May 11, 1875, July 28, 1881, October 11, 1884, May 1, 1888; *Eau Claire News*, April 20, 1890; *Eau Claire Weekly Leader*, October 29, 1893; *Eau Claire Sunday Leader*, June 8, 1895.

Council's willingness to employ a variety of policies regarding economic development, not confining itself exclusively to caretaker policies. In many respects it may seem surprising that such an active policy orientation could emerge at a time when the economy's horizontal differentiation was slight, the social structure's vertical differentiation great, and political culture more traditional than mixed. Since economic development policies carried implications for caretaker decisions, perhaps it is appropriate to describe them first. One of the first significant economic development policies in Eau Claire has already been mentioned—the building of the Dells dam in 1876-77 under the aegis of a private corporation but assisted by city money secured by bonding. In a sense the bonding for the dam set a precedent: though private groups might initiate, own, or manage improvements, the city government was expected to cooperate by providing money and moral support. Since there was such overlap in personnel among manufacturing, commercial, and political leaders, this kind of cooperation was rarely successfully challenged. The City Council was, for the most part, eager to cooperate when business leaders wanted to provide money in 1881 for the Chippewa Valley and Superior Railway to obtain a right of way. Or again, the City Council was most obliging in providing a cash subsidy to the Eau Claire Pulp and Paper Company in 1882. Elsewhere, James B. Smith has described in detail the way in which organizations of Eau Claire businessmen, over the years, boosted the city by attracting "new" businesses and/or manufacturers.[15]

Private sector booster organizations varied during this period in name, in method, and in success. With the cooperation of the City Council, the Board of Trade (intermittently active from 1879 to 1890), the Eau Claire Commercial Syndicate (from 1887 to 1892), and the Commercial Association of Eau Claire (after 1896) helped to implement policies to create a more diversified economic base. Personnel overlap among these organizations as well as with the City Council was common. Sometimes the private activity succeeded without involvement of the City Council, but during the 1880s and 1890s the city carried out two basic policies to recruit industry: direct subsidies and tax rebates. The extent of a subsidy or tax rebate was generally determined by the number of jobs which a firm would provide.

Eau Claire's efforts to attract manufacturers were considerable, though for the most part it was the city's private businessmen who bore the burden of the recruitment of businesses from other parts of the country. Rather than initiating and conducting negotiations on its own behalf, city government usually acted in response to the activities of businessmen. In a few

15. Smith, "Movements for Diversified Industry in Eau Claire, Wisconsin."

instances the City Council attempted to handle the recruitment of business without the aid of business groups, but usually with little success. It is impossible to assess the consequences of Eau Claire's economic development policies. Perhaps Eau Claire's population growth would have been the same had the government pursued no economic development policies. Companies assisted by bonuses or tax rebates employed over half the people in manufacturing by 1907, however, suggesting that the presence of new companies was important to the city's economic strength. Another aspect of promoting economic development was urging good roads, to tie cities to hinterland markets, and Eau Claire leaders were active in urging road improvements as part of their interest in tying their city to the development of northern Wisconsin.[16]

Economic development policies that cost money were not wholly without critics, however. As mentioned above, John Bailey made his mark in Eau Claire politics by stressing how the City Council had served as handmaiden to the lumber lords without providing adequate benefits for ordinary citizens. Others contended that simply to advertise Eau Claire's advantages would be enough to attract new firms to the city, that good railroad connections, availability of prime manufacturing sites, and a large work force would be sufficient to attract capital investment. Some argued that low taxes were what attracted industry and that one would never have low taxes with bonus payments. And still others suggested that money spent on schools, sewers, and sidewalks would make Eau Claire such a desirable city that manufacturers would be certain to arrive without special rewards. Other concerns were whether bonuses or tax rebates should be given only to attract firms to Eau Claire or should be given to assist firms already on the scene.

Since bonus expenditures were offered at the time that the lumber industry was beginning to collapse, there was even less money for caretaker policies after 1885. As a result, many municipal services in the 1880s and 1890s were neglected—though the demand for services was escalating. Even with financial "bankruptcy" appearing to be a real possibility, Eau Claire resorted during these two decades to considerable bonding in an effort to finance better streets, sidewalks, sewers, and schools—issuing so many bonds that the state limit on bonding was breached.

The municipal authorities were much more attentive to the maintenance of bridges and the containment of fires than to anything else. Floods of 1880 and 1884 had cut the town in half, and bonding to repair and main-

16. A more detailed analysis of this process is ibid. See also *Eau Claire Free Press*, April 21, 1885, January 9, February 2, 12, 1886, December 21, 1889; *Eau Claire Telegram*, February 25, 1895; *Eau Claire Weekly Free Press*, December 10, 1896.

tain bridges took precedence over any other activity. Since Eau Claire had two rivers running through it, bridge problems were particularly acute. With bridges consuming so much public money, it is not surprising that their construction called forth considerably more public concern than did other city activities. A new bridge, or the relocation of an old one, was likely to spark emotional council debate, though for the most part bridges were items of only minor controversy.[17]

Fire, for a community with saw mills and a paper company which would burn very quickly, was also a major concern. Most dwellings and commercial buildings were wooden for an obvious reason: lumber was cheap. Since bridges, streets, and sidewalks were all wooden, fire was a much worse menace than flooding in terms of the scope of the population affected. Reminded of this by the high fire insurance rates that prevailed, Eau Claire's City Council was relatively generous with the fire department.[18]

Other caretaker responsibilities were rarely above minimal levels. Although a Board of Health existed, it was generally inactive. The city engaged in sewer building and street paving in the 1880s, but had to curtail such activities for lack of funds. Schools were certainly not impressive in construction or quality. The 1889 merger of the three school administrations was brought about to conform to a new state law requiring general district school systems and the resultant Board of Education in Eau Claire promptly announced that the city would not honor compulsory education requirements for lack of space. The Board of Education did, however, immediately inaugurate a substantial building program. By the end of the century, although the school system had expanded, it would still not contain all eligible pupils.[19]

Eau Claire had a privately owned waterworks, and even that was realized only after years of discussions. Within a few years of the 1885 completion of the waterworks, complaints about the quality and quantity of the water were numerous. In Eau Claire, however, there was concern not only for breaking the franchise but for the possibility of municipal purchase. Even though the Eau Claire city government usually had serious financial difficulties, it was more used to assuming responsibilities for important services than most municipal governments in Wisconsin.[20]

17. *Eau Claire Free Press*, June 16, 1880, February 26, March 8, 1881, June 29, July 8, July 22, September 13, October 2, 1884.
18. *Eau Claire Weekly Leader*, March 20, 1892.
19. *Eau Claire Free Press*, January 23, 1890; *Eau Claire Sunday Leader*, October 19, 1895.
20. *Eau Claire Free Press*, March 11, 20, 1880, February 16, 1881, July 23, 1883, January 3, 1884, February 5, 6, 1885, February 20, 1890, February 9, 23, 1893; *Eau Claire Weekly Leader*, October 2, 1892; *Eau Claire Sunday Leader*, July 29, August 5, 1893; *Eau Claire*

Even with rather modest caretaker's expenses, the Eau Claire city government, by 1895, had exhausted its funds and issued script to the sum of $125,000. Financial troubles were exacerbated by the "defaulting" of the city treasurer just at the time that the city reached the bonded debt limit. Rather rigid economy was thereafter the order of the day.[21]

The Eau Claire City Council, throughout this period, expended fairly sizable amounts on the poor. The demand for welfare support was particularly vigorous in Eau Claire when the slackening supply of lumber combined with the panic of 1893. And while the response of the City Council was meager by present-day standards, the welfare program was broader in scope than in most cities of comparable size.

The City Council of Eau Claire did not spend a great deal of time on morality legislation or social control. Even after the "rough and tumble" loggers had left the city, public officials turned a blind eye to saloons, to gambling, and to "sporting houses," though these were constant issues of public concern. Despite the strong prohibition party influence, the City Council usually approved almost every saloon license application. So long as the council, as distinct from the electorate, set the liquor license fees, they were low. Fees, ostensibly reserved for the aid of the poor, were also used for general city purposes and thus were very welcome. No doubt the fact that Eau Claire had once been a major center for single lumbermen had done much to generate tolerance for moral diversity.

JANESVILLE

The types of changes that took place in Janesville during the late nineteenth century were perhaps more typical of the experiences of small cities than events in Eau Claire. Janesville was not a boom town, was not made up so disproportionately of foreigners, and did not have a city government that moved from boom to bankruptcy in less than a decade. Its population did not fluctuate wildly; its political leaders quit from boredom not scandal.

Structural Dimensions

Economic Structure

The changes that took place in Janesville were a reflection of the

---

Weekly Free Press, November 29, December 12, 1895, January 23, 1896, August 22, 1899; *Eau Claire Evening Free Press*, February 15, 22, April 2, 5, May 24, July 21, 1900.

21. *Eau Claire Telegram*, May 2, 1895; *Eau Claire Weekly Free Press*, May 17, 1895; *Eau Claire Sunday Leader*, July 2, 6, 1895.

general process of late-nineteenth-century adjustment in Wisconsin's economy, and its role in the national goods and services network. For the most part, but not exclusively, these changes bore upon agriculture, both its giving place to manufactures and to the shifts internal to agriculture. From 1870 to 1900 Wisconsin almost doubled in population, and what had been a frontier economy was replaced by a mix of manufacturing, commerce, and agriculture. Many Wisconsin cities reflected these overall changes, but there were differences from one city to another, according to natural advantages, to hinterland characteristics, to communications advances, and to local promotions and fortuitous circumstances. The transportation and communications revolution is demonstrated by the change in the role of wheat in Wisconsin's economy. During the 1860s agriculture was of first importance in Wisconsin's economy, with lumber second. A major agribusiness, the processing of wheat constituted two-fifths of all the state's manufacturing. Wheat could be grown easily and processed with few people, minimal technology, and little capital into flour of low quality. Its low quality did not make it less necessary to local purchasers, however, and even more distant customers bought Wisconsin flour so long as there were no better alternatives.

For the farmer, wheat was a highly desirable cash crop as long as land was cheap and labor costs low: capital outlays were minimal, little care of crops was required, and wheat could be marketed in bulk. In a relatively short time, however, this ideal picture was shattered: the phosphates in the soil were depleted and crops were less bounteous; the influx of more farmers drove the cost of land up and made land-extensive farming uneconomical.

After the Civil War Wisconsin industries were chiefly concerned with provisioning the local population. This meant that most sizable communities had flour mills, textile mills, breweries, furniture shops, iron foundries, harness making and repair shops, meat packers, leather goods—all necessary to supply the local farmers. For a long time communities were relatively self-sufficient hamlets, existing primarily to service a local population. But the national demand for Wisconsin products—especially lumber for building—put a speedy end to the relative isolation and self-sufficiency of frontier communities. Railroads had reached most sizable Wisconsin communities by 1875, the timing depending on whether the community was in the south, center, or north of the state, and the railroads carried away local products and brought the products of the east.

At the end of the Civil War, many manufacturing firms in middle-sized midwestern cities operated behind a protective banner of high freight rates on eastern goods. Because of high transportation rates, many eastern

producers tended to ignore midwestern markets for many products. At the end of the nineteenth century, however, transportation rates from eastern cities declined, and eastern firms were increasingly able to sell their products in the Midwest, causing many local industries to stagnate.[22]

Often, local Wisconsin industries were challenged and declined as a result of goods brought by the railroad. Rough products of local textile mills were acceptable for local consumption only until better products, often from the east, were available in considerable quantity. Flour from winter wheat yielded to spring wheat flour, and the local milling industry gave way to Minnesota mills. Of course, local industries were not quick to declare themselves obsolete as competitive products from other regions became available. The greater the percentage of an item's sale price attributable to transportation costs, the more likely a local industry was to persist in a competitive situation. Too, industries could often emphasize "buy at home" campaigns. As Wisconsin communities became integrated into a national economy, however, an upper limit was placed on the size of communities, with the hinterland increasingly consuming products from all parts of the country.

While much of Janesville's economy was tied to local consumption, the economy, over time, was integrated more and more into markets outside the city. With the increasing diversity of products and services, there was by 1900 a somewhat diversified economic structure based on both commerce and manufacturing. In contrast to 1870 a greater horizontal differentiation characterized the economic sector by the end of the century. Janesville, located just over the Illinois border, approximately ninety miles north of Chicago, seventy miles west of Milwaukee, and forty miles south of Madison, had a relatively stable, somewhat diversified economy by 1900. From the founding of the city to the turn of the century, Janesville's economic specialty had been agribusiness—both the processing of agricultural products and the servicing industry required for agriculture.

The city had been settled in the first half of the nineteenth century by New Englanders. Located on the banks of the Rock River—a good source of power for manufacturing establishments—and in the heart of fertile agricultural land, Janesville was primarily a market and supply center for

22. For a discussion of this theme, see Edgar M. Hoover, *The Location of Economic Activity* (New York: McGraw-Hill, 1948); Allen Pred, *The Spatial Dynamics of U.S. Urban Industrial Growth, 1800-1914* (Cambridge, Mass.: The M.I.T. Press, 1966); James B. Smith, "Lumbertowns in the Cutover: A Comparative Study of the Stage Hypothesis of Urban Growth" (Ph.D. diss., University of Wisconsin, 1973); Norman L. Crockett, *The Woolen Industry of the Midwest* (Lexington: University of Kentucky Press, 1970); Kurzhals, "Initial Advantage and Technological Change in Industrial Location."

farmers. The surrounding land was suitable for winter wheat, which was converted to flour in Janesville's numerous mills. By 1850 Janesville was a minor milling center. The coming of the first railroad in 1856 gave further impetus to the milling industry, reinforcing the agricultural base of the community. The fact that two major railroads (the Chicago and North-western Railway and the Chicago, Milwaukee, and St. Paul Railway) passed through Janesville was vital for its early growth and prosperity. For a short time, improvements in transportation linkages to the outside world had the effect of thrusting Janesville, with its fertile hinterland, even more into an agricultural role. Of course, local industry also developed, as manufactures too expensive to transport considerable distances were produced locally for a profit. For example, local agricultural machine industries were operating on a small scale, at the same time that Janesville was becoming a milling center. Over time, these businesses expanded and endured. By the 1880s the manufacturing of farm implements had become important to Janesville's economy, as the agricultural yield of southern Wisconsin demanded many kinds of machinery—especially plows, thrashers, and reapers.

The limitations on wheat growing and processing have been briefly described above. Rock County, of which Janesville was the county seat, had been one of the three most productive wheat-producing counties in Wisconsin and was hit moderately hard around 1870 by the lessening of demand for winter wheat products. The rise of the superior Minnesota grain-processing facilities meant that after the 1870s the flour produced in Janesville was only for local purposes. In addition to the flour mills and farm machinery, Janesville had industries to service farm and town dweller: brick yards, boot and shoe companies, iron shops, woolen mills, carriage and wagon businesses, cooperage firms, leather shops, breweries, and saddlery and harness shops. Each of these enterprises employed only a few workers and was strictly local.

With the demise of profitable wheat export, farmers around Janesville turned to tobacco on a bigger scale, so that Janesville had about thirty tobacco warehouses in 1885. Another support of the economy was the production of wool. Of the wool sheared in the area, some was used in local woolen mills, some exported.

Janesville benefited, too, from the dairy industry, as it became more specialized and profitable in the last quarter of the nineteenth century. Butter and cheese became major products of Rock County, as Janesville was near to major markets, had the proper type of soil, grasses, and water necessary for the production of butter and cheese.

But the biggest single employers in Janesville, along with the agricultural

implement companies, were the cotton mills, the first one established in 1874. Some 75 percent of the workers in Janesville's cotton mills were women (who received low wages) and in 1889 47 percent of the people employed in manufacturing as wage earners were women. For a while, Janesville had a higher percentage of women in its labor force than any other city in Wisconsin. Considered from a national perspective Janesville, among middle-sized communities, was far from being a manufacturing city. But in terms of other Wisconsin cities of its size, Janesville ranked fairly high in manufacturing. Ten percent of the population was employed in manufacturing throughout the decade of the eighties, and 13 percent by 1900.

Tied closely to its hinterland by the material-processing and material-service nature of its manufactures, Janesville continued to be successful in agribusiness due to the fertility of Rock County soils, the proximity of the Rock River, and the fact that major railroads passed through the town. Although Janesville was heavily dependent on agribusiness, it developed a somewhat diversified economic base. Relying on an agricultural hinterland which was becoming increasingly complex, Janesville was not seriously affected by panics and recessions of the late nineteenth century, although local firm failures were common (see table 2.4).

Table 2.4. Janesville: Capitalization of Firms, 1875–1900

	1875	1900
Primary sector		
Timber-using	—	4.3%
Farm-product-processing	3.4%	1.5
Secondary manufacturing		
Wood-using	1.7	3.3
Sawmill machinery	—	—
Other metal-using	.5	13.3
Other	12.3	21.2
Wholesale trades	4.9	9.9
Retail trade, service	75.6	45.4
Utilities	1.6	1.1
Total	100.0%	100.0%
Total capitalization	$1,914,000	$3,938,000

Source: See table 2.1.

If Janesville's fairly stable economy could be explained in terms of its hinterland ties and diversification, so could its relative lack of dynamism. Janesville's location within the triangle of Chicago, Milwaukee, and Minneapolis tended to limit the growth and prosperity of the city despite the access afforded by the railroads, the power of the river, and the available

work force. It lacked the advantage of a Lake Michigan location, as cities on the lake could import coal and other necessities more cheaply.

In terms of economic autonomy Janesville passed through the same processes as Eau Claire, although more gradually. Economically, during the last third of the century, Janesville moved from supplying a small hinterland to providing products for a much larger area. Strictly local enterprises vanished on any significant scale. As Janesville was called upon to participate more and more in nationwide economic competition, it lost momentum in population growth. In many ways, the loss of economic autonomy for Janesville was tied up with loss of population expansion. Loss of autonomy and inability to compete economically meant, for many years, constricted funds for municipal purposes. In general, the economic autonomy of Janesville was modest after the coming of the railroads. By 1870 its self-sufficiency was open to challenge and the days of a hamlet-type economy were over. With the passage of time, economic autonomy eroded further and further, though the continued agricultural productivity of the local area furnished a certain economic set of arrangements that national networks and shifts never dislodged.

Social Structure

At the same time that more complexity developed in the economic structures of Janesville, there were changes in the social structures, especially in the direction of less vertical differentiation. At no time was Janesville ever so stratified as Eau Claire in its boom days, and by the end of the century the two cities had rather similar occupational profiles.

During the last thirty years of the nineteenth century, the component groups in the social structure of Janesville shifted moderately. As a bustling small market center, Janesville had a sizable middle class of professionals, store keepers, retailers, tobacco buyers, etc. The percentage of the population that was middle class increased slightly over thirty years, as the manufacturing and service sectors of the economy began to account for a greater percentage of the total values of goods and services. Much of the placidity of Janesville may be attributed to slow population growth, turnover of the least skilled, and some gradual upward social mobility as the economy diversified.[23]

Table 2.5 shows the shift among heads of households away from unskilled work, into skilled and semiskilled tasks. At the same time it should be noted that 60 percent of the population was blue collar both in 1870 and 1905. Too, among white collar workers there were more clerks

23. For an analysis of changes in social structure in Janesville, see Edward M. Lang, "The Common Man" (M.A thesis, University of Wisconsin, 1968).

Table 2.5. Occupations of Heads of Families in Janesville: 1870, 1880, 1905[a]

	1870	1880	1905
Professionals	5.7%	5.5%	5.6%
Proprietors managers, and officials	30.8	32.0	20.8
Clerks	3.9	4.3	11.0
Skilled and semiskilled laborers	32.2	26.9	46.4
Unskilled laborers	27.4	31.3	16.2
Total	100.0%	100.0%	100.0%
N =	1595	1355	2468

Source: These data were compiled from federal census manuscripts for 1870 and 1880, and from tabulated State of Wisconsin materials for 1905. These materials are on deposit at the Wisconsin State Historical Society, Madison, Wisconsin.

[a]Persons whose occupations were not listed in census manuscripts are omitted from this table. The number is 312 in 1870, 141 in 1880.

and fewer managers, owners, and proprietors as time passed. Together these data seem to suggest, in relative terms, the growth of a lower middle strata and movement from a pyramidal pattern toward a cone-shaped pattern.

Although immigrant groups over time tended to hold less desirable jobs than those of the native-born, Janesville was not a community of great extremes of wealth. There was no great pool of unemployed people, although most people lived in modest circumstances, with the Irish invariably at the bottom of the social structure.

As table 2.6 indicates, the native-born population cohort in Janesville was always larger than the foreign-born or native-born-of-foreign-parents cohorts. Between 1880 and 1905 a sizable semirooted group (the native-born of foreign-born parents) had developed, and seemingly fitted into the community with minimum disruption.

Throughout the period, slightly more than half the residential dwellings of Janesville were owned by their occupants. This was so even though there was considerable turnover in population. Of course, Janesville was not unique in this respect, as we know from studies of other areas that population turnover was very considerable in the nineteenth century, a factor which may have kept Americans from being so conscious of rigidities in the stratification system. It was often those at the bottom of the stratification system who moved on, and geographical mobility kept collective protest among mill workers in Janesville, and in dozens of other communities, to a minimum. As Herbert G. Gutman has written, "men as

Table 2.6. Ethnic Characteristics of Heads of Families in Janesville: 1870, 1880, 1905

	1870	1880	1905
Foreign-born			
Irish	21.5%	19.8%	3.2%
English	10.0	9.6	2.3
German	6.4	7.2	7.6
Canadian	3.0	3.0	2.5
Other	3.8	4.9	9.6[a]
Total	44.7	44.5	25.2
Native-born of foreign-born parents	1.8	8.1	33.8
Native-born of native-born parents			
New England	15.6	12.0	4.0
Middle Atlantic	30.3	23.8	13.1
Wisconsin	2.6	6.1	15.5
Other	5.0	5.5	8.4
Total	53.5	47.4	41.0
Grand total	100.0	100.0	100.0
N =	1983	1577	2826

Source: These data were compiled from federal census manuscripts for 1870 and 1880, and from tabulated State of Wisconsin census materials for 1905. These materials are on deposit at the Wisconsin State Historical Society, Madison, Wisconsin.

[a]Includes 6.4% Swedes and Norwegians.

well as women who expect to spend only a few years as factory workers have little incentive to join unions."[24] In Janesville they did not become actively involved in shaping challenges to power.

By the 1890s there were ten labor unions in Janesville, three of them specifically for railroad employees. The others were craft unions for barbers, bricklayers, and masons, cigar-makers, leather workers, painters, tailors, and typographers. Although strikes were not unknown, they were few, brief, and not too acrimonious, a characteristic of which many in Janesville were proud.[25] The craft orientation of labor unions, the lack

24. Herbert G. Gutman, *Work, Culture and Society* (New York: Alfred A. Knopf, 1976), pp. 29–30. For a discussion of urban areas with much more labor activity, see Alan Dawley, *Class and Community: The Industrial Revolution in Lynn* (Cambridge, Mass.: Harvard University Press, 1976), pp. 225–26.

25. For data on strikes in Janesville and elsewhere in Wisconsin, see issues of the *Wisconsin Bureau of Labor Statistics, Biennial Reports* (Madison, Wis.) during the latter part of the nineteenth century. For a discussion of labor strife elsewhere, see Herbert Gutman, "The Worker's Search for Power: Labor in the Gilded Age," in *The Gilded Age: A Reappraisal*, ed. H. Wayne Morgan (Syracuse: Syracuse University Press, 1963), pp. 28–68; and Dawley, *Class and Community*.

of a shared common tradition among the labor force, the ethnic diversity within the community, the city's economic complexity, the possibility of homeownership, the likelihood of moving to a different city, all served to diffuse whatever potential the amount of vertical differentiation in Janesville might have had for shaping political outcomes. Even in times of pyramidal social structure, with many unskilled workers, Janesville's political culture and process seemed to reflect few tensions arising from distribution of status.

Political Structure

Political structures in Janesville altered modestly over time, with patterns changing in a fashion similar to those in economic and social structures. Government became more complex, but only slightly. The governmental sector was so small in 1870 that adding a very few people or specifying a few roles more precisely could enlarge public or professional employment by hundreds of percents.

Janesville had a mayor-council form of government, with the mayor (until 1893) selected annually in the spring, generally from a field of two. Usually, the mayoral candidate was nominated by the Republican or Democratic party in convention. Third-party candidates appeared a few times, most often with Prohibitionist backing, but won too few votes to be taken seriously. The two major parties were able to absorb the new groups that entered the community, and throughout the late nineteenth century the parties were relatively free of ethnic hostilities. Probably the flexibility of the two major parties was responsible for the lack of any effective third party, and in turn the lack of third-party challenge may have acted to retard municipal growth of responsibility. Two parties without challenge were not stimulated to outbid each other with new ideas.

Characteristic of oligarchy, there was considerable continuity in leadership over the years. In the twenty-seven mayoral elections held from 1870 to 1899 the person chosen mayor had served a previous term in that office eleven times. Moreover, there were only thirty-one different people who ran for mayor as Republicans or Democrats during the thirty-year period. Overall, a relatively small cast of people were overtly concerned with being, or wanting to be, mayor.

Usually the mayor was a prominent businessman. Among the mayors were the owner of the gas works, a bank executive, and an owner of a box company. A business oligarchy was able to dominate the political life of Janesville because it was mostly businessmen who were willing to

serve in office, who had money and time to invest in the community, and who were most admired in Janesville. Too, given the modest amount of labor organization, there were no sources for serious challenge to the business oligarchy.

The City Council, made up of two aldermen elected from each ward and having sixteen members by 1900, had about a dozen committees that did its main work. Four of these were important, and appointments to them were negotiated by the mayor and council members in private sessions before the first public meeting of the new council took place. Aldermen varied greatly in the length of time they stayed on the council: some men stayed for as long as a decade. Most aldermen only served a term or two, and usually they left the council because they chose not to seek re-election rather than because they were retired by their constituents. Campaigns, if indeed they can be called that, were very brief. Because most people in a small city knew the leading figures, there was no need for extensive campaigns. Politics was very personal. Business elites were also social and political elites, in frequent interaction with one another.

Municipal elections in Janesville were also the mechanism by which members of the Board of Education were chosen. The candidates for these posts also bore party labels. Board of Education members were often not opposed, and incumbents were frequently returned. Usually people of considerable social standing occupied the positions on the Board of Education, which for the most part worked amiably with the City Council. The board met and reported regularly, and kept the council at bay about both personnel and budget by the simple device of showing how economically schools were administered. The Board of Education worked closely with the superintendent of schools and gave way to his presumed expertise—except when his policies threatened to result in great expense. In general, however, Janesville citizens were quite willing to accept professionalism in educational administration, so long as education-related persons were sufficiently deferential to city councils.

Friction between the County Board of Supervisors and the City Council was rather common, and at times, even intense. The Janesville City Council was persuaded that it was paying to support county indigents, an obligation that seemed unfair to council members who argued that Janesville had no paupers. Too, when the county set tax assessments, many in Janesville thought themselves overtaxed.[26]

There was also occasional friction between the city Board of Health and the council, as the health officer sought more independence. After

26. *Janesville Gazette*, February 26, 1874.

1882, the Board of Health reproved the council over and over for short-comings in health ordinances and faults in health ordinance enforcement. Generally, the aldermen took remedial action, but the health officer was a regular source of unease. Not surprisingly, most doctors were reluctant to accept appointment to the Board of Health. The loads on the office were heavy in an era before water treatment, sewers, or indoor plumbing, when slaughterhouses might discard carcasses anywhere, when the preferred method for handling household garbage during cold weather was to throw it on the lawn and hope a pig might eat it during the spring thaw, when people who had moved from farms wished to raise pigs, cows, and chickens in the city, and when there was often need for quarantine of persons with infectious diseases. In such an age those on the Board of Health were engaged in a constant campaign to educate not only the electorate but also the mayor and council members.[27] They tried to emancipate themselves from political perspectives by drawing on expertise, but there was little acceptance of their special role.

During the thirty-year period in question, the tone and style of the political process in Janesville did change somewhat. Over time, more and more professionals and quasi-professionals were used to manage and serve the city, as horizontal differentiation increased. For example, a city engineer was appointed after careful recruitment from another city in 1889. Street care, which had for many years been the responsibility of one alderman in each ward, was assigned to the superintendent of streets. The fire department moved in the direction of greater rationalization, with regular inventories and updating of equipment, and higher salaries for firemen. The one-man police force passed into history. In 1881 the city council created a municipal court, though within ten years Janesville citizens began to think it was not efficient enough. Some of these changes were voluntary, while others were mandated by state law requirements.

What often appeared to be simple organizational changes in city government required changes in the city charter, and these changes necessitated action by the Wisconsin legislature. Because charter changes frequently involved considerable bickering, charter amendment was not undertaken lightly, so that some structures and practices while outdated, lasted unchanged for years. For example, it was common that the number of voters in wards was quite unequal for years before ward redistricting took place. Usually, what seemed to be fairly important financial considerations were necessary before city leaders undertook charter revisions.

Even with an increase in the level of professionalization and with greater adherence to formal procedures in politics, much of Janesville's politics remained the province of amateurs. A good illustration of this

27. Ibid., May 9, June 6, October 11, 1877, May 8 and 10, 1880.

was the handling of water works construction in 1885. Fatigued with fifteen years of fruitless discussion about who should own and build waterworks, in 1885 Janesville citizens elected five water commissioners. These men, all inexperienced, were charged with producing an extensive water works system, and in just over a year did so. Keeping in touch with both citizens and council, they explored technical problems relating to the construction of a water works, arranged for bids and contracts with nonlocal companies, and assisted in drafting a complicated ordinance. All this was done without fanfare and with reasonable confidence. Janesville thus followed a fairly common practice for small cities in the late nineteenth century—blending amateur/volunteers and professionals in solving problems.

Political autonomy in Janesville was in some ways less established than in Eau Claire, even in 1875. Janesville, as one of two similarly sized cities in Rock County, was forced to be concerned with the policies of county government and evolved a set of coping mechanisms to defend city interests and treasury. State manifestations of interest in locally funded services were sometimes resented, sometimes welcomed. To the Board of Health a state citation for lack of a pesthouse seemed helpful. To a financially poor Board of Education, having the high school termed unfit was a mixed blessing. From the state's censure might come the coerced momentum to plan and execute a new structure, but how was the money to be raised? State authorities were little concerned with roads or bridges, two high expense areas, so erosion of autonomy stemmed mostly from state efforts to control closed or semiclosed institutions and efforts extended only very marginally to the private sector. Industrial accidents and poor work site practices brought record keepers and scoldings, but no effective sanctions. Finally, the loss of political autonomy proceeded slowly, in part because the state usually had nothing to offer small cities. Occasionally there were state institutions to be sited, but there were only small regular state funds disbursed. For the deaf and blind there were special state monies for education, but with few eligible pupils financial incentives were small.

Still, during the late nineteenth century the state moved into areas of policy that affected local units, for example, outlining guidelines for election conduct and passing compulsory school laws. The effort of the state government was to establish some threshold levels for procedures in urban units, as well as to affect the substance of policy somewhat.

Political Culture

Politics in Janesville were rather serene. Fiscal and personal excesses sometimes manifest in the politics of Wisconsin cities were hardly existent

in Janesville. The slowness of economic and population growth, the lack of sharp class conflict for most of this period, and the low profile of a city government with few functions all contributed to this sense of quiet. There was a mixed political culture throughout the period, with a bit more expectation of rationalism and efficiency as the nineteenth century expired.

Several of the aspects of slow growth have already been discussed, as well as various of the factors which contributed to a low potential for community friction. Although by 1905 Janesville was inhabited roughly one-third each by foreign-born, by native-born persons with foreign-born parents, and by native-born persons with native-born parents, the native-born fraction in 1870 and 1880 had been larger (54 and 48 percent, respectively). Janesville's institutions were established by settlers from New England and the Middle Atlantic states, and the English and Germans who came to Janesville folded into that system and orientation. The immigrants came to Janesville in several medium-sized waves, rather than one large mass. Such gradualism made it easier for institutions to absorb newcomers. (Table 2.6 shows the birthplace of heads of families for three points in time.)

Janesville's political culture expressed a fusion of New England pietism and German Lutheranism, with emphasis on seriousness and duty. The Scandinavian elements of the city gave support to such attitudes, so much so that the more ritualistically oriented Irish could raise no effective challenge. Perhaps it was the ethnic diversity, more than any other factor, that was responsible for Janesville's having a mixed political culture.

By the 1890s Janesville had dozens of voluntary societies (apart from very numerous church organizations), with Masons, Odd Fellows, and temperance societies the most common kinds of organizations. There were many more church-related or sponsored societies than secular organizations, which is suggestive of the prominent role of religion in Janesville. Secret and benevolent societies were especially popular. Each of the larger ethnic groups had its special clubs, which celebrated American as well as foreign holidays—thus tending to keep ethnic consciousness alive. Because membership in these organizations cut across many occupations, however, they did not exacerbate community cleavages—except on the issue of prohibition. Rather, voluntary organizations which kept alive traditional customs, rituals, and beliefs tended to provide citizens with a sense of identity and meaning. In sum, these organizations in Janesville— as in many communities of comparable size—acted as stabilizing institutions and facilitated adjustments to a rapidly changing world.

Like many other middle-sized cities of the late nineteenth century, Janesville had a business-oriented and business-dominated government,

an oligarchical form of government. But diverse kinds of business were represented, not just a single type. Unlike governments in some other cities, Janesville's city government was virtually unchallenged by labor or minority groups. Even issues of liquor control, which elsewhere were the basis for considerable cleavage, raised only modest difficulties in Janesville. Nevertheless, prohibition had considerable strength in Janesville, and it was not unusual for a prohibition speaker to attract five and six hundred people. But much of the wrath of Janesville's leading prohibitionists was directed elsewhere in the state rather than at groups within the city.[28]

And to a greater extent than most business governments, Janesville's officials took seriously the aim to govern as little and to spend as little as possible. Lack of serious political differences was also cause and effect of lack of spending: since the city was concerned with decreasing debt, taxes were low. People expected little of government and brought few pressures to bear on it, resulting in a political system which generated few disputes.

Usually the man elected mayor had served on the council and had lived in Janesville at least a decade. The winner usually carried the office of mayor by less than 60 percent of the popular vote, and the office shifted from Republican to Democrat in an almost balanced way, giving the impression of competition. In fact, however, the office was not much sought. The actions of the mayor were quite dependent on cooperation with the City Council, and being mayor required many hours of work without salary. Mayors did become disgruntled with the office: one announced his retirement before the end of his term but was coaxed into remaining. Another simply moved away and mailed his announcement of resignation.

Like the mayor, aldermen were usually candidates of the two major parties, and party lines shaped votes on important issues and appointments. Evidently this partisanship did not preclude harmony, for wrangling—especially partisan wrangling—was unusual in the council. This superficial harmony was characteristic of many small towns, where it was believed that permitting disagreements to erupt would cause intolerable and permanent cleavages.

It is difficult to judge how seriously the people of Janesville took the selection or activities of officeholders. Usually party conventions for nominating were held only a few days before the election (a practice altered by Wisconsin's Cooper law in the 1890s, which mandated candidate selection fifteen days before elections), and even after the conventions were held, nominees frequently changed. It was not uncommon for two

28. Ibid., November 11, 1872, May 5, November 4, 1873, February 10 and 11, 1890.

or three people to refuse the mayoralty nomination. Despite the personal and noncompetitive aspects of politics, a high percentage of those registered to vote did so. For example, it was normal for more than 70 percent of the registered electorate to vote in a municipal election. True, only men were allowed to register, and there were restrictions on the newer immigrants in terms of voting. Overall, the political culture reflected a blend of traditional aspects such as personalism, informalism, and low expectations with moderate participation. The particular blend manifest in Janesville's political culture owed a great deal to the socioethnic structures and the economic oligarchy. And the political culture derived from, and supported, governmental structures small in scale, low in professionalism.

Public Policy

The public policy carried out in Janesville during the last third of the nineteenth century was the epitome of fiscal conservatism. During this period it was quite common for politicians to present as their own novel idea the need for economy, and in Janesville such rhetoric was the rule. There was widespread agreement in the political arena that government should do as little as possible, in particular spend only such modest amounts as might be required to allow the private systems—economic and social—to function. Such fiscal prudence emphasized caretaker policies to the virtual exclusion of amenities and economic development. Accordingly, the administration of charity and welfare took place through private coordinating agencies. The charity coordinating agency, Janesville Associated Charities, which emerged in the 1880s, was intended to draw together activities hitherto carried out very informally, either through social or service clubs, or through emergency aid drives.[29] City officials were delighted to have private groups assume responsibility for the poor not because such a policy was necessarily good for the poor, but because welfare provision was considered clearly a public responsibility.

To some extent this fiscal prudence was rooted in hard fact, for Janesville was not a wealthy city compared to other middle-sized towns. Between 1880 and 1890 the property valuation per capita actually decreased. Perhaps Janesville's unwillingness to spend was not unreasonable, since the resources of the city expanded somewhat less rapidly than the population.

Janesville's elected officials never forgot the bankruptcies of the 1870s and assumed that communities with large bonded debts would be "caught" in subsequent panics. Rather than risk such a prospect, Janesville worked

29. John A. Fleckner, "Poverty and Relief in Nineteenth-Century Janesville," *Wisconsin Magazine of History* 6 (Summer 1978): 279–99.

for years to reduce its debt to zero—finally reaching that goal in 1886. The consequences of the drive to reduce debt were most discernible in the school system, which by the early 1890s was suffering from wretched physical facilities.

Despite the fact that early in its history Janesville made considerable sacrifices to establish an education system which was superior to most midwestern cities of its size, the city during the latter part of the century had a lower debt rate, had lower taxes, paid teachers lower salaries, and had more overcrowded schools than most Wisconsin and Illinois cities of comparable size. Ironically, citizen awareness of the shortcomings of the schools and pressure for remedial spending came at a time when the city's financial problems were critical, making school building into a heated political issue during the depression of the nineties.

The implications of caretaker policies are fairly obvious: most services and facilities existed modestly, if at all. Janesville had a fire department, bridges, downtown sidewalks, some street paving, some sewer facilities, street lights, a street railway, a police force, waterworks, schools, and so on by the late 1800s, but the level of service was well below the demand. Since fire was perceived as a serious threat, allocations for fire control were more generous and less disputed than others. Indeed, Janesville, like many cities of the late nineteenth century, perceived fire as one—if not the most—serious problem confronting the city, and for good reason. Even though lumber was used less frequently for construction than in Eau Claire and Green Bay, Janesville, within only a few years, lost a textile mill, the Wisconsin School for the Blind, its opera house, a hotel, its largest and most expensive church, and numerous residences in fires and also recorded several casualties.[30]

Over the thirty-year period Janesville's fire department was permitted to spend sufficient money to stay abreast of most technological break-throughs. Within the city council the "fire committee" was one of the four important ones. Preoccupation with fire was hardly surprising in a city where the amount paid in fire insurance premiums was greater than the cost of city government. Fire, then, was the one area in which caretaker policies were defined to include the spending of fairly liberal sums of money. And it was concern with the danger of fire that did much to encourage city oligarchs to improve the city's water facilities.[31]

Likewise, the bridges joining the two sides of town across the Rock

30. *Janesville Gazette*, February 1, April 23, 1873, May 16, 1874, August 22, 1877, September 5, 1879, April 4, 1893, March 31, April 14, 1894; Lang, "The Common Man," pp. 18–19.

31. *Janesville Gazette*, May 27, 1878, April 21, 1893.

River were not items of controversy. It was generally agreed that bridges were essential in a town cut in half by a river. Bridge construction was undertaken with more concern for economy than durability, however, and the result was constant repair.

The problem of obtaining a waterworks, however, required a decade and a half of discussion. Perhaps the most divisive political issue in Janesville during the late nineteenth century was whether the city should own and operate a waterworks or whether there should be a privately owned and operated waterworks.

As the city oligarchs preferred that the facility be privately owned, an out-of-state company was granted a franchise to operate the waterworks, but the company's operations during the depression of the nineties were sharply criticized by many citizens. The company was under investigation within four years of its organization on several counts: (1) the low quality of water for human consumption; (2) the inadequate quantity of water for fire fighting; (3) the difficulty of procuring additional water mains; and (4) the high rates for water charged to customers. As the waterworks company was privately owned, considerable rhetoric centered around municipal ownership, thus ensuring more responsive management but involving the assumption of a long-term debt and enlarging the functions of government, choices which Janesville citizens always tried to avoid.[32]

For the most part new policies or modifications in policy emerged from the City Council only when interested parties placed great pressure on local government. New fire equipment was acquired, fire personnel was added, "pesthouses" delayed, according to pressure from very small groups of interested persons, not in response to any long-range plans. Long-range plans and the implementation thereof cost money, and Janesville's officials were leery of spending. For example, the existing sewer lines were magnifying rather than reducing the city's waste problems by 1893. Several solutions were proposed. The price tag for systematic improvement was several hundred thousand dollars, however—a sum that was viewed as intolerable for the almost destitute city, and the issue of sewage was "solved" by doing nothing. The council as guardian of city monies held itself in a defensive posture: its aim was to keep money from the county and the state, from those who might claim poverty, or from those who might bring suit.

Obviously, since council membership varied greatly over time there were exceptions to these tendencies. But overall, Janesville's city govern-

32. Ibid., May 16, July 5, 16, 19, August 2, September 17, 23, October 1, November 6, 1878, March 24, November 20, December 18, 1894.

ment had little sympathy for publicly funded amenities. A YWCA group established and operated a public library for many years before convincing the city to take over its support at a modest level. Demands for city park projects met a less fortunate fate: about once a year some trivial sum was spent for tree trimming or park signs, but overall, if there were parks, they were to be in their natural state. Gazetteers and city directories of the period point with pride to lovely homes and churches, not to city buildings or schools, as showplaces. Both a hospital and pesthouse, viewed by local doctors as necessities, were treated as nonessential for most of the period. There was always some concern that spending for sidewalks or sewers could place intolerable burdens on the poor. Even no-cost policies like containing and eliminating pigs, cows, and chickens in the city were seen as diminishing the ability of the poor to survive, by forcing them into dependence on a cash economy.

For the most part the Janesville city government also maintained a very low profile in the area of economic development. Though public officials expressed discontent from time to time with the lack of growth in the city's economy, they did little of real substance to change things. In 1888 a subscription fund was begun for attracting industry to Janesville, but the city government refused to contribute to the fund or even to assume an active role in its administration. Nor did Janesville, like many cities, have a tax rebate policy for industry. Perhaps it is not surprising that public authority gave so little attention to economic development; private groups with such interests (Board of Trade, Business Men's Association, etc.) were quite weak and intermittent in their activities, and generally failed to pressure local government to carry out policies designed to advance the economic fortunes of the city, preferring to act independently of governmental authority. The one way in which Janesville's public monies were spent on economic development was to assist railroads. Bonding for railroads took place in both the 1870s and 1880s. Though the city was far from anxious to assist the railroads financially, it had little option since railroads were considered necessary to support manufacturing by importing raw materials and by exporting textiles as well as agricultural products.[33]

Whereas Eau Claire's spectacular growth between 1870 and 1885 convinced its elites that it had a great future as a metropolis, Janesville's very modest growth led to few expectations among civic leaders. Indeed, its elites rarely expected Janesville to become a great metropolis. And whereas other cities experienced a crisis as the lumber industry declined,

33. Ibid., December 12, 1884, October 6, 13, 1885, November 19, 1887; Fleckner, "Poverty and Relief in Nineteenth Century Janesville."

Janesville's changing economic base was never perceived in crisis proportions. Thus its elites felt little pressure to recruit external industry.

Insofar as policy for public order and morality was concerned, Janesville city government carried out modest activities. Liquor license fees
were set low, but saloons had to pay double (for retail and bulk licenses)
and the resultant revenue could be used for general city purposes.

When confronted with spending on policies designed to promote
public order and morality, Janesville was able to have its cake and eat it
too. Liquor license revenue was supposedly set aside for the poor, and in
the 1870s Janesville remitted most of such collections to the county for
assistance to the poor. At a later date, liquor license fees were not remitted
and became a considerable source of city income, along with taxation
and modest state and county aid. Thus, vice control, in the shape of high
liquor license fees, had the potential for transferring some of the tax
burden to the saloons. Although the fees for saloon licenses varied from
1870 to 1885, after 1885 cities held elections to determine the amount to
be charged for licenses: $200, $350, or $500, and election results were
binding for three years. For a number of years the amount of the license
was one of the major issues which confronted the City Council. Usually
Janesville chose $200, and then required saloons to pay twice: once for a
retail license, once for a bulk license. With some sixty saloons each paying
$400, a tidy sum was available for city purposes. When double licensing
was finally eliminated in the 1890s, however, financial problems resulted.

Of course, saloon license fees were only one aspect of the broad problem
of temperance, which was more long-lasting than incendiary. Petitions
for stricter enforcement of closing hours and age limits for entering saloons
were presented to the council over a long period of time—sometimes
bearing over one thousand signatures. The mayor—or council—would
listen, and promise, and on occasion there would be stricter enforcement
of laws regulating saloons.

Throughout the late nineteenth century the police force, relative to
other cities of comparable size, was one of the smallest in the country:
there was only one policeman. That there was only one policeman is
suggestive that cleavages in Janesville were modest relative to other cities,
that the problem of social control was of much less concern than was to
be the case many years later. In social control, as in economic development
and amenities, Janesville policies approached the minimum.

Although the city government of Janesville had a rather low profile
throughout this period, some aspects of its style changed. There was
more of an assumption by the turn of the century that government was
the guardian of public interest, rather than private interest. Thus the City
Council was willing to engage in litigation with the waterworks' owners

in order to obtain better service. Too, the City Council became more conservative in the granting of other utility franchises. Gradually, orientations toward accountability and efficiency increased: contractors made use of better quality materials on street railways, auditors made regular checks of treasurer's books, and so on.

Though public policy remained caretaker-oriented, the levels of publicly financed services increased in Janesville in the late nineteenth century. This process was not particular to Janesville, or to Wisconsin, but represented the consequences of changes in technology affecting public health, transportation, communication, etc. And as cities assumed new responsibilities, citizens developed higher expectations, resulting in a process that would fundamentally alter the role of local government in the twentieth century.

The technological changes and increasing complexities of late-nineteenth-century America both caused the state government to increase its supervisory role in some municipal activities, and the city to develop new authority to regulate life on a day-to-day basis, authority to regulate the location of telephone and telegraph wires as well as sanitation and railway track, to remove and regulate garbage, animals, and other health hazards, and to establish, manage, and regulate quasi-public organizations such as libraries, hospitals, and welfare organizations.[34]

GREEN BAY

Green Bay, a much older community than the two described above, had certain natural advantages—its location at the mouth of the Fox River as it emptied into Lake Michigan being paramount. It had been in existence many years prior to 1870, and its institutions were better established. Still, the processes which were common in other middle-sized cities in Wisconsin worked out in much the same way in Green Bay during the last third of the century.

Structural Dimensions

Economic Structure

Although its lake location was an advantage to Green Bay, and shaped

34. Ibid., May 5, 1873, May 14, 1874, March 20, 1884, August 31, 1888, September 19, 1894; Morton Keller, *Affairs of State: Public Life in Nineteenth Century America* (Cambridge, Mass.: Harvard University Press, 1977); J. R. Herryman, "Constitutional Restrictions upon Legislation Concerning Villages, Towns, Cities, and Counties," *American Law Review* 22 (1888): 403–18.

its economy somewhat toward maritime activities, the freezing of Lake Michigan for several months a year limited the city's ability to become a major port. When furs in the region were virtually exhausted in the early nineteenth century, lumber became the primary base of Green Bay's economy. Once the forests within Green Bay's environs were depleted (about 1870), it was clear that wood-processing and wood-working industries would survive but not many sawmills could. At the time that other parts of the state were able to tap massive supplies of logs and move into full lumber production, Green Bay—out of necessity—developed wood-processing industries more sophisticated than milling. The lumber-based industries that developed during the late nineteenth century were shingles; ship staves; cooperage; furniture; sash, door, and blind companies; and carriages and wagons. Shingle making, however, was by far the most important industry in the economy.[35] Several of the wood-based industries of the 1870s were oriented toward local consumption, as were most of the nonwood industries: flour mills, boot and shoe makers, brick yards, iron foundries, leather working businesses, breweries, harness makers. Lumber or wood-based industries remained the backbone of Green Bay's export economy until 1900, but their dominance decreased during the latter years of the century. In sum, by the end of the century Green Bay had developed a fairly diversified manufacturing economic base.[36]

Aware that exclusive dependence on wood products conflicted hopelessly with booster aims that Green Bay rival Chicago, Green Bay business leaders left few stones unturned in their efforts to diversify the economic base in the late nineteenth century, to develop a more horizontally differentiated economy. Reasonably well-favored by railroads, from 1880 to 1900 Green Bay flirted with a host of schemes for enhancing its economic prospects: sugar beet growing and processing; flax cultivation and processing; the manufacturing of machines; resort development to attract the well-to-do during the summer; and finally, supplying products for the whole of northern Wisconsin, which was erroneously thought to have considerable potential for settlement. Although most of the schemes to develop Green Bay into a major metropolis came to naught, other kinds of economic activity were brisk enough to keep Green Bay growing,

35. *Green Bay Gazette*, March 11, 1880, April 27, 1883, October 1, 1889, September 13, 1898.

36. For additional information on Green Bay, see Deborah B. Martin, *History of Brown County* (Chicago: The J.S. Clark Publishing Co., 1913); Donald A. DeBats, "The Political Sieve: A Study of Green Bay, Wisconsin, 1854-1880" (M.A. thesis, University of Wisconsin, 1967); and Lee F. Pendergrass, "Businessmen and Politicians in the Urban Development of Green Bay, Wisconsin, 1866-1882" (M.A. thesis, Univesity of Wisconsin, 1968); *Green Bay Gazette*, April 2, 1898.

and moving steadily away from exclusive dependence on primary lumber products.

While attempting to lure new manufacturers, Green Bay did not neglect to seek federal money for deepening its harbor channel. Both lines of endeavor were reasonably successful. There were numerous congressional appropriations for harbor improvement, and new industries came: a box company, a food factory, and a machine company. By 1895 there were sixty-nine factories in operation, and the Bradstreet agent who visited Green Bay in 1897 commented on its favorable economic climate and prospects, indicating that among Wisconsin cities, Green Bay was the least affected by economic cycles. Although the percentage of the population engaged in manufacturing almost doubled between 1890 and 1900, Green Bay ranked only seventeenth in the value of manufactures among Wisconsin cities in 1900 (in population, it was eighth) (see table 2.7).[37]

Table 2.7. Green Bay: Capitalization of Firms, 1875–1900

	1875	1890	1900
Primary sector			
Timber-using	10.8%	32.4%	33.2%
Farm-product-processing	.8	3.1	5.3
Secondary manufacturing			
Wood-using	.9	.4	.1
Sawmill machinery	—	—	.2
Other metal-using	—	7.2	1.4
Other, mainly			
alcoholic beverages	8.2	7.6	8.0
Wholesale trades	7.4	5.6	17.6
Retail trade, service	71.9	39.8	31.9
Transportation	—	3.9	2.3
Total	100.0%	100.0%	100.0%
Total capitalization	$1,451,000	$3,035,000	$5,662,000

Source: See table 2.1.

There had, of course, been fluctuations in Green Bay's economic condition between 1870 and 1900. Certainly, the decline of lumbering had hurt Green Bay, as had the depressions of the 1870s and 1880s. But the increasing diversity of the economy and the mixture of commerce

37. *Green Bay Gazette*, January 6, 1887, February 27, October 17, 1888, December 17, 1890, February 21, 1891, March 28, 1895, February 17, 1897, February 4, 1898; *Green Bay Advocate*, March 11, 1875; United States Office of the Census, 1900, Census of the United States, *Manufactures* (Washington, D.C.: U.S. Government Printing Office, 1900), pt. 2, table 5; *Report of the Commissioner of Labor Statistics* (Madison: State of Wisconsin, 1891–92), table D.

and manufacturing made for overall prosperity and growth (see table 2.7). As a distribution center, Green Bay profited with the growth of the dairy industry in the state. Meantime, local railroad payrolls were sizable, and water shipping continued to expand in the 1890s. Finally, the economic resources of Green Bay, though concentrated, were not so skewed as in other lumber towns such as Marinette or Eau Claire. The Green Bay rich were highly visible, very active—and generally anxious to put their money and energies to work locally, but seldom willing to invest their fortunes in cities elsewhere.[38]

Green Bay's economic autonomy had always been shaped by its water location; it had been a pass-through point for trappers trading their furs, later a sawmill town exporting lumber, and over time a ship and railroad nexus city. To put it differently, Green Bay had never been an isolated self-sufficient hamlet. With the virtual disappearance of primary products, Green Bay was ever more forced into a national goods and services network.

Social Structure

During the last third of the nineteenth century, as the economy became more complex, the distribution of occupations in Green Bay shifted. A smaller percentage of the population was in proprietor-manager-official groups, and a large fraction consisted of those who were skilled and semi-skilled workers (see table 2.8). Over time Green Bay became more, not less, "blue collar," and simultaneously within blue collar ranks, the skilled and semiskilled came to outnumber the unskilled. This pattern of distribution is similar to that of Janesville, though more slanted toward blue collar occupations. As more and more workers made their livelihoods with skilled and semiskilled work, there were, overall, smaller social distances within the city, and a gentle movement away from a pyramidal distribution as a cone-shaped pattern emerged.

Occupational distributions, as measures of social status or vertical differentiation, were made more complex by questions of ethnicity in Green Bay. Green Bay was predominantly foreign or second-generation foreign for most of the late nineteenth century (see table 2.9). More specifically, in 1905 only 21 percent of the Green Bay heads of families were native-born of native-born parents. Very heavy foreign-born representation was the usual pattern in Green Bay. The Germans (including Prussians) constituted the largest immigrant group, followed by the

38. *Green Bay Gazette,* October 17, 1888, August 7, 1891, January 27, 1892, April 5, 1894.

Table 2.8. Occupations of Heads of Families in Green Bay: 1870, 1880, 1905[a]

	1870	1880	1905
Professionals	4.2%	3.6%	3.1%
Proprietors, managers, officials	27.6	29.0	18.9
Clerks	10.8	6.1	9.3
Skilled and semiskilled laborers	26.8	27.8	38.5
Unskilled laborers	30.6	33.5	30.2
Total	100.0%	100.0%	100.0%
N =	1114	1594	3850

Source: These data were compiled from federal census manuscripts for 1870 and 1880, and from tabulated State of Wisconsin materials for 1905. These materials are on deposit at the Wisconsin State Historical Society, Madison, Wisconsin.

[a]Persons whose occupations were not listed in census manuscripts are omitted from this table. The number is 50 for 1870, 83 in 1880.

Table 2.9. Ethnic Characteristics of Heads of Families in Green Bay: 1870, 1880, 1905

	1870	1880	1905
Foreign-born			
Prussian, German	23.4%	37.2%	11.3%
Belgian	14.4	15.4	10.5
Canadian	8.0	4.4	2.9
Irish	6.1	3.0	8.0
Other	16.4	12.5	8.0
Total	68.3	72.5	40.7
Native-born of foreign-born parents	—[a]	8.0	38.2
Native-born of native-born parents			
Wisconsin	4.4	4.7	11.6
New England	6.5	2.6	1.0
Midwest[b]	4.3	2.4	2.2
Other	16.5	9.7	6.4
Total	31.7	19.4	21.2
Grand total	100.0%	100.0%	100.0%
N =	815	1450	4622

Source: These data were compiled from federal census manuscripts for 1870 and 1880, and from tabulated State of Wisconsin census materials for 1905. These materials are on deposit at the Wisconsin State Historical Society, Madison, Wisconsin.

[a]Not tabulated separately for 1870.

[b]Nine states in 1870, six states in 1880, three states in 1905.

Belgians. Those two nationality groups alone, including those foreign-born as well as those native-born of foreign-born parents, made up one-half of Green Bay's family heads by the end of the nineteenth century. Also fairly well represented were the Irish, and to a lesser extent the Danes, the Poles, and Hollanders.[39]

Among these immigrant groups the Belgians and Irish were Catholic, as were many of the Germans and Poles. Of Green Bay's eight churches in 1874, three were Catholic. New Catholic immigrant groups tended to stay in existing churches briefly, then form their own churches. As a result, Green Bay had six Catholic churches, including one Polish, one English, one French, one German, and one Dutch-Flemish by the end of the nineteenth century.[40] The ethnic church model helped keep ethnic groups separate, and may have helped prevent an ethnic/native dichotomy from developing in the community.

Among immigrant groups there were considerable differences in occupational status within the pyramidal social structure as well as within the political structure. Of the two largest groups the Germans were better represented among the economic and political elites. There were German mayors, German owners of the largest business firms, and a number of German professionals. Belgians became aldermen, not mayors, owned mostly small businesses if any at all, and were much less represented in the professions. Whereas the Prussian-Belgian differences had been considerable in 1860, by 1880 differences between those two groups had narrowed somewhat, though more recent immigrant groups were disproportionately represented among unskilled laborers.[41] By 1905 there was little difference in the extent to which the foreign-born, the native-born of foreign-born parents, and the native-born held jobs in the professional-managerial ranks.

It is difficult to know how much mingling of ethnic groups occurred, and in what context. Seemingly, ethnic groups were relatively untouched by public "Americanizing" institutions such as schools. Immigrant children generally attended parochial schools, Catholic as well as Lutheran. On the other hand, residential patterns did not reflect strict segregation of ethnic groups. People born in different countries lived in the same neighborhoods, and, more often than not, lived in homes they owned. In 1905 at least 60 percent of the foreign-born heads of families in Green Bay owned their

39. State of Wisconsin, *Census Report* (Madison: The state, 1885), pt. 2, pp. 633-34; State of Wisconsin Census 1905, unpublished but available at the Wisconsin State Historical Society, Madison, Wisconsin.

40. *Green Bay Gazette*, September 29, 1888, May 3, 1892; *Green Bay and Fort Howard Directory, 1874; Green Bay City Directory*, 1900.

41. *Green Bay Gazette*, September 22, 1892; De Bats, "Political Sieve."

homes. Property owning acted as an assimilation mechanism in that ownership made foreigners somewhat more concerned with local public policy, particularly policies regarding taxes, sidewalks, sewers, and paving.[42] The immigrants of Green Bay were perceived as regular citizens, unlike the woodsmen of Eau Claire or the female textile workers of Janesville.

Ethnic origins were kept alive in Green Bay not only through church affiliations, but also through voluntary societies. German voluntary societies (whether secret or benevolent) retained German names (for example, *Turn Verein, Armen Verein, Germania Kranken Unterstuentzungs Verein).* Still, the relatively large size of Green Bay's first- and second-generation immigrant community, the settled nature of the community (as contrasted with Eau Claire), the diversity of immigrant groups, and, most important, that immigrants had founded the city—all tended to minimize serious differences among ethnic groups.[43]

Compared to the other two cities Green Bay had many more social organizations, religious and secular. Stemming from the longer history of settlement and the variety of ethnic groups, these organizations tied citizens to the city's problems and prospects. In a larger community ethnicity differences might have meant the emergence of separate social pyramids. But the smallness of Green Bay, especially as economic enterprises grew larger, made this impossible.

Political Structure

In one major way Green Bay was uncharacteristic of middle-sized cities in Wisconsin and the nation at large during the late nineteenth century: politics were nonpartisan. Though county and state politics were partisan, there were no local Republican or Democratic parties. In most regards political structures were the familiar ones: a mayor elected annually and a council of aldermen elected from wards. Over time, as the city grew and eventually merged with neighboring Fort Howard in 1895, aldermanic districts were modified and the council grew. In Green Bay, as in Janesville and Eau Claire, there was always a lag between the perception of need for council boundary change and the actual change. City charter changes required action by the state legislature, and were not undertaken lightly.

42. State of Wisconsin, *Census Report* (Madison: The state, 1905).
43. *Green Bay and Fort Howard Directory, 1874* (Appleton: Reid and Miller, 1874); *Wright's Directory of Green Bay* (Milwaukee: A.G. Wright, 1900). The Green Bay newspapers in the latter part of the nineteenth century were filled with discussions about "ethnic" organizations.

During the late nineteenth century there were many local elections in Green Bay, even as in the other two cities. There were essentially two types of issues that called for special elections: funding for municipal improvements and setting of liquor license fees. Waterworks, bridge, and school bonds often by law had to be submitted for referenda, and liquor referenda were commonplace.[44] Councils were reluctant, even when able, to become involved in expensive building programs. Too, the upper limits for council bonding were set low to ensure some degree of citizen control. Small cities of this type certainly could not call upon enough ready cash to build schools or bridges, so recourse to the electorate was a regular feature.

Green Bay's government accomplished most of its work through City Council committees, and for the most part, mayor and council cooperated on issues of economy, street paving, bridge construction, and merger with neighboring Fort Howard. After the merger, with Green Bay imposing its institutions on smaller Fort Howard, there was a bit of chafing between the two "sides of town." But appointive offices were shared on the basis of informal agreement, and there was no serious friction. There was, however, concern with financial decisions made in the county, with the paucity of county services, and with money transferred out of Green Bay to the county.[45]

Among the City Council, Board of Education, and Board of Health there were rather strong differences of opinion as the nineteenth century drew to a close. Though the City Council appointed the Board of Education, most often choosing people of considerable social status, it usually allowed the school supervising body relative autonomy in its operations. There was a great deal of overlap among City Council members, Board of Education members, and leadership of the Business Men's Association, and there was little concern for professionalism in education. The Superintendent of Schools was not a strong figure, and those who held the job usually moved on after several years, to be replaced by someone from an outside school system (in Wisconsin or Illinois). Fiscal shortages in the 1890s caused tension, however, when the Board of Education refused to stop spending and asked for more money from an already pressed City Council.

Contrary to the Board of Education, the Board of Health enjoyed

44. *Green Bay Gazette*, August 29, 1885, July 9, 1886, January 19, 1888, November 8, 1889; *Green Bay Advocate*, September 17, 1890.

45. Merger activities and consequences were widely discussed throughout 1895. See the *Green Bay Gazette*, especially March and April issues; and *Green Bay Advocate*, April 10, 1890.

quite a bit of autonomy from the City Council and assumed a very energetic stance, even when people were likely to be annoyed by its activities. The doctor or doctors on the Board of Health made presentations one after the other to the City Council, requiring city ordinances bearing on public health. In an era in which many urban dwellers had come recently from self-sustaining farms, animals in town were common, and their control involved health authorities and elected officials in disputes with people used to having cows and pigs on their property. Similarly, food standards (especially for milk) were set by the Board of Health, as well as minimal sanitation standards. The responsibilities of the Board of Health were clearly acknowledged as quite distinct from the general kind of policy set by the City Council.

During the thirty-year period in question the structure of city government in Green Bay changed somewhat, as more political roles with clear responsibilities were created by the City Council. Usually, these specialized services involved applying some expertise, and there were increasing calls for better-trained persons for posts.[46] That Green Bay was a port, requiring more than a minimum of engineering expertise for improvement and upkeep, probably contributed to more appreciation for the niche of expert in public bureaucracies. Like Eau Claire and Janesville, Green Bay experienced some decline in political autonomy in the late nineteenth century. State regulators manifested a very modest presence, and state resources remained small if increasing. Meantime, Green Bay had always used its congressmen to get federal port appropriations, with similar success over time.

Political Culture

With a mixed political culture, tending more toward the traditional than the legal-rational, Green Bay citizens participated only moderately in politics, held generally low expectations of municipal government, and were likely to accept a very personalized politics. Political issues, not so absent as in Janesville, were not causes for much ire.

One important underpinning of the traditional emphasis in political culture was ethnoreligious-based ritualism. Although the residents of Green Bay were drawn from a variety of nations, very few of them shared the intense pietistic religious perspective that was common in Janesville. The pietists of late-nineteenth-century America, with a personal, vital, and fervent faith in a transcendent God, were oriented to conversion, change of heart, and personal piety—to emphasis on right behavior both

46. *Green Bay Gazette*, April 21, 1897.

for self and for others. Those with ritualistic perspectives (especially Catholics) accepted life in terms of resigned stewardship in a world that man might not change. Ritualistic perspectives emphasized doctrine and liturgy, adherence to external forms and symbols of religion. Supernatural values and secular activities were, to the ritualists, separate things; daily activities which were sinful to pietists carried no such stigma for ritualists. For the "ritualists" there was, thus, less desire to "work" the political process for moral ends, to challenge and reshape it, to set a different communitywide tone. From time to time political elites in Green Bay were questioned, or the fruits of the political system were challenged. But overall, with a majority of the population more inclined to accept than to manipulate authority, citizen political mobilization was uncommon.[47]

Another reason that politics in Green Bay, whether mayoral or aldermanic, was rarely acrimonious was the virtually total overlap between business and political elites. The business-political elites took some pains to stay in touch with other citizens. For example, they frequently organized public meetings in anticipation or support of City Council decisions. Overall, they succeeded in their aim of keeping a broad political base. Occasionally, there were charges about shoddy election practices, but for the most part criticisms of city government were restrained.

Thus, the relative harmony of the City Council meetings could be explained by the fact that many important issues were handled by the Business Men's Association. True, the City Council handled expenditures for streets, bridges, and schools, but it did not bear responsibility for bonuses and encouragement to out-of-town business firms for locating in Green Bay. These the various businessmen's associations provided.

Some citizens believed that lack of partisanship encouraged "better people" to seek political office. As a consequence of the nonpartisanship, there was a slight tendency for Green Bay to have more upper middle class officeholders than the other cities. Most Green Bay citizens, like those in many middle-sized American cities in the late nineteenth century, seemed to reason that a business government was the best government and that if the mayor were a successful businessman or professional man, the prospects for the city would be improved.[48]

Election campaigns in Green Bay were short, with candidates announcing their availability through newspaper "cards," or in response to

47. See Paul Kleppner, *The Cross of Culture* (New York: The Free Press, 1970), pp. 69–91, for a fuller discussion of this issue.

48. *Green Bay Gazette*, March 31, 1886, March 19, 1891, February 25, April 9, 1896, February 4, 1897.

calls or petitions. Such short notice and nonpartisanship discouraged high levels of voter turnout or intense political participation. Partly as a consequence, there was considerable continuity of personnel in the office of Green Bay's mayors. In the twenty-one elections between 1880 and 1900 only seventeen different men attempted to become mayor. For example, James Elmore ran in 1890, 1891, 1892, 1893, 1894, and 1895; Charles Hartung in 1885, 1886, 1887, 1888, and 1889. This lack of turnover, both among incumbents and challengers, was tied, in part, to the lack of parties. There were, after all, no regular instruments for dislodging mayors or for discouraging perennial challengers. Aldermen, too, were challenged and turned out of office infrequently: they usually resigned their positions for lack of time or interest rather than because of defeat or challenge.[49]

From time to time there was bickering over the adequacy of representation for different ethnic groups—with the Belgians complaining one year of lack of representation, and in another year rumors mounting that several candidates belonged to the American Protective Association. Elected city officials were less Catholic and less immigrant than the city population in general, though in ethnic distribution and wealth they tended to reflect the ethnic diversity of the city better than the mayors. And while the very wealthiest men in the city seldom served as mayor, the mayors were from the economic elite. In terms of political leadership Green Bay was in this period first a simple, later a multiple-element, oligarchy.[50]

Ethnicity was very important in Green Bay politics, however, Clubs for state and national elections were often formed along ethnic lines, and speeches were made in German as late as the 1890s. Locally, referenda were sometimes printed in several languages, and minor patronage appointments might depend on ethnicity.[51]

There was no strong organized labor group in Green Bay politics. True, the Federation of Labor was organized in Green Bay in 1894, but it remained somewhat ineffective. Since Green Bay workers were not employed in two or three large factories and did not have a common type of work (as did Eau Claire lumber and sawmill men), the conditions supportive of union activism were not very great. Newspaper editorials

49. Ibid., April 3, 1880, March 25, 1884.

50. Ibid., November 11, 1880, March 31, June 19, 1882, February 13-15, 1886, January 17, 1889, November 6, 1894, October-November, 1898; Green Bay Advocate, October 21, 1880; Green Bay Weekly Gazette, November 24, 1880; De Bats, "Political Sieve."

51. Green Bay Gazette, April 7, 1875, March 27, 1882, May 3, 1884, October 23, 1890, September 30, 1892; Green Bay Weekly Gazette, October 20, 1880; Green Bay Advocate, October 16, 1900.

often boasted of the paucity of strikes. During the last five years of the nineteenth century several new unions were organized, and there was more activity by the older unions. Since the workers in unions were for the most part skilled craftsmen, considered respectable middle class citizens by other townspeople, their organizations were not viewed as threats to economic or other elites.[52]

In 1900, however, organized labor began to speak with a more unified voice, and supported John Dillon's decisions to run for mayor. Dillon, president of the Coopers' Union and president of the Federated Trades Council, which had 800 members, was also an organizer for the American Federation of Labor. Dillon ran as a general reform candidate, with enthusiastic labor union support, against the incumbent mayor and another reform candidate. He finished second, after a campaign filled with emotional rhetoric that did not mobilize any more voters than other mayoral elections. And even that election was engaged primarily over personalities, not issues.[53]

Prohibition activity was perpetually present in Green Bay but not particularly divisive or successful. This was, first, because of the population mix. Green Bay lacked the pietistic New England and Scandinavian element often associated with temperance fervor in Wisconsin. Second, there was not a sizable "rough-and-tumble" working class in Green Bay, so there was not much concern for preserving social order through temperance control. Third, the Catholics, against whom prohibition sentiment was often directed, had been among the early founders of Green Bay, and for this reason they enjoyed higher social status than Catholics in Eau Claire and Janesville.

The political culture of Green Bay for most of the late nineteenth century was not supportive of challenge. The oligarchical economic-political elite links were questioned more as labor elements became active after 1895 and as city size (and merger) altered some of the small town interaction patterns. Traditionalism in decision making, however, survived well beyond 1900.

Public Policy

The public policies adopted and implemented in Green Bay were not markedly different from those described in Janesville: in both instances caretaker activities tended to dominate all other concerns. Energies in the

52. *Green Bay Gazette*, September 17, 1886, March 23, May 2, 1891, January 3, September 5, 1894, March 8, 1896; *Green Bay Advocate*, June 13, 1895.
53. *Green Bay Advocate*, March 23, March 30, April 3, 1900.

private sector in Green Bay were much more mobilized, however, leading to a rather different set of outcomes for the city.

The mayors and common councils of Green Bay were very concerned with following a conservative fiscal policy, especially after the city experienced great financial embarrassment in 1878-79. Hit by the aftermath of the 1873 Panic and saddled with large bonded debts, the city found itself with a number of unpaid tax bills, and eventually, tax sales. When money became available in the 1880s, Green Bay officials redeemed 20 percent of the bonded indebtedness, refinanced other debts to secure lower interest rates, and vowed never again to rely heavily on debt. For the balance of the nineteenth century the city government was most prudent as to bonding as well as to current expenditures: even after the city's economy began to flourish in the late 1890s the habit of frugality persisted, and caretaker policies were the only ones pursued.[54]

To some extent Green Bay found itself inhibited in city spending by railroad bonding incurred at an earlier date. But whatever the reasons, Green Bay citizens had little enthusiasm for adding to municipal possessions if it meant higher taxes. Thus, schools were antiquated, while water works and utilities had to be handled privately, if at all. Capital spending outlays, if they were to be approved, had to be short-term, and of proven necessity. Long-range planning tended to be more controversial because it usually involved more citizens and generally called for more money. For example, the development of an adequate school system was thought to lie beyond what could be afforded. Even if Green Bay's public high school building was the worst in the state, as the newspaper insisted, the city repaired it cheaply rather than replace it. Public schools were crowded and often obnoxiously dirty, despite the fact that approximately one-third of the pupils attended parochial schools. Perhaps there was reduced citizen pressure for a better school system because a large number of children attended private schools.[55]

If resources were doled out to schools grudgingly, such was not the case with the fire department. Since there was constant fear of fire, as in Eau Claire and Janesville, the city made serious efforts to provide adequate financing for a fire department. By the late 1890s newspapers gave the impression that there was a very efficient and well-equipped fire depart-

54. For the reaction of Green Bay's elites to the financial problems of the 1870s, see Pendergrass, "Businessmen and Politicians in the Urban Development of Green Bay"; *Green Bay Gazette*, March 4, 1880, January 14, 1882, May 18, 1883; *Green Bay Advocate*, January 5, 1882.

55. *Green Bay Gazette*, January 24, 1880, July 24, 1883, January 7, 1884, April 5, 1886, April 3, 1893, June 23, 1894, June 17, 1899; *Green Bay Weekly Gazette*, August 17, 1875.

ment. Compared to the school authorities, the fire department was the epitome of professionalism and modernization.

There were intermittent city council flirtations with long-range planning, particularly in reference to a citywide sewage system. As early as 1883 the City Council and the Business Men's Association agreed on a comprehensive sewer plan, but enacting it, with consequent large tax loads for the city, was another matter. Nevertheless, a rudimentary system of sewers was built toward the end of the century.[56]

In carrying out caretaker responsibilities, the City Council was much concerned with bridge upkeep and location, as well as with street lights and paving. As a river divided the city, the problem of maintaining bridges was perpetually an issue; while the poorly paved roads were incessantly in need of repair. Probably no subjects occupied so much attention as those involving the condition of sidewalks, streets, and bridges.

After 1890 there was considerable concern in Green Bay about the granting of municipal franchises. That Green Bay would have an electric street railway was taken for granted, and likewise that private auspices would own and operate it. But Green Bay's council was anxious to grant a franchise that would secure for the city the greatest benefits. The caution mentioned above was peculiar neither to Green Bay nor to street railways. Whereas in the 1870s and 1880s most Wisconsin cities had been willing to grant franchises quite freely, by 1890 many had become quite wary. Eager as they were for services, they were aware that a franchise could be a burden to a city rather than a benefit. The rampant boosterism, which often led to multiple utility companies and to foul water supplied by legally unassailable water companies, was checked toward the end of the nineteenth century by concerns for quality, by threats of franchise revocation if service were not improved. When franchises were to be granted, competitive bids from companies throughout the United States were welcome. And if companies holding franchises delivered inadequate services, cities sought redress in the courts and in the legislatures.[57]

Green Bay's most serious franchise problems arose in conjunction with the waterworks. The most important aspect of waterworks performance was the quantity of water available for putting out fires; second on the list was fitness of water for drinking and other personal services. With the waterworks providing an intermittently unsatisfactory volume of water, the Green Bay City Council alternately harangued and cajoled the company holding the franchise.

56. *Green Bay Gazette,* January 18, 1883, January 17, 1885. By 1897-98 Green Bay, despite an incomplete system, considered itself a city with sewers.

57. This theme is given excellent treatment in a number of other Wisconsin cities during this period in Thelen, *The New Citizenship; Green Bay Gazette,* June 4, 1885, August 25, 1886, February 1, 1887. In Green Bay, franchise investigations were undertaken in 1895.

Even more troublesome, if less vital, was the coming of an electric street railway. One company after another made promises or began work, but the net effect year after year was the lack of service.

Although the policies in Green Bay were very much typical caretaker, in one regard they were a bit unusual for cities of this size. Green Bay's City Council, stimulated by a very active Board of Health, was much more vigilant of community health than elsewhere in Wisconsin. The Board of Health, headed by a doctor elected by the City Council, walked a fine line between working for voluntary cooperation and for enforcement through ordinance or other authority. By 1891 the Board of Health also employed a policeman and a plumbing inspector. Examples of Board of Health activity were public demonstrations of dry earth closets, school vaccinations, demands for a new pesthouse, better water supply and sewage facilities, milk inspection, issuing of burial licenses, the quarantining of diseases, and the limiting of animals roaming over the city. For the most part the Board of Health had little difficulty getting council cooperation. On the other hand, the doctor on the Board of Health made no friends because of his job: few people wanted regulations enforced. Sanitation regulations were often expensive, and quarantines were inconvenient.[58]

Always hovering in the background for Green Bay was the willingness of some of its well-to-do citizens to aid the city. The Business Men's Association and its forerunners sought to lure industry and railroads to Green Bay. During the late 1860s boosters had been able to convert their faith that municipal improvements would lead to urban development into cash for railroad bonding. Later organizations turned their enthusiasm to the attraction and development of industry. New industry, with work for the idle and increased opportunities for upward mobility, also meant a broadened tax base. The Business Men's Association was unremitting in its endeavors to assure the economic development of Green Bay: its activities were addressed to manufacturers, service-oriented industries and associations, and agriculture, as well as the railroads. With a private association raising subscriptions and bonus money, the City Council did not have to allow for such grants in annual budgets or in debt calculation. In addition, wealthy citizens provided a hospital, a library, and a park for the city.[59]

58. *Green Bay Gazette*, September 1, 1883, July 25, August 5, August 12, 1884, January 22, October 30, November 3, 1885, February 20, 1888, December 14, 1893, March 15, 1894, January 11, June 11, 1895, January 20, 1898; *Green Bay Advocate*, August 28, 1900.

59. *Green Bay Gazette*, January 21, 28, July 27, 1875, January 6, 1881, December 1, 1882, September 13, December 15, 1883, December 2, 1884, April 23, December 30, 1885, February 26, June 25, December 22, 1886, March 3, 1887, April 24, August 9, 1888, Sep-

As these examples indicate, both amenities and some necessities were made available as a result of private aid. Actually Green Bay was somewhat more oriented toward amenities than the other two cities described. Only slowly recovering from its illusion that it might rival Chicago or Milwaukee as a major port, Green Bay citizens often talked of the appurtenances of first-class cities, with particular emphasis on parks. Green Bay even appropriated occasional public monies for park care (fencing, flowers, etc.). Still, such amenity activity, both private and public, was very modest: the private park subscription fund lapsed in the mid-1880s for lack of support, and in the 1890s the city government puzzled for four years over how to finance Washington Park without finding a workable solution.[60]

Similarly, in the area of economic development policies, Green Bay's public authorities did just enough to demonstrate that they were not insensitive to business growth but not much more. Green Bay did not repeat the large-scale railroad bonding of the 1870s, but used its public authority to help the railways purchase right-of-ways. In the 1890s Green Bay's council and citizens (in referendum) declared their willingness to support bonds (in order to secure a new state normal school). The effort to attract a new school to the city was unsuccessful, however. For the most part, it was private sources which sought federal appropriations for the harbor and Fox River waterway, new federal buildings, new industry, conventions, state fairs, and so on. Their efforts were usually successful, especially when harbor needs were involved.[61]

Issues and policies of morality, though time-consuming for the Green Bay Council, were rather unremarkable. Green Bay usually had about ninety saloons, and there were modest debates about the proximity of saloons to churches and schools, about enforcement of laws prohibiting the sale of alcohol to minors, and the like. Liquor license fees, a subject of considerable controversy, were usually low, whether set by council or popular vote, though neighboring Fort Howard chose high fees. The police force made infrequent raids on houses of prostitution and token efforts to control saloons. Arrests for serious crimes were few. The police force was supervised rather carefully by the City Council, but not taken as seriously as the Fire Department or the Board of Health. There were

tember 14, 1894, October 13, December 5, 1895, April 29, 1897, May 3, 1899; *Green Bay Advocate*, January 9, 1890.

60. *Green Bay Gazette*, September 6, 1882, August 11, 1884.

61. Ibid., January 18, 1882, October 25, 1883, April 29, June 14, October 11, 1893, January 20, 1894, November 12, 1895, May 14, 1896; *Green Bay Advocate*, January 16, 1882.

occasional charges of corrupt practices within the police department, and, as a result, there were a few coerced changes in personnel.[62]

Green Bay in the late nineteenth century is a salutary reminder of how weak public government systems were at that time, and how private, not public, systems bore the loads and demands of citizens.

CONCLUSION

We have attempted, by discussing these three Wisconsin cities during the last third of the nineteenth century, to demonstrate how the conceptual analytical scheme developed in the first chapter can be employed to illuminate a set of historical changes.

In particular, we have shown for each of these communities how shifts in economic, social, and political structures related to changes in political culture and public policy, how shifts in occupational distribution and ethnic integration affected supply and demand of services. Discussion of a larger number of cities representing a wider geographical area and over a longer time span would allow even better illustration of the conceptual approach outlined. For these three cities, however, structures, processes, and policies shifted, even in a brief time span, in the direction of the change outlined in chapter 1. That is, economic structures shifted from emphasis on primary products, and the economic autonomy of communities declined. By 1875 each of these three communities had passed beyond the stage of being a small community with a primitive economy. Even so, the high prevailing transportation costs meant that each of the three communities produced a whole range of commodities for consumers. Like most cities in the early stages of industrialization, they had industries based on food processing, wood products, and textiles, industries requiring low level skills and unsophisticated technology. High transfer costs protected these fledgling industries to some extent. With the reduction in transportation costs, local industries were eventually rationalized and tied more closely into a regionwide network of goods and services. To survive, industries usually had to specialize in an economic activity in which they enjoyed an advantage even with transportation costs equalized. By the turn of the twentieth century, industries which were specialized had developed in all three cities, and a more sizable manufacturing sector was developing. The tertiary sector—with emphasis on professional, administrative, and personal services—was still very small.

Social structures changed in that occupational differentiation increased,

62. *Green Bay Gazette*, May 15, 1875, January 17, May 3, 1880, January 17, 1885, August 27, 1898, February 27, 1899, April 28, 1900.

though not at the same pace in all communities, given their somewhat different points of passage through the processes of economic change. As the cities moved away from their dependence on a primary product base, social structures shifted from the pyramid model toward the cone shape. This process of change was most rapid in Eau Claire, although it began at a later point in time.

The essentially oligarchic political systems remained throughout this period, with intermittent challenges. Had Eau Claire been a community with only 2500 people, it might have been an autocratic company town, but its population size made almost inevitable sufficient differentiation to support a number of individuals as political dominants. And by the turn of the century, there was neither sufficient tertiary sector employment nor enough horizontal differentiation to support much departure from oligarchic-based models.

The three communities followed much the same pattern in terms of political structure, increasing their use of professionals and enlarging their modest municipal bureaucracies in the context of oligarchy. To some extent, these changes were responses to external forces: the pressure of state legislation and bureaucracies, the examples of other cities, the increasing awareness of technological means for solving problems. At the same time, changes in local political structures were responses to localized shifts in information and in the political culture. The pietism that became identified with political reform provoked counter-reactive political activity from those who did not want to be "saved" or "cleansed." Both those who wanted to use politics to save others and those with little interest in reformism were drawn into the political process: they would vote, balance tickets, and criticize the city government according to its departure from some ideal role. Identifications such as "loggers from the pineries," "immigrants," and "boardinghouse residents" faded; to some extent, communalities of expectation for waterworks to fight fire and make pure water available replaced earlier distrusts. The fervor of prohibition floundered a bit, and in some places labor politics emerged.

All of these changes were not without impact in the policy area. With extreme financial pressures resulting from the agricultural depression of the 1890s, none of the cities was able to move far from a caretaker base. Economic development, sponsored by municipal government funds and energies in Eau Claire, fell to private hands in Green Bay, hands which managed very capably. Janesville's economic development activity, public and private, was quite modest.

The ethnic diversity and the rapid population turnover in these communities contributed to an oligarchical political structure. The ethnic diversity prevented class solidarity among the low income population—the

majority of the citizenry. At the same time, the communities were still sufficiently small and at a low enough level in the stage of capitalism so that the elites were relatively cohesive, sharing a common set of values. Moreover, the elites tended to remain in the communities while sizeable percentages of their population emigrated out each year. These three communities are consistent with other findings about late-nineteenth-century communities which demonstrate that those "people who had a 'stake' in a community—those people most interested in maintaining the stability necessary to ensure their continued security or success—were the people most likely to stay around long enough to achieve and maintain community control."[63]

By 1900 intense concern for social control policies had moderated in those cities in which it previously had been strongly felt. The major change, insofar as policy was concerned, was the broadening of the definition of caretaker. In 1870 caretaker policies required very little activity—perhaps some planking for the downtown streets, bridges to deal with the water bodies dividing towns, and modest concern with education, police, and fire problems. During the ensuing thirty years the expected minimal levels of services changed drastically: each city was expected to have public health protection; schools of varying levels; paved streets; sidewalks; sturdy bridges; waterworks for fire protection and potable water; responsive fire departments; police authority; street lights; electric light companies; and the like. More optional, but not far from basic, were street railways, fire alarm systems, and telephone companies. City governments were, of course, not expected to provide or finance all of these; they were, however, expected to exercise sufficient control of franchises to ensure that reputable companies would provide service on adequate levels. Street railways were to be completed, not abandoned halfway for lack of funds, leaving torn-up streets. Utility poles were not supposed to be unattractive or unstable. Utility rates were supposed to be reasonable, expansions of service to be feasible. If cities, in their initial enthusiasm for long-term franchises, had made citizens victims of what appeared to be rapacious private companies, then it was expected by 1900 that city governments would secure redress. Franchises would have to be broken or purchased, and those seeking new franchises had to be prepared for close questioning. More vigorous demands for providing public services

63. See Richard S. Alcorn, "Leadership and Stability in Mid-Nineteenth Century America: A Case Study of an Illinois Town," *Journal of American History* 61 (December 1974): 686. For a discussion of cohesion and conflict at the community level, see Lee Benson, *Philadelphia Elites and Economic Development: Quasi-Public Innovation During the First American Organizational Revolution* (Wilmington, Del.: Regional Economic History Research Center, Eleutherian Mills-Hagley Foundation, 1978).

were made on municipal governments by 1900, and the amateurs in politics struggled with restricted funds to satisfy outraged citizens.

On some major dimensions, these three cities were rather similar. When they are compared on a variety of policy measures with the other 275 middle-sized cities in the United States, the three appear very similar to one another. For example, in total per capita municipal expenditures in 1903, they ranked 215, 174, and 194 (Green Bay, Janesville, and Eau Claire). The raw figures make the point even more clearly: Green Bay spent $8.53 per capita, Janesville $9.57, and Eau Claire $9.09. In terms of indebtedness per capita, the three cities ranked between 222 and 246. When the average value of productive possessions (governmentally owned property which produced income) per capita is considered, they ranked between 208 and 248. On two measures, highly related to one another, they were spread farther apart: on unproductive possessions (property which was nonincome producing), the ranks were 117, 56, and 176. And on expenditures per pupil in public schools, the ranks were 205, 110, and 211 (Green Bay, Janesville, and Eau Claire, respectively).[64]

These particular measures, reflecting so much similarity among the three cities, are drawn from 1903, and it will be recalled that we have already suggested that the three became more alike over time. Comparable data available for the same measures for 1880 and for all other cities of similar size reveal somewhat greater diversity among the three Wisconsin cities. The cities, however, ranked closely together on a number of indicators throughout the late nineteenth century for a variety of reasons. They were similar in their stage of development and somewhat comparable in per capita income. Moreover, they were in the same state, subject to many of the same state laws and inspection procedures.

As table 2.10 indicates, the demographic differences among the cities (as to the fractions of the population that were female, young dependents, and militia-aged males) became smaller over time. The published aggregate data are not, unfortunately, available in time series at a more refined level. One can posit that the consistently smaller young dependent population in Janesville had to do with the fact that single women were employed in mills. Presumably women without children, in transient employment without strong unions, would be less demanding of government and willing to accept caretaker-only policies, even if schools were quite poor. The decade of the 1890s, when service demands began to be expressed, ended with an upturn in local wealth and some prospects for moving away from the low-profile government ideology. The picture is more complex, however. Janesville had long had a sizable sector of the

64. The sources on which these ranking are based are described in chapter 3.

work force in white collar occupations, and yet did not have the range of services we ascribe to middle class demands. The demographic and other socioeconomic variables are only part of the very complex explanation of policy, even for what we think of as simpler times. The conceptual framework of chapter 1 helps us to sort the important basic variables, but for their enrichment and for ultimate understanding we need the specifics of the situational context provided in this chapter.

Table 2.10. Comparison of Three Cities, 1870–1900

	Eau Claire	Janesville	Green Bay	Measure of difference
Males of militia age as percentage of population				
1870 (18–45)	—	19.5	20.7	—
1880 (18–44) (County)	27.1	21.0	17.4	9.7
1890 (18–44)	23.2	21.9	20.7	2.5
1900 (18–44)	18.0	21.9	19.8	3.9
Female percentage of population				
1870	—	50.8	49.6	—
1880 (County)	45.0	49.5	48.8	4.5
1890	48.9	51.8	49.5	2.9
1900	51.0	51.6	51.4	.6
Young dependent percentage of population				
1870 (5–18)	—	30.6	30.8	—
1880 (5–17) (County)	26.9	26.9	33.5	6.6
1890 (5–20)	32.6	30.6	36.5	5.9
1900 (5–20)	36.9	28.8	35.0	8.1
Percentage of workers in white collar occupations				
1870	22.9	40.4	42.6	19.7
1880	18.9	41.8	38.7	22.9
1905	32.8	37.4	31.3	6.1
Property valuation per capita				
1880	$350	$445	$215	1 to 2.1
1890	$312	$403	$239	Ratio 1 to 1.7
1900	$486	$656	$602	1 to 1.3

There were peculiar combinations of circumstances affecting some aspects of policy—for example, the rough and ready aspect of Eau Claire,

leading to social control policy discussions, and the linkage between Green Bay nonpartisanship and private sector problem solving. Within the overall oligarchic pattern, there was—even for three cities in the same state—enough variety to suggest that some diversity of behavior might flow from similar structural patterns. This is, of course, why one needs to move from the general to the specific and back again, to enrich both the abstract and applied perspectives.

The most striking characteristic of these three cities was the importance of the economic marketplace in shaping their structures and social processes. At neither the state or local levels were there any effective public institutions charged with social planning. Instead, there was a widespread belief that those individuals with the most wit, energy, and wealth should shape society's most important outcomes in the private sector. With technological changes proceeding at a "whirlwind" pace, however, few people had a clear vision of what kind of community could and should emerge in this region. As a result, drift, custom, inertia, unplanned activity characterized the social and political process of these three cities. A kind of "bastard pragmatism" dictated instant solutions to every problem. The emphasis was on the present—rarely with any thought of the future. The political process was often dominated by details of narrow social significance: the size of contracts for schools and jails, the location of bridges and streets, the number and cost of liquor licenses. And it was in the private sector that economic dominants made the most important decisions about the local quality of life.[65]

---

65. See Hurst, *Law and Economic Growth*, for a discussion of the political process in Wisconsin during the late nineteenth century.

3

The Impact of Voting Behavior
on Public Policy

THEORETICAL PROBLEM

THE SEARCH for the determinants of public policy has become a major concern of social scientists in recent years, with attention being focused on nation-states as well as on numerous subnational units of government such as states, counties, and cities. There has been very little effort to explain public policy at earlier points in time, as most of the analysis has been confined to the most recent past. As a result, we have a very inadequate understanding of the following questions: May we assume that the determinants of policy outcomes in the contemporary world can be generalized to earlier points in time? Or, if they cannot, how do the determinants of policy change over time? Obviously, these questions may be answered only as a result of systematic studies of earlier points in time, and this chapter is designed to shed some light on these questions.

The questions which cut across much of the scholarly literature tend to focus on the following: How much control over public policy does the electorate exert? How much autonomy do political elites have in the shaping of public policy? How important are the social and economic characteristics of a society in shaping its public policy?

The foregoing chapters developed and applied a conceptual framework for community outcomes, mainly in the government-policy area. A large number of indicators, at input, process, and output stages, were discussed in the first chapter, with efforts to specify linkages among them. The second chapter, rooted in specific historical materials, helped to clothe the conceptual approach with reality, discussing the interplay of forces in different varieties of oligarchic communities through processual analysis, particularly as this interplay relates to policy outputs. But to confront

119

the questions raised above, for a large number of cities, a somewhat different research strategy is used. In this case, explanation proceeds from a large cross-sectional historical data set rather than from an in-depth processual model. There are many theoretical areas of overlap with the strategies, and each gains strength from the utility of the other.

While there are many answers to these questions, most of the recent literature on the determinants of public policy clusters around four general positions: (1) the elitist model of decision making; (2) the electoral approach to policy; (3) the socioeconomic determinants of policy; and (4) an eclectic explanation of policy outcomes. And though the following abbreviated description of these explanations does very little justice to any single position, there is some utility in differentiating these central tendencies in the literature.

The Elitist Model of Decision Making

The basic position here is that political elites are relatively immune to electoral pressures. There are several variants on this position, some taking the view that the electorate are ill-informed—perhaps irrational—while others, having a more charitable view toward the electorate, nevertheless believe that it is impossible for public choices to be managed through elections. For example, Kenneth Arrow, an economist, assumes the voter to be rational but argues that inasmuch as voters vary in resources, occupations, ideologies, ages, as well as on many other variables, individuals have different priorities on issues. One voter may give a priority ranking to issues of A, B, C, and D, another voter may rank the same issues as D, C, B, and A, while a third voter may rank the same issues as B, A, D, C. For these reasons, preferences can rarely be aggregated into democratic collective choices, especially in a large and complex society. Because there are so many alternatives among which voters might choose on any issue, it is only when the electorate is confronted with a choice between mutually exclusive policies that public choices are likely to be decisive. Voting is then an "all or nothing" proposition. On most occasions, however, the voter focuses his attention on candidates, and he is unable to discriminate those candidates' positions which he approves from those to which he objects. Moreover, the voter has even greater difficulty in influencing the performance of local officials who are appointed rather than elected.[1]

1. An inventory and categorization of the literature on electoral behavior during American history is J. Rogers Hollingsworth, "Problems in the Study of Popular Voting Behavior," in *American Political Behavior: Historical Essays and Readings,* ed. Lee Benson et al. (New York: Harper & Row, 1974). Some of the issues discussed in this chapter are examined

Meanwhile, a vast, empirically based literature demonstrates that most voters lack a consistent and firmly held position on most issues of public policy and that very few voters have an understanding of the policy position of public officials.[2] Moving beyond these findings, a number of scholars contend that electoral behavior is a ritualistic enterprise which has virtually no impact on policy formation. For example, Alfred de Grazia echoes this sentiment when he writes, "the electoral process is symbolic and psychological in meaning rather than a device for the purpose of instructing delegates" on policy issues.[3]

It was in the context of this kind of thinking that Joseph Schumpeter argued "democracy means only that the people have the opportunity of accepting or refusing the men who are to rule them."[4] Scholars who take this view certainly are not arguing that political elites are immune from pressure groups and other forces; rather, they are merely concluding that the electorate plays little role in shaping policy.[5]

The Electoral Approach to Policy

Economists who have tried to fit the models of economics to voting behavior have been the most sophisticated advocates of this view. But the electoral approach to policy has long been widely accepted. James Buchanan, Gordon Tullock, and Anthony Downs are economists who have applied the economic theory of marketplaces to government, by regarding

---

in abbreviated form in J. Rogers Hollingsworth, "The Impact of Electoral Behavior on Public Policy," in *History of American Electoral Behavior*, ed. Joel Silbey et al. (Princeton, N.J.: Princeton University Press, 1978). An excellent discussion of the normative questions involving representative government is Hanna F. Pitkin, ed., *Representation* (New York: Atherton, 1969). Also see Kenneth Arrow, *Social Choice and Individual Values* (New York: John Wiley and Sons, 1951); L. L. Wade and R. L. Curry, *A Logic of Public Policy: Aspects of Political Economy* (Belmont, Calif.: Wadsworth Publishing Co., 1970).

2. For a perceptive discussion of the literature on this position, see John C. Wahlke, "Policy Demands and System Support: The Role of the Represented," *British Journal of Political Science* 1 (July 1971): 271-90. Robert R. Alford and Roger Friedland contend that elected officials shape the views of voters, rather than voters shaping the views of political elites. See "Political Participation and Public Policy," *Annual Review of Sociology* 1 (1975): 429-79.

3. Alfred de Grazia, *Public and Republic* (New York: Alfred A. Knopf, 1951), p. 170. For a general development of this view, see Murray Edelman, *The Symbolic Uses of Politics* (Urbana: University of Illinois Press, 1964).

4. Joseph A. Schumpeter, *Capitalism, Socialism, and Democracy* (New York: Harper and Brothers, 1947), p. 285.

5. See Peter Bachrach, *The Theory of Democratic Elitism: A Critique* (Boston: Little, Brown, 1967). A challenge to the view that the electorate has little influence on elite behavior is Morris P. Fiorina's "Constituency Influence: A Generalized Model and Its Implications for Statistical Studies of Roll-Call Behavior," *Political Methodology* 2 (1975): 249-66.

public policy as part of an exchange relationship, as elites exchange public policies for electoral support.[6] Buchanan and Tullock make this succinct statement: "we have . . . assumed that decisions are made by popular vote. Where we have discussed elected legislatures, we have assumed that the legislator simply votes according to the majority preference in his districts."[7] The electorate thus transmits orders to the elected, "ideally something of an automatic mechanism—indeed a sort of slot machine by which votes inserted at one end turn out laws at the other."[8]

Elected officials are assumed, in this view, to be "in touch with the circumstances, feelings, and needs" of their constituents,[9] especially in local politics. When elites or elected officials fail to represent the wishes of constituents, they will be replaced by voters, who are central and influential persons in shaping policy.[10]

The Socioeconomic Determinants of Policy

Whereas advocates of the two previous positions attempt to explain policy by focusing on political activity, this mode of analysis shifts attention away from the electorate, pressure groups, and political elites. Because this approach assumes that government lacks autonomy, the political

6. For the political theory involving this view, see Charles E. Lindblom, *Politics and Markets* (New York: Basic Books, 1977); C. B. Macpherson, *Democratic Theory: Essays in Retrieval* (London: Oxford University Press, 1973); James M. Buchanan and Gordon Tullock, *The Calculus of Consent* (Ann Arbor: University of Michigan Press, 1962); James M. Buchanan, *Public Finance in Democratic Process* (Chapel Hill: The University of North Carolina Press, 1967); Anthony Downs, *An Economic Theory of Democracy* (New York: Harper & Row, 1957); Wade and Curry, *Logic of Public Policy;* R. L. Curry and L. L. Wade, *A Theory of Political Exchange* (Englewoods Cliffs, N.J.: Prentice-Hall, 1968); Norman Frohlich et al., "A Test of Downsian Voter Rationality: 1964 Presidential Voting," *American Political Science Review* 72 (March 1978), 178-97; and William Riker and Peter Ordeshook, *An Introduction to Positive Political Theory* (Englewood Cliffs, N.J.: Prentice-Hall, 1975).

7. Buchanan and Tullock, *Calculus of Consent,* p. 338. Also see p. 298. In the studies by Downs and Buchanan and Tullock the rational voter is analogous to the rational man inherent in many economists' models. He is one who knows what he wants, what his choices are, and what his resources are.

8. John Dearlove, *The Politics of Policy in Local Government* (London: Cambridge University Press, 1973), p. 27.

9. D. N. Chester, *Central and Local Government* (London: Macmillan and Co., 1951), p. 342.

10. Peter O. Steiner, "Public Expenditure Budgeting," in *The Economics of Public Finance,* ed. Alan S. Binder et al. (Washington, D.C.: The Brookings Institution, 1974), p. 271; James H. Kuklinski, "Representativeness and Elections: A Policy Analysis," *American Political Science Review* 72 (March 1978): 165-77. For a modified, complex, and sophisticated statement of this view, see Sidney Verba and N. H. Nie, *Participation in America: Political Democracy and Social Equality* (New York: Harper & Row, 1972); and Dearlove, *Politics of Policy in Local Government,* p. 39.

system receives very little research attention. In this explanation, government political structures are relatively unimportant in affecting the nature of public policy, for policy making is mechanistic and deterministic in nature, shaped by the social and economic world.[11]

Applying this approach to policies in American states, Thomas R. Dye summarizes the position: "Economic development shapes both political systems and policy outcomes, and most of the association that occurs between system characteristics and policy outcomes can be attributed to the influence of economic development. Differences in the policy choices of states with different types of political systems turn out to be largely a product of political variables. Levels of urbanization, industrialization, income and education appear to be more influential in shaping policy outcomes than political system characteristics."[12] At least implicitly, the view here is that the political process functions as a neutral mechanism to transform the demands from the socioeconomic environment into public policy.[13]

11. For discussions of this and related literature, see J. Rogers Hollingsworth and Ellen Jane Hollingsworth, "Expenditures in American Cities," in *The Dimensions of Quantitative Research in History*, ed. William O. Aydelotte et al. (Princeton, N.J.: Princeton University Press, 1972), pp. 247-89; Richard I. Hofferbert, "State and Community Policy Studies: A Review of Comparative Input-Output Analyses," in *Political Science Annual*, ed. James A. Robinson (Indianapolis, Ind.: Bobbs-Merrill Company, 1972), pp. 3-72; Alford and Friedland, "Political Participation and Public Policy"; Terry N. Clark, "Community Power," *Annual Review of Sociology* 1 (1975): 271-95; John H. Fenton and Donald W. Chamberlayne, "The Literature Dealing with the Relationships between Political Processes, Socio-economic Conditions and Public Policies in American States: A Bibliographical Essay," *Policy* 1 (Spring 1969): 388-404; Herbert Jacob and Michael Lipsky, "Outputs, Structure, and Power: An Assessment of Changes in the Study of State and Local Politics," *Journal of Politics* 30 (May 1968): 510-38; H. Heclo, "Policy Analysis," *British Journal of Political Science* 2 (January 1972): 83-108; Bernard H. Booms and James R. Halldorson, "The Politics of Redistribution: A Reformulation," *American Political Science Review* 67 (September 1973): 924-33; Robert C. Fried, "Party and Policy in West German Cities," *American Political Science Review* 70 (March 1976): 11-24; Robert C. Fried, "Comparative Urban Performance," in *Handbook of Political Science*, ed. Fred L. Greenstein and N. W. Polsby, Vol. 6 (Reading, Mass.: Addison-Wesley, 1975).

Early and very influential statements of the socioeconomic determinant view are Richard Dawson and James A. Robinson, "Inter-Party Competition, Economic Variables, and Welfare Politics in the American States," *Journal of Politics* 25 (May 1963): 265-89; Richard Dawson, "Social Development, Party Competition and Policy," in *The American Party System: Stages of Political Development*, ed. Richard Chambers and Walter Dean Burnham (New York: Oxford University Press, 1967), pp. 203-37; Thomas R. Dye, *Politics Economics, and the Public* (Chicago: Rand McNally, 1966), and "Governmental Structure, Urban Environment, and Educational Policy," *Midwest Journal of Political Science* 2 (August 1967): 353-80.

12. Dye, *Politics, Economics, and the Public*, p. 293.

13. Dearlove, *Politics of Policy in Local Government*, pp. 73-74.

There are several complementary generalizations inherent in this approach to policy explanations.[14] For example, the literature suggests that communities of higher socioeconomic status have large numbers of citizens who demand a variety of governmental services, who are more sophisticated in judging the quality of educational services, and who know how to make their demands felt in the political system. In contrast, communities with low socioeconomic status have more people whose demands on local government are somewhat more limited, who are less capable of judging the value of community services, and who are less able to mobilize political support.

A second socioeconomic explanation of policy involves the concept *social heterogeneity*. For example, several scholars have argued that the degree of social heterogeneity in a community is a good indicator of its capability of mobilizing resources. The assumption is that the presence of a great deal of heterogeneity produces many political cleavages, which in turn create conflicting political demands among the citizenry, forcing political elites to increase the level of expenditures for community services, to satisfy first one group, then another.

Another group of scholars argue that policies may be explained by the amount of stability in a community. The argument here is that the more stable a community—the older the community and the less mobile its population—the greater the probability that multiple "centers of power" will have established well-developed relations with each other, relations which facilitate the mobilization of community resources.

Several scholars have argued that the social and economic interaction of a community with its environment is an important variable for understanding policy analysis. The more interaction a community has with its environment, the more services it is called upon to provide, not only for the immediate community, but for people outside the community as well. The more economic activity a city has in its hinterland, the more capacity it has to respond to the demands for greater services. There is an abundance of literature bearing on these points, much of it related to the delineation of zones and to the patterning of hierarchies of cities.

And finally, a few scholars have attempted to explain public services by occupational variables. Having a large sector of the work force in primary activities (mining, lumbering, fishing) has generally been associated with low levels of community amenities. Conversely, communities with large numbers of professional people—cities which are suburbs, educational

14. For additional bibliographical references to the literature on the relationship between the socioeconomic characteristics of cities and public policy, see Hollingsworth and Hollingsworth, "Expenditures in American Cities," pp. 347-89.

centers, or state capitals—are more likely to have been characterized by generous civic spending.

The implications of widespread manufacturing employment are mixed and somewhat dependent upon whether manufacturing is predominantly processing or fabricating. Overall, emphasis on manufacturing serves as a depressant to municipal expenditures, according to recent scholarship.

A Multiple-System Approach to Policy Outcomes[15]

This explanation is somewhat eclectic, as it assumes that there is some validity to each of the above positions, but that none is very satisfying. First, there is the assumption that the socioeconomic environment plays an important role in shaping the political system and policy outcomes. Certainly, public goods cannot be made available unless there is an adequate resource base. Advocates of the multiple-system position, however, also contend that it is imperative to explain the linkages by which socioeconomic variables get translated into public policy *via* the political system. In other words, many aspects of the total social system—socioeconomic as well as political—must be considered if the policy process is to be understood.

Second, this position assumes that the relationship between political variables and policy is vastly more complicated than the second and third explanations suggest. Critical is the contention that a great deal of political interaction is too subtle to be revealed in quantitative analysis as presently practiced.

Third, there is the contention that at all levels of political activity, the political choices of individuals are constrained by the actions of others. Policy is the result of the give and take among people with different perspectives and goals. Just as the movement of each marble in a bowl depends on the position of movement of each other marble, so in politics decisions are the result of a complex network of conflicting views.[16] Even if voters do not generally have consistent and firmly held views on matters of public policy, elites generally feel that they and their records are highly visible to their constituents. Because the office holder believes that the eyes of the public are on him and that voters cast their ballots according

15. This view is generally not stated with considerable clarity, but sources that express this position with varying degrees of explicitness are Stuart H. Rakoff and Guenther F. Schaefer, "Politics, Policy, and Political Science: Theoretical Alternatives," *Politics and Society* 1 (November 1970): 51-90; Wahlke, "Policy Demands and System Support"; Dearlove, *Politics of Policy in Local Government*.

16. Roland N. McKean, *Public Spending* (New York: McGraw-Hill, 1968), p. 12.

to his actions, he does attempt to shape his views on issues which he believes to be salient to large segments of his constituency.

With this body of literature, however, there is no systematic and predictable relationship between various determinants of policy and outcomes. At some points in time and in some places, socioeconomic variables are of utmost importance, while on other occasions, electoral behavior and/or political elites appear to be more decisive in shaping outcomes. And in some instances, the literature suggests that policy explanation is none of the above but is a combination of idiosyncratic phenomena.

This approach to the study of policy is not merely a residual category, however, but is consistent with a study of reality which Abraham Kaplan, Paul Diesing, and other philosophers of science have called a "pattern model of explanation." It is an explanation that is evaluated by means of elaborate contextual validation. It requires a blend of both of our research strategies, the comparative variable analysis and the historical specification approach.[17]

RESEARCH GOAL

The primary purpose of this chapter is to assess the adequacy of the electoral approach to policy, though we are hopeful that the data presented below will provide useful insights into the validity of the other three explanations of public policy. To do this, it is, of course, desirable to develop refutable hypotheses and to test their validity empirically. For several reasons this is a difficult task, however. In the first place, each of the above four positions has been expressed in different ways by various authors, making an empirical testing of hypotheses implicit in any one of the explanations somewhat complicated. Second, the empirical testing of basic hypotheses in social science research is rarely possible in any *pure* sense. Even if the difficulties of testing hypotheses are immense and should not be minimized, neither should the problem be overstressed. And in our judgment the basic arguments in each of these positions can be empirically tested.

During the past two decades there have been a number of studies of public policy in state and local government in contemporary America,[18] but many of the studies are combined analyses of policies in state and local

17. For the literature about this view, see Kuklinski, "Representativeness and Elections"; Abraham Kaplan, *The Conduct of Inquiry: Methodology of Behavioral Science* (San Francisco: Chandler Publishing Co., 1964); Paul Diesing, *Patterns of Discovery in the Social Sciences* (Chicago: Aldine-Atherton, 1971).

18. For example, see the literature cited in Hollingsworth and Hollingsworth, "Expenditures in American Cities."

governments. In part this stems from the increasing integration of those governments. Because we very much need to improve our understanding of public policy for earlier points in time, in urban settings, and for middle-sized cities, this study focuses on American cities ranging in size from 10,000 to 25,000 in 1900. There were 278 such cities. Urban politics are the appropriate focus for studies of the determinants of public policy at the turn of the century, for at that time cities provided the majority of governmental services. As table 3.1 shows, three-quarters of civilian expenditures were by local authorities in 1902, with federal and state expenditures only 10 and 15 percent, respectively.

Table 3.1. Percentage of Expenditures by Level of Government

Expenditures	1902	1929	1940	1948
Civilian				
Federal	10%	8%	42%	35%
State	15	22	22	31
Local	75	70	36	34
Total (including military)				
Federal	29	25	50	69
State	12	18	19	15
Local	59	57	31	16

Source: The method of computing the percentages and sources for the data in this table are discussed in R.A. Musgrave and J.M. Culbertson, "The Growth of Public Expenditures in the United States," *National Tax Journal* 6 (June 1953): 97–115, esp. table 4 and appendices. This table includes only expenditures from funds raised by the level of government doing the spending. This kind of analysis can become quite complicated, and some scholars have inadvertently counted inter-governmental expenditures twice, and even occasionally three and four times, as funds are transferred to multiple levels of government. For example, in *The Politics of Taxing and Spending* (Indianapolis, Ind.: The Bobbs-Merrill Co., 1969), p. 157, Ira Sharkansky reaches quite different conclusions from the one presented here, as he frequently counts the same expenditure twice. As a result, the percentages of expenditures at various levels of government usually sum to more than 100 in his analysis, occasionally to more than 120 percent.

Carrying out analysis of policy for smaller urban units is desirable not only because the vast majority of spending occurred at the local level. There are many historical case studies of the politics of large cities, but very few for smaller cities, in which a substantial percentage of United States residents lived. Moreover, smaller cities had much more autonomy within states than larger ones. The constraints by state and national governments on decision making in small cities were modest, in that statuatory requirements and limitations existed on only a limited scale and fiscal transfers and grants were small. Local units of smaller size, overall,

raised their own monies and assigned their own priorities. In the early twentieth century most smaller urban units did not have either separate taxing districts (for schools, for sanitation) or separate spending authorities. The city government raised the revenue and directed its expenditure.

Government processes were relatively uncomplicated at the turn of the century for cities of this size, as chapter 2 has illustrated. It is often thought that the defining and settling of public questions can be more easily studied for less complex urban units, that small societies offer better opportunities for grasping basic patterns. Thus, one might expect popular voting behavior to influence policy in cities of this size even if it is difficult to demonstrate that electoral behavior has an impact on policy in larger cities.

CONCEPTS AND DATA

Indicators of Public Policy

Most of this chapter focuses on public expenditures per capita for 1903 as a basic indicator of public policy. It is, of course, desirable to make distinctions among different types of policies, as socioeconomic as well as electoral variables had more impact on some policy sectors than on others. We must be mindful, however, that the range of urban policies, especially in middle-sized cities, was quite restricted at the turn of the century. Aside from focusing on the determinants of all expenditures on a per capita basis, the analysis also assesses the determinants of the largest categories of expenditures, also on a per capita basis: education, fire, health, police, and highways and sanitation. These five categories made up the bulk of the expenditures for the 278 cities. Municipal spending for outlays (capital expenditures such as school, fire station, and hospital construction, etc.) were not included in the analysis because of their considerable variation from year to year.

Budgets are not, of course, wholly adequate as policy indicators. Yet in that they represent authoritative allocation of values via government decisions, "budgets remain the best unit for identifying and analyzing urban outputs that we have yet been able to find."[19] Budgets, as indicators of the scope of government in the lives of citizens, vary from place to place in scale and components. Budgets reflect government priorities and, in many cases, aspirations. As Phillip C. Burch suggests, expenditures constitute the "alpha and omega" of politics, the very heart of governmental activities.[20]

19. Quoted in Robert C. Fried, "Communists, Urban Budgets, and the Two Italies: A Case Study in Comparative Urban Government," *Journal of Politics* 33 (August 1971): 1014.

20. Phillip C. Burch, *Highway Revenue and Expenditure Policy in the U.S.* (New Brunswick, N.J.: Rutgers University Press, 1962), p. 34.

Limits do inhere in expenditure data, limits that must be recognized. To begin with, expenditures may not be good indicators about the quality of public services. Measuring the quality of public services has proved very difficult for social scientists concerned with the contemporary world, and the problems are much more extreme for earlier time periods. When hopeful breakthroughs occur, they often do stem from budget data, as recent cost benefit analysis in health and education illustrates. Second, price level variations from city to city and region to region existed. At the turn of the century there was much more divergence among regions in economic development, of course. A dollar had one value in Madison, Wisconsin, another in Macon, Georgia. To give some recognition to regional variation factors, some of the analysis below is reported for regions as well as for the whole group of cities. Within regions, there was less variation in price and cost levels.

Third, budget data tell us little about policy content. To overcome this handicap, we have supplemented statistical data with information from secondary sources and from an in-depth longitudinal study of several cities. Thus, this study makes an effort to limit expenditure data sets to policy contents and their variation.

Cross-sectional statistical analysis is the basis for most of this chapter, though for participation and competition measures, data from several years are used (1895-1903). A detailed longitudinal analysis, aside from the data reported earlier, was not undertaken for two reasons. First, given the absence of reliable population figures for the years between the federal censuses, it was impossible to ascertain fundamental per capita expenditure figures on a year-after-year basis. Population fluctuated greatly from census to census in smaller urban units that were on frontiers, in extractive areas, or suburban in status. Changes in population of 50 percent or more was not uncommon. One could interpolate population on the basis of federal census figures for ten-year intervals, but such a proce-dure seems quite inappropriate for an era of such population fluctuation and for analysis based upon statistical techniques as sensitive as regression. Second, to gather systematic electoral and expenditure data for many cities was a herculean task, so much so that collecting data for more points in time became unreasonable. It is just such enormous time invest-ments that account in large measure for the lack of attention by American scholars to budget/expenditure data at the local level. Longitudinal analysis carried out by the authors, however, does support the results reported herein.[21]

21. J. Rogers Hollingsworth, "The Impact of Electoral Behavior on Public Policy," in *History of American Electoral Behavior*, ed. Joel Silbey et al. (Princeton, N.J.: Princeton University Press, 1978).

Region

Social scientists find working with the concept of region very difficult. Robert L. Lineberry and Edmund P. Fowler have suggested that "region as a variable is an undifferentiated potpourri of socio-economic, attitudinal, historical, and cultural variables."[22] Because the electoral process was different in southern cities from that in cities elsewhere in the nation, we present data separately for southern and nonsouthern cities (See the appendix for a regional designation of each of the 278 cities.). And elsewhere we divide the cities into six different regions for analysis.

Electoral Variables

In an effort to measure the impact of voting behavior on public policy, we will explore relationships suggested by other social scientists concerned with contemporary public policy. Their hypotheses about the electoral behavior and public policy relationship often involves (1) the competitiveness of elections; (2) the level of turnout; and (3) the type of election (that is, partisan or nonpartisan).

The following model, or a variation of it, is often proposed: the higher the level of political activity among the electorate, the higher the level of political outputs. Increases in voter turnout mean more generation of demand by competing groups and responses by political elites to those demands. Less voter turnout, less participations, mean that elites can maintain their position with less activity; they need not make efforts to satisfy so many competing interests.

Much research cast in this mode of thinking attempts to assess the impact on public policy of the level of competitiveness of partisan activity and the level of voter turnout. In *Southern Politics* V.O. Key expressed the classic form of this view, which many other scholars have echoed and refined.[23]

22. Robert L. Lineberry and Edmund P. Fowler, "Reformism and Public Policies in American Cities," *American Political Science Review* 61 (September 1967): 707. In *Regionalism in American Politics* (Indianapolis, Ind.: The Bobbs-Merrill Co., 1970), Ira Sharkansky presents a very penetrating discussion of regionalism in American politics.

23. V. O. Key, *Southern Politics in State and Nation* (New York: Alfred A. Knopf, 1951), pp. 298-314. Also see Silbey et al., eds., *History of American Electoral Behavior*, pp. 343-45; Duane Lockard, *New England State Politics* (Princeton, N.J.: Princeton University Press, 1959), pp. 320-40; John H. Fenton, *Politics in the Border States* (New Orleans: Hauser Press, 1959), and *Midwest Politics* (New York: Holt, Rinehart, and Winston, 1966); Eugene C. Lee, *The Politics of Nonpartisanship* (Berkeley: University of California Press, 1960).

Similar assumptions deal with the type of election: partisan or non-partisan. Scholars usually argue that nonpartisan electoral systems discourage enduring political alignment and thus have reduced voter participation. Less participation stemming from nonpartisanship, and lower turnout, means a lower level of policy outputs by government.[24]

Usually studies with systematic measures of the impact of party competition and turnout on public policy in the United States focus on contemporary state politics (since 1960). For the most part the studies have not found meaningful relationships between electoral behavior measures and policy outputs when socioeconomic variables are controlled.[25]

Aside from the Richard Dawson study of welfare policies, partly focusing on the state level since 1914, there have been no efforts to assess the electoral behavior impact on public policy for early American history or for American cities at any era.[26] Given the relative ease of data collection for state level electoral variables and the extreme difficulties encountered in amassing historical urban data sets, however, it is small wonder that analysis has been at the state level. Reservations as to whether states are too heterogeneous for good tests of relationships between electoral behavioral variables and policy outcomes have thus been more voiced than tested.

To gather local political data for cities at the turn of the century five basic techniques were used: (1) reading local or metropolitan newspapers; (2) selection of material from case studies of individual cities when possible; (3) corresponding with librarians and city clerks in each of the 278 cities of this size; (4) heavy reliance on reports of the U.S. Commissioner of Education and special reports of the U.S. Census Office, especially *Statistics of Cities with Population 8,000 to 25,000: Bulletin 45* and *Statistics of Cities with Population over 25,000: Bulletin 20* (both published in 1907); and (5) analyzing in depth the political process of several cities, 1870-1900.

The electoral data were sufficiently fragmentary or inconclusive as to merit excluding 45 percent of the 278 cities of this size from this part of the analysis. Thus, the statistical analysis of electoral behavior focuses on the 154 cities for which it was possible to collect adequate political data. Cities included in our political analysis had available the following information: election data for voter turnout, data adequate for constructing an index of competitiveness, and data on the form of election and government.

24. Lee, *Politics of Nonpartisanship.*
25. See the literature cited in note 11.
26. Dawson, "Social Development, Party Competition, and Policy."

Table 3.2 compares the social and economic characteristics of the universe of cities (N=278) with those for the 154 cities for which electoral data are available. In their social and economic characteristics the two sets of cities are very similar, as well as in terms of regional distribution of cities.

Table 3.2. Comparison of Selected Characteristics of 278 and 154 Middle-Sized Cities, 1900

Variable	N = 278	N = 154
Mining[a]	0.22%	0.18%
Percentage of population change, 1890–1900	38.8 %	35.0 %
Percentage Protestant	59.8 %	60.1 %
Suburb[b]	0.10%	0.07%
Per capita wealth	$797.10	$814.52
Municipal expenditures, per capita	$ 11.31	$ 11.67
Education expenditure, per capita	$ 3.65	$ 3.79
Highway expenditures, per capita	$ 2.07	$ 2.11
Police expenditure, per capita	$ 0.72	$ 0.71
Fire expenditures, per capita	$ 0.96	$ 1.00
Health expenditures, per capita	$ 0.16	$ 0.16

[a]Mining was coded as follows: 0 = no mining, 1 = either coal or iron mining, 2 = both coal and iron mining.
[b]Suburb was coded as follows: 0 = not suburb, 1 = suburb.

Competitiveness

There has been considerable discussion over the time span and appropriate offices to be used in constructing an index of competitiveness.[27]

27. For different approaches to measuring competitiveness, see David G. Pfeiffer, "The Measurement of Inter-Party Competition and Systematic Stability," *American Political Science Review* 41 (June 1967): 457-67; Paul T. David, "How Can an Index of Party Competition Best Be Derived," *Journal of Politics* 34 (May 1972): 632-38; Mark Stern, "Measuring Interparty Competition: A Proposal and a Text of a Method," ibid., 34 (August 1972): 889-904; A John Berrigan, "Interparty Electoral Competition, Stability, and Change: Two Dimensional and Three Dimensional Indices," *Comparative Political Studies* 5 (July 1972): 193-210; Dawson and Robinson, "Inter-Party Competition, Economic Variables, and Welfare Policies in the American States"; Richard I. Hofferbert, "The Relation between Public Policy and Some Structural and Environmental Variables in the American States," *American Political Science Review* 60 (March 1966): 73-82; Dye, *Politics, Economics and the Public;* Robert T. Golembiewski, "A Taxonomic Approach to Political Party Strength," *Western Political Quarterly* 9 (September 1958): 495-519; Austin Ranney and Wilmoore Kendall, "The American Party Systems," *American Political Science Review* 48 (1954): 477-85; Joseph A. Schlesinger, "A Two-Dimensional Scheme for Classifying the States According to Degree of Inter-Party Competition," *American Political Science Review* 49 (1955): 1120-28.

For this study the competitiveness index is the average percentage of the vote of the winning candidates for the two most powerful political offices for the city in each city election from 1895 to 1903. The mayor was almost invariably one of these offices. Normally, elections were held annually or every two years in cities of this size. In constructing the index two offices at several points in time were used. The lower the percentage the more competitive the city, so that a city with an index of fifty was much more competitive than one with an index of ninety.

Turnout

At the turn of the twentieth century the requirements for voting were much more varied. In some states poll taxes, literacy laws, and stiff residence requirements severely restricted the suffrage. There are many problems involved with ascertaining the size of the actual legal electorate. For example, women were denied the franchise in state and national elections, but in some cities permitted to vote locally. Women were sometimes denied municipal election franchise, but permitted to vote for boards of education. In some areas immigrants were allowed to vote once they met minimal residency requirements, but in other areas they were denied the franchise. Practices of exclusion in southern cities also varied widely. To identify all the local variation in practice was impossible.

To circumvent these problems, turnout is measured as the average percentage of the city population which voted in local elections during the 1895-1903 period. For the most part, 1900 is used as the year for computing the city's population, although in a few instances reliable state or local census figures are used if available. This index gives us information about the level of actual voter participation, although it does not adjust for disfranchising conditions. Thus it is a useful measure for studying popular participation comparatively, as the legal requirements for voting do vary from place to place and across time.[28]

Form of Election

The terms *partisan* and *nonpartisan* described the form of the ballot. The measure is designed to test the hypothesis that the existence of party label on the ballot is associated with higher levels of policy outputs and

28. For a turnout measurement similar to the one used here, see Peter Flora, "The Development of Education in the Process of State Formation and Nation Building: A Comparative Analysis" (paper presented to the European Consortium for Political Research in Mannheim, Germany, April 1973). Other measurements of turnout are Daniel N. Gordon, "Immigrants and Municipal Voting Turnout: Implications for the Changing Ethnic Impact on Urban Politics," *American Sociological Review* 35 (1070): 665-81; and Dawson, "Social Development, Party Competition, and Policy."

turnout than when a nonpartisan ballot is employed. Even so, one must recognize that in some American cities formally partisan cities were occasionally nonpartisan in fact, and some formally nonpartisan cities were de facto partisan.

FINDINGS

Policy Parameters

Although most policy spending was undertaken by local, rather than state or federal sources, cities at the turn of the century spent relatively modest sums per capita—$11.31 per resident as an average (see table 3.3). Some regions spent substantially more than others, and there was vast variation in spending from one city to another. At one end of the continuum, Brookline, Massachusetts, spent roughly $40.00 per inhabitant; at the other, Galena, Kansas, spent less than one-tenth as much ($2.94). In general, the cities of the Northeast and the West spent more than those in other regions.[29]

Regardless of the per capita municipal expenditures, education in each region was the function which accounted for the most spending. Even so, the cities of the South spent somewhat lower proportions of their budgets on schools, only half as much per capita as cities of the Northeast (see table 3.11). Although there was an overall lack of standardization in school systems, elementary schools usually enrolled children at the age of six or seven, with some open to children of four or five. Otherwise, the school systems had little else in common. For example, the school systems of California and Massachusetts were required to operate for at least 180

Stimulating discussions about turnout are Jerrold G. Rusk and John J. Stucker, "the Effect of the Southern System of Election Laws on Voting Participation," in *History of American Electoral Behavior*, ed. Silbey et al., pp. 198-250; J. Morgan Kousser, *The Shaping of Southern Politics* (New Haven, Conn.: Yale University Press, 1974); Walter Dean Burnham, *Critical Elections and the Mainsprings of American Politics* (New York: W. W. Norton, 1970), chap. 4; and Stanley Kelley et al., "Registration and Voting: Putting First Things First," *American Political Science Review* 61 (June 1967): 359-79.

For discussions on variations in voting requirements, see the studies cited in Rusk and Stucker, as well as Albert J. McCullock, *Suffrage and Its Problems* (Baltimore, Md.: Warwick and York, 1929), table 4, pp. 54-59; Frederick D. Ogden, *The Poll Tax in the South* (Tuscaloosa: University of Alabama Press, 1958); the extensive bibliography in C. Vann Woodward, *The Origins of the New South*, rev. ed. (Baton Rouge: Louisiana State University Press, 1972); and Alan P. Grimes, *The Puritan Ethic and Woman Suffrage* (New York: Oxford University Press, 1967).

29. For data on these cities, see U.S. Bureau of the Census, *Statistics of Cities Having a Population of 8,000 to 25,000: 1903* (Washington, D.C.: U.S. Government Printing Office, 1907).

Table 3.3. Governmental Expenditures

	All cities (N = 278)	North-east (N = 52)	Middle Atlantic (N = 68)	Lakes (N = 78)	South (N = 38)	Plains (N = 28)	West (N = 14)
	Average expenditures for functions, by region						
All expenditures	$11.31	$14.78	$10.47	$10.20	$10.30	$9.58	$14.95
Education	3.65	4.37	3.53	3.77	2.07	3.32	5.86
Highways	2.07	2.93	1.91	1.75	1.85	1.64	2.85
Police	0.72	0.81	0.61	0.60	0.94	0.72	0.96
Fire	0.96	1.06	0.61	1.06	1.02	1.03	1.45
Health	0.16	0.22	0.20	0.13	0.14	0.10	0.15
	Ratio of regional expenditures per capita to those of all cities						
	1.00	1.31	0.93	0.90	0.91	0.85	1.32
	Percentage of budget by function						
Education	0.32%	0.30%	0.34%	0.37%	0.20%	0.35%	0.39%
Highways	0.18	0.20	0.18%	0.17	0.18	0.17	0.19
Police	0.06	0.05	0.06	0.06	0.09	0.08	0.06
Fire	0.08	0.07	0.06	0.10	0.10	0.11	0.10
Health	0.01	0.01	0.02	0.01	0.01	0.01	0.01

days; Colorado and Mississippi had school for twenty weeks; Illinois for 110 days; Montana for three months. Local school boards were usually left the initiative to institute longer school years. Many states set their school terms in response to their perception of the role children played in agriculture—there was no harm for children to be in school so long as foregone farm labor had little value. Less agriculturally oriented states tended to disregard the time rivalry between farm and school to a greater extent. Local school boards also decided the length of the school day in most states, the amount of tolerance for truancy, the salaries, training, and number of teachers, and the subjects offered. Some school districts were far more concerned with the specifics of education than others: some insisted on the teaching of the evil effects of alcohol and narcotics, of the Bible and other denominational material, of state history. Most states had some form of compulsory education requirements, but there was considerable variation in the ages to which requirements applied. The language of the West Virginia statute was not atypical: "every youth between the age of 6 and 21 shall have a right to receive instruction at the free primary schools."[30]

For the cities in this study, the second-largest budget fragment was devoted to "highways and sanitation." Under the general rubric of "highways and sanitation" many things were grouped: expenditures for street lighting, street cleaning, "other street expenses," refuse disposal, and general management. The largest categories of expense were "other street expenses," repair work, and street lighting. Whereas virtually every city had expenditures for street lighting, expenses for sewers and sewage disposal were not only much smaller, but much less common. Although the amounts spent on highways and sanitation per capita varied from region to region, the percentages of budgets spent on those functions were quite similar. Brookline, Massachusetts, spent more ($9.72 per resident per capita) on highways and sanitation than any other city of its size; Mt. Carmel, Pennsylvania, the least ($0.42).

Although in some states, counties were charged with controlling the roads, they usually did not maintain them, and to the city fell the task of making passable the approaches to town. At the turn of the century rural road surfacing was usually graded dirt, with cities more likely to use asphalt and brick rather than the traditional materials: granite blocks, cobblestones, or planks. Still, some cities, even by the turn of the century, had no paved streets. Since many of the cities in this study were located on rivers, or divided by rivers, bridge expenses were commonplace—and

30. U.S. Commissioner of Ecucation, *Report of the Commissioner of Education for the Year 1904* (Washington, D.C.: U.S. Government Printing Office, 1905), p. 512.

probably more critical than other road expenses. A town with a muddy main street might not have been pleasant, but an unbridged river in a city was intolerable.

Street lighting, which had gained widespread acceptance by 1900, accounted for a third of the expense of highways and sanitation. Not a single city in this group was without some form of street lighting, with electric lights being the most common form of lighting, followed by gas lights. A few communities still used oil lamps. The ubiquitous use of street lights is a good clue to municipal activity by the turn of the century: cities were expected to provide services and amenities.

Fire expenses were often fairly high. For example, Brookline, Massachusetts, spend $3.50 per resident per capita for fire control, and only two or three communities spent nothing. At the turn of the century fires were a considerable economic threat, as well as a salient political issue. Most construction, whether commercial or residential, was frame, and as the famous Chicago fire of 1871 had illustrated, once a fire began, half a city might be wiped out before it could be brought under control or before it burned itself out. Concord, New Hampshire, had over two hundred fires in 1903, and hundreds of thousands of dollars of property were destroyed in other cities. In some instances, losses were in excess of a million dollars.

All the same, fire equipment was rather modest. Most cities of this size had one or two steam engines, and most cities had fire hydrants, though half the time they were not municipally owned. Whether fire hydrants were municipally or privately owned depended on whether the waterworks was municipally owned or not. Other kinds of fire equipment at that time included cisterns, fire alarms, and even boats. Most cities had firemen on their payrolls, and some had hundreds of volunteers. In describing the advantages of their city, sketches in almanacs, city directories, and state gazeteers generally focused particular attention on the high quality of fire departments.

One-third of the 278 cities spent more money on police than on fire, although overall fire expenses were greater. Since even recent statistics on crime are the subject of so much criticism and uncertainty, those of the turn of the century must be treated very cautiously. It was southern cities, however, that reported the largest numbers of arrests, while mining cities in Pennsylvania and some lumber cities of Wisconsin and Michigan reported that hardly anyone was ever arrested. Police forces were unusually small—perhaps a dozen men—and standards of professionalism were only beginning to be felt in middle-sized and small cities.

Insofar as civil spending for health was concerned, efforts in some cities were so modest as to be token. Outside the New England, the Middle Atlantic, and the Lakes states, only a few cities spent more than $5,000 a

year on health. In general, the magnitude of the health problem in the southeastern part of the United States was not reflected in higher spending. Usually health expenditures covered the salary of a health officer, whose major concern was with food and water safety, sanitary conditions, contagious disease, hospitals, pesthouses, and the registration of births and deaths.

Electoral Parameters

The average turnout figure, or the percentage of the total population that voted between 1895-1903, in the 154 cities for which we have electoral data, was 17 percent (see table 3.4). This seemingly low turnout figure must be evaluated with the realization that children as well as most blacks and many women did not vote. If the number of people who voted was considered as a percentage of males twenty-one and older, voter turnout is higher: 55 percent. In this study, however, the turnout percentage of the whole population is used in the subsequent analysis.

Table 3.4. Levels of Voter Turnout in 154 Cities

	All cities (N = 154)	North- east (N = 33)	Middle Atlantic (N = 28)	Lakes (N = 48)	South (N = 17)	Plains (N = 17)	West (N = 11)
Percentage of population voting in local elections	17	15	16	20	11	17	18
Voters as percentage of male population 21 and over	55	50	55	63	39	62	53

So far as competition for high office was concerned, using a scale similar to Dawson's for differentiating the level of competitiveness from high (59 or less), through medium (60 to 74), to low (75 and over), the index of competitiveness of 59 for all 154 cities was relatively high (see table 3.5). Significantly, the cities in no region ranked low on the index, though southern cities, as expected, were the least competitive. Regardless

Table 3.5. Index of Competitiveness

All cities (N = 154)	Northeast (N = 33)	Middle Atlantic (N = 28)	Lakes (N = 48)	South (N = 17)	Plains (N = 17)	West (N = 11)
59	60	58	57	69	59	55

of their legal form of government, most cities had partisan politics, though southern cities reported nonpartisan status more frequently than cities in other regions.

Walter Dean Burnham and others have commented on the low level of competitiveness in American state politics during this period.[31] But at the urban level these data tend to indicate that the degree of competitiveness was greater than previous studies of American state politics would have suggested. Perhaps the differences in levels of competition between local and state politics may be explained by the fact that people probably participated at higher levels in local politics because they understood local issues better than those elsewhere and because they perceived that local decisions had more effect on their lives than those made at higher levels.

Statistical Analysis

In a previous study we demonstrated that clusters of socioeconomic variables measuring social heterogeneity, urban stability, interaction with the environment, and type of economic activity had little impact on explaining the variation in the expenditures of middle-sized cities at the turn of the twentieth century.[32] In table 3.6 we include the most powerful variable for each of these concepts, and again we observe that these variables had little impact on explaining all expenditures or in explaining expenditures in any single policy area. In contrast, our indicator on the socioeconomic status of a community—per capita wealth—is the most efficient socioeconomic variable for explaining the level of expenditures for these cities throughout the nation and in each region. In addition, per capita wealth is the most powerful variable for explaining the level of spending for each of the five policy areas for all 278 cities and in cities in each of the regions. Of course, it is not surprising that per capita wealth would have a significant impact on expenditures, as public expenditures were dependent on a community's resource capacity. On the basis of another regression equation, we are able to report that for every $100.00 that per capita wealth increased in the 278 cities, the total expenditures rose by $0.75.

At this point, we wish to assess the impact that electoral behavior has on expenditure levels: specifically, does electoral behavior exert any influence on levels of expenditure once one controls for the level of wealth in a community?

31. Burnham, *Critical Elections and the Mainsprings of American Politics;* Dawson, "Social Development, Party Competition, and Policy."

32. Hollingsworth and Hollingsworth, "Expenditures in American Cities."

Table 3.6. Effect of Socioeconomic Variables on Public Expenditures[a]

Independent variables for 278 cities	All expenditures	Education expenditures	Highway and sanitation expenditures	Fire expenditures	Police expenditures	Health expenditures
Percentage of population consisting of Protestants	−344.99 (− 4.95)[d]	− 1.87 (− 7.07)[d]	− .85 (− 4.76)[d]	− .04 (− .30)	.03 (.34)	− .01 (− .34)
Mining activity	−196.26 (− 4.93)[d]	− .13 (− .84)	− .49 (− 4.82)[d]	− .24 (−3.49)[d]	− .10 (− 2.36)[b]	.04 (1.89)
Percentage of population change, 1890–1900	.30 (.90)	.00 (.98)	.00 (1.56)	.00 (− .55)	.00 (2.00)[b]	.00 (− .71)
Suburb	258.97 (4.18)[d]	.48 (2.07)[b]	.39 (2.43)[b]	− .21 (−1.88)	.24 (3.72)[c]	.05 (1.55)
Wealth	.66 (14.89)[d]	.00 (10.44)[d]	.00 (14.16)[d]	.00 (6.75)[d]	.00 (10.02)[d]	.00 (5.01)[d]
R²	.58[d]	.43[d]	.54[d]	.19[d]	.37[d]	.11[d]

[a] t-statistics appear in parentheses below the regression coefficients.
[b] Significant at .05 level.
[c] Significant at .01 level.
[d] Significant at .001 level.

When we examine table 3.7 we observe that the three participation variables (competitiveness, turnout, and form of election), either individually, or as a group, have virtually no influence on any of the major kinds of municipal spending. As only ten cities had nonpartisan governments, it is not surprising that this variable has little association with spending. But that more direct measures of participation (for example, turnout and competition) should have virtually no association with spending is rather surprising.

Elsewhere, we have examined the relationship between electoral variables and slightly different categories of urban expenditures, but on a regional basis,[33] and there, also, the electoral variables have no impact on expenditures except in the South.

Here also, the most interesting coefficient in table 3.8 is the relationship between turnout and education expenditures in southern cities ($r = .73$). In the South, public education was less developed than in any other region, and education was viewed not as a necessity but as an amenity. And the greater the political participation (that is, turnout) in local elections, the more the political elites in southern cities were encouraged to spend on schools.

In the policy-making process allocative authorities decide to spend more money in certain policy sectors and not in others. Because expenditure data reveal the priorities of governments, one might expect the participation variables to assist in explaining the priorities of spending by sectoral categories. Table 3.9 shows, however, that when the five categories of spending (education, highways and sanitation, fire, police, and health) are considered as a percentage of total expenditures in the 154 cities, the participation variables also have virtually no explanatory power.

Over time, what kinds of relationships can one expect to find between increases in competition and turnout, and changes in levels of expenditures? Data to answer this kind of question, be they electoral, policy, or population data, are extremely difficult to collect for cities of this size in the late nineteenth century. For three cities (Eau Claire [1875-1900], Green Bay [1870-1900], and Janesville, Wisconsin [1870-1900]), however, we do have longitudinal data which are reliable. In another study we have attempted to discover if increases in the level of political activity bring about higher levels of political outputs when viewed longitudinally, and we found that there is virtually no impact on changes in level of spending when turnout and competition levels change over time. To put it another way,

33. Hollingsworth, "Impact of Electoral Behavior on Public Policy." This essay raises similar questions to the ones presented here, though the present chapter is much broader in scope.

Table 3.7. Relationship between Electoral Variables and Expenditures[a]

Independent variables for 154 cities	All expenditures	Education expenditures	Highway and sanitation expenditures	Police expenditures	Fire expenditures	Health expenditures
Competitiveness	- .04 (- 1.06)	- .03 (- 2.12)[b]	- .01 (- .63)	.00 (- .55)	.00 (- .64)	.00 (.33)
Turnout	-1.02 (- .21)	.37 (.23)	- .51 (- .46)	- .27 (.71)	.95 (1.68)	- .04 (- .22)
Partisanship	1.57 (1.19)	.52 (1.16)	.45 (1.44)	.04 (.35)	- .23 (- 1.47)	.07 (1.65)
R^2	.02	.05	.02	.00	.04	.02

[a] t-statistics appear in parentheses below the regression coefficients.
[b] Significant at .05 level.

Table 3.8. Effect of Electoral and Wealth Variables on Education in Southern and Nonsouthern Cities[a]

Independent variables for 154 cities	Education in southern cities		Education in nonsouthern cities	
	Electoral variables only	Electoral variables combined with wealth	Electoral variables only	Electoral variables combined with wealth
Competitiveness	.00 (- .09) [- .44]	- .01 (- .41) [- .44]	.00 (- .10) [.01]	.01 (1.03) [.01]
Turnout	11.91 (2.94)[c] [.73][c]	9.42 (2.30) [.73][d]	-1.36 (- .87) [- .07]	- .97 (- .79) [- .07]
Partisanship	.06 (- .13) [- .08]	- .13 (- .32) [- .08]	.15 (.29) [.02]	- .05 (- .12) [.02]
Wealth	Inapplicable	.00 (1.64) [.48]	Inapplicable	.00 (9.03)[d] [.61]
R²	.53[b]	.62[b]	.01	.39[d]

[a]t-statistics appear in parentheses below the regression coefficients; zero order correlation coefficients appear in brackets.
[b]Significant at .05 level.
[c]Significant at .01 level.
[d]Significant at .001 level.

Table 3.9. Relationship between Electoral Variables and Expenditure Sectors As a Percentage of All Expenditures[a]

Independent variables for 154 cities	Education as a percentage of all expenditures	Highway and sanitation as a percentage of all expenditures	Police as a percentage of all expenditures	Fire as a percentage of all expenditures	Health as a percentage of all expenditures
Competitiveness	− .15 (− 1.93)	.02 (.55)	.01 (.74)	− .02 (− .63)	.00 (.34)
Turnout	6.15 (.59)	− 2.55 (− .49)	− 1.63 (− .62)	7.35 (1.41)	− .68 (− .42)
Partisanship	− .19 (− .06)	1.64 (1.14)	− .37 (− .51)	− 3.12 (− 2.15)[b]	.65 (1.44)
R^2	.04	.01	.01	.05	.02

[a] t-statistics appear in parentheses below the regression coefficients.
[b] Significant at .05 level.

our data reveal no differences between longitudinal and cross-national data in pattern.[34]

Other scholars have suggested that turnover of political elites in office is associated with changes in public policy, but a detailed analysis of several cities has failed to reveal any significant relationship between public policy and turnover of either public officials or party following a local election. Significantly, the failure of this study to support such a hypothesis is consistent with Jack Walker's study of policy content in American state politics, in which he found that turnover had only a slight impact on public policy.[35]

Our data, as well as the secondary literature, reveal that there was a different political process operating in cities of the American South. Whereas the three electoral variables have a negligible effect on most policy sectors across the country, turnout does have a significant effect on educational expenditures in southern cities. Turnout alone explains 53 percent of the variance in southern educational expenditures, which is the same as the three political variables combined. While our most powerful socioeconomic variable is generally much more robust than the three political variables combined, this is not the situation with education expenditures in southern cities. Wealth explains only 23 percent of the variance in educational expenditures ($r = .48$). And wealth combined with the participation variables increase the explanatory power for southern educational expenditures to 62 percent (see table 3.8). Or, after wealth has explained all of the variance in education spending it can, participation variables uniquely explain an additional 39 percent. On the other hand, after participation variables have been entered in a regression equation, the addition of wealth explains only an additional 9·percent of the variance. Thus, the level of turnout in southern cities is a much more powerful variable in shaping the level of educational experiences than per capita wealth. Wealth per capita is the variable which most determined the level of total municipal expenditures as well as individual policy categories, with the exception of education in southern cities (see table 3.10).

CONCEPTUAL AND CONTEXTUAL PERSPECTIVES

Perhaps it is appropriate to make several additional observations about this kind of research strategy, for the problem of understanding the determinants of public policy is somewhat more complicated than the presentation thus far suggests.

34. Ibid.
' 35. Jack L. Walker, "The Diffusion of Innovations Among the American States," *American Political Science Review* 63 (September 1969): 889-99.

Table 3.10. Combined Effect of Per Capita Wealth and Electoral Variables on Expenditures[a]

Independent variables for 154 cities	All expenditures	Education expenditures	Highway and sanitation expenditures	Police expenditures	Fire expenditures	Health expenditures
Competitiveness	- .02 (- .61)	- .02 (- 1.89)	.00 (- .14)	.00 (- .08)	- .00 (- .33)	.00 (.47)
Turnout	- .60 (- .16)	.49 (.36)	- .42 (- .45)	- .24 (- .74)	.98 (1.84)	- .03 (- .20)
Partisanship	.54 (.51)	.22 (.58)	.23 (.88)[c]	- .03 (- .35)	- .30 (- 2.03)[b]	.07 (1.46)
Wealth	.01 (9.46)[c]	.00 (7.33)[c]	.00 (7.87)[c]	.00 (7.28)[c]	.00 (4.53)[c]	.00 (1.86)
R^2	.39[d]	.30[d]	.31[d]	.27[d]	.15[d]	.04

[a]t-statistics appear in parentheses below the regression coefficients.
[b]Significant at .05 level.
[c]Significant at .01 level.
[d]Significant at .001 level.

First, one must not interpret the findings of this chapter as suggesting that political variables are of no consequence in shaping policy outcomes. *While electoral variables may be relatively unimportant in shaping policy outcomes, other dimensions of the political system are of considerable importance in shaping the policy process. It is only through political-system variables that socioeconomic characteristics get translated into public policy.* There is not a clear, predictable one-to-one relationship between socioeconomic variables and public policy outcomes, as these correlations, and others in similar studies, leave much of the variance in levels of expenditures unexplained. Give the theoretical framework, data sets, and methodology available to scholars, this situation will probably not change greatly in future research. Very likely, the strength of electoral and socioeconomic variables in shaping public policy is reduced by situational variables which reflect the idiosyncracies and contextual characteristics of particular communities (for example, the personalities of particular leaders, the existence of highly partisan issues, fortuitous events such as fires, floods, etc.). In understanding the process by which socioeconomic variables get translated through the political process into public policy, we need to incorporate idiosyncratic and contextual variables into our analysis. It is especially important that we focus on political elites and comprehend how they perceive and respond to the social and economic context within which they operate. Before policies are formulated, elites must have a realization of community needs, and partly because men perceive their environments differently, policy choices and priorities vary from city to city.

Second, the findings presented thus far do not suggest that regularly scheduled elections are unimportant in a political system, though they do encourage us to be more explicit in explaining the functions of elections and in specifying the nature of the interaction between electoral behavior and the making of public policy.

Third, it is important to note that the findings presented above about electoral data pertain only to regularly scheduled elections. In the late nineteenth century, however, voting behavior in referenda was extremely important in shaping public policy in middle-sized cities. With rapid technological innovations occurring, the world of urban Americans was a changing one. The availability of electricity, streetcars, public sanitation facilities, and water works frequently confronted cities with options which were to be settled by special referenda. Voters frequently accepted or rejected bonding issues, lowered or raised liquor license fees, permitted or disallowed liquor to be sold, agreed or disagreed to public ownership of local utilities, and generally registered these decisions in referenda elections. In sum, voters played an extremely important role in shaping

public policy through special elections in which it was possible to make mutually exclusive choices.[36]

The influence of regularly scheduled elections on public policy was modest, however, as indicated by our cross-sectional and longitudinal data. This is somewhat better understood when one notes that campaigns were brief in duration. It was not at all unusual for elections to be held only three or four days following the parties' nomination of candidates. Sometimes newspaper editorials demanded longer campaigns, and in response several states passed laws requiring that local campaigns be at least fourteen days long. But in most middle-sized cities campaigns lasted for only a few days, a fact which severely limited discussion of public policy issues and undoubtedly minimized the impact of elections on policy. During campaigns, however, it was common for citizens to be preoccupied with candidates' reputations for honesty, fair play, courage, and prudence. And it was over issues involving personal morality that local campaigns during regularly scheduled elections were generally waged, even though these issues frequently symbolized ethnocultural cleavages within the community.

Because middle-sized cities had very limited resources, public decisions rarely involved amenities. The policy-making process was generally one involving modest incremental changes, excepting those occasions when referenda were submitted to voters. Most decisions were made in the city council, often as a result of recommendations of an appropriate committee of the council. With the passage of time, however, problems involving education, public health, waterworks, street railways, electricity, fire, police, and libraries became increasingly complex, leading many cities to create boards with special governing powers, thus removing the substance of policy even a further step from the electorate.

Two competing attitudes toward public policy existed in many cities. On the one hand, most citizens, especially the more influential ones, had a strong sense of loyalty toward their community. Taking great pride in their city, social and economic elites hoped that their community would keep abreast of the progress in the fields of education, public health, communication, and transportation. Newspapers reflected the intense urban rivalry which existed, referring to the progress achieved elsewhere and exhorting their communities to emulate other cities.

On the other hand, newspaper editorials and city council discussions

36. This subject is discussed in chapter 2 above and in Donald A. DeBats, "The Political Sieve: A Study of Green Bay, Wisconsin, 1854-1880" (M.A. thesis, University of Wisconsin, Madison, 1967).

constantly referred to the community's limited fiscal resources and urged the utmost caution in budgetary affairs. Because the elites of most communities were aware of innovations taking place in other cities, there was a process of constantly expanding expectations. There was, however, a perpetual gap between expectation and performance, as city governments were severely constrained by limited financial resources. For this reason, it is not difficult to comprehend why the wealth of a community was the most efficient predictor of what its level of expenditures was likely to be.

And yet it was the intense and boastful municipal rivalry which was of utmost importance in helping us to understand the policy-making process in American cities. Sensitive to changes taking place elsewhere, in large as well as small, in foreign as well as in American, cities, elites were frequently willing to legitimate policies once they had been adopted in urban areas which served as a positive reference group. Once a policy gained the stamp of legitimacy, it had a momentum of its own. An important qualifying phrase here is the term *reference city*. Cities received their cues from multiple sources, as all cities did not choose to play in the same league. Cities usually competed with communities in the same region, but the elites of some cities received directions or cues from several groups of cities. For example, Michigan and Wisconsin cities competed vigorously with one another, but at the same time they attempted to follow the lead of the most "advanced" cities of New York, Connecticut, and Massachusetts. Even so, lumber towns such as Manistee and Menominee were in a category of their own, and their elites received and responded to very few cues from eastern cities. In Indiana and Illinois most cities also followed the lead of cities in New York and Massachusetts, though in the southern part of these midwestern states, the elites often seemed to be more in tune with southern cities than with those of the Midwest. For example, the expenditure patterns and the content of policy in a city such as Cairo, Illinois, resembled those of southern cities more than those of northern Indiana and Illinois. On the other hand, Massachusetts cities, being far more advanced in the areas of public health, education, and technology than cities of comparable size in other regions, usually took their cues from larger cities in Europe and America. Meantime, southern cities recognized that their resources and tradition placed them in a different category from that of cities in other regions, and partly for that reason they were less inclined to take their cues for policy changes from other parts of the country.

Table 3.11 reveals that southern cities were operating in a league vastly different from those elsewhere. First, southern cities appropriated a much smaller share of their budgets for education than cities elsewhere—

Table 3.11. Comparisons of City Expenditures by Region

Region	Ratio of education spending to $1.00 for highways and sanitation	Ratio of education spending to $1.00 for fire	Ratio of education spending to $1.00 for police	Percentage of budget for education
Northeast	1.49	4.12	5.40	30%
Middle Atlantic	1.85	5.79	5.79	34
Lakes	2.15	3.56	6.28	37
Plains	1.95	3.11	4.46	33
South	1.03	1.87	2.03	19
West	2.06	4.04	6.10	39
All cities (278)	1.76	3.80	5.07	32

indeed about half the percentage appropriated by cities in the Plains and Lakes regions. Second, the ratio between police and educational expenditures was much closer in southern cities than in those elsewhere, suggesting that policy makers in southern cities placed much greater emphasis on police as an agency of social control than was the case in cities outside the South.

Perhaps a brief discussion of several policy areas will demonstrate the difference between the kind of political process in southern cities and those elsewhere. Outside the South there were, of course, variations in educational expenditures, both per capita and per student, as well as differences in educational policies. Over time, however, there was a narrowing of differences in expenditures as well as in the substance of policy. For example, many states were still opposed to public high schools as late as 1865, but by the late 1880s every state outside the South was strongly committed to free public high schools, and middle-sized cities were increasingly offering two high school programs, a "practical" one for students whose formal education was to terminate with high school and a classical curriculum for college preparatory students. The public school systems in most nonsouthern cities provided, by the end of the century, kindergartens and evening schools.

Despite rapid changes in educational policy during the latter part of the nineteenth century, however, an analysis of regularly scheduled elections in a number of cities has failed to discover a single local election when educational policy was a campaign issue. This is somewhat different from state electoral politics, in which language for instructional purposes became a major campaign issue in several midwestern states during the early 1890s. But in local politics, educational policy was generally shaped by local school boards, the personnel of which were sometimes appointed, sometimes elected. Even when the school boards were elected, the moral character of those standing for election, rather than their position on policy matters, generally shaped the outcome of campaigns.

In the South, however, there were very different patterns in the substance of educational policy, as well as in the interaction between electoral behavior and policy. As suggested above, the elites in southern cities had a perception of social needs which was distinctively regional, and they made little effort to follow the lead of cities outside the South, with the result that there was much less commitment to public high schools, kindergartens, or night schools. For example, the middle-sized cities of Alabama, Arkansas, Florida, Kentucky, North Carolina, South Carolina, and West Virginia had no public kindergartens, while only one city in each of Mississippi and Georgia had one. And in contrast to the strong commitment to public night schools which existed in northern cities, Fort

Smith, Arkansas, and Columbus, Georgia, were the only two middle-sized southern cities with public night schools.[37]

From a fiscal point of view southern cities could hardly afford a high quality system of public education for one race, and to provide quality education in a dual system of schools for blacks and whites was an impossibility. By 1900, however, southern cities were attempting to maintain two systems of schools, with the result that expenditures per pupil were substantially lower than they might otherwise have been. In such a system, investment in education for blacks suffered the most. In Florida, North Carolina, and Tennessee there were no public high schools for blacks in middle-sized cities, and only one city in each of South Carolina, Mississippi, and Florida had a high school for black students. On the other hand, each of the southern cities did have a public high school for white children by 1900.

Unlike the pattern outside the South, electoral behavior had a significant impact on education policies in southern cities. Table 3.8 indicates that the electoral variables had more impact on educational expenditures in southern cities than on any kind of expenditure in cities outside the South. An examination of newspapers in those southern cities with a high level of voter turnout suggests that they generally had moderate levels of black voting. This information, when analyzed with a scattergram of southern cities and considered alongside the correlations in table 3.8, tends to suggest that where blacks did vote, more expenditures were mobilized in the educational sector than in those cities where blacks did not vote and/or turnout was low.

Another study treating the effect of black voting on education is that of Richard Freeman. Using state and county level data, he demonstrates that the disfranchisement process at the end of the nineteenth century had a substantial impact on educational expenditures for blacks. Prior to disfranchisement, the states of Alabama, Georgia, Louisiana, Mississippi, North Carolina, South Carolina, and Virginia spent almost equal amounts per child enrolled in public schools, regardless of color. By 1915, more than a decade after disfranchisement, the black-white differentials on educational expenditures were considerable. For every dollar spent on a black child, the following sums were spent for educating a white child: Alabama

37. For excellent data on educational policies for American cities during the latter part of the nineteenth century, see the annual reports published by the U.S. Commissioner of Education, 1875-1900. For the discussion of one southern city which refused to follow the models of eastern and northern development but which instead adopted western models, see Ira Don Richards, "The Urban Frontier: Little Rock in the Nineteenth Century" (Ph.D. diss., Tulane University, 1964).

$6.46, Georgia $4.85, Louisiana $9.08, Mississippi $5.36, North Carolina $2.77, South Carolina $9.82, and Virginia $3.58.[38]

While the limited voting of blacks influenced both the level of spending per capita and per child enrolled in schools, the economic environment of southern cities obviously shaped educational outcomes. For example, a smaller percentage of black than white children would have attended school even if governments spent the same money per child regardless of race. Given the low per capita income of black families, black children, particularly those over age twelve, found it much more difficult to forego earnings than white children. Partly because there were so few black children who could afford to forego earnings and to attend high school, southern school officials found it convenient to avoid the establishment of public high schools for blacks, thus guaranteeing that blacks who could afford to forego earnings would be denied a public high school education.[39]

In the other spending areas the policy-making process was somewhat comparable to that involving education: (1) southern cities tended to deviate from patterns elsewhere; (2) very little evidence, based on our cross-sectional and longitudinal analyses exists that regularly scheduled elections had a systematic influence on the level of spending; and (3) variation both in the way that elites perceived the needs of their cities and in the resource base of communities tended to promote variation in policy. Issues in these policy areas were rarely touched upon in local campaigns. City councils made relatively low annual increments in these policy areas, generally as a result of little acrimony but usually with some concern about what neighboring as well as pace-making cities were doing.

Just as boards of education tended to gain greater autonomy vis-à-vis city councils in shaping educational policy, a similar process occurred in regard to boards of health and public health policies. And because

38. See Richard B. Freeman's *Black Elite: The New Market for Highly Educated Black Americans* (New York: McGraw-Hill, 1976), which is a study on education in the Carnegie Commission's Program on Higher Education.

39. For further discussion of these problems, see William Landes and Lewis Solmon, "Compulsory Schooling Legislation: An Economic Analysis of Law and Social Change in the Nineteenth Century," *Journal of Economic History* 36 (March 1972): 54-81; Forest Ensign, *Compulsory School Attendance and Child Labor* (Iowa City, Ia.: Athens Press, 1921); Barry Chiswick, "Minimum Schooling Legislation and the Cross-Sectional Distribution of Income," *The Economic Journal* 79 (September 1969): 495-507; Richard K. Smith, "The Economics of Education and Discrimination in the U.S. South: 1870-1910" (Ph.D. diss., University of Wisconsin, 1973); Irving Gershenberg, "The Negro and the Development of White Public Education in the South: Alabama, 1880-1930," *The Journal of Negro Education* 39 (1970): 50-59.

policies in these areas were increasingly removed from the control of the electorate and their elected representatives and were placed in the hands of professionals and the better educated members of the community, innovations in education and public health were probably diffused more rapidly among cities than would have been the case had there been full discussion of each policy issue during political campaigns and in city council meetings. Southern cities lagged behind cities elsewhere not only because of limited resources but because of their relatively low levels of professionalization and bureaucratization—all of which influenced their elites' perception of needs in these policy areas.[40]

IMPLICATIONS FOR THE STUDY OF PUBLIC POLICY

For these middle-sized cities at the turn of the century, socioeconomic variables clearly shaped public policy. The strength of the most robust variable—per capita wealth—varied from one policy sector to another as well as across regions. In contrast, the electoral variables—excepting educational policy in southern cities—had very little systematic effect on the level of expenditures. And our analysis of the policy context suggests that elites and cultural variables were important in shaping outcomes, but that their importance probably varied from region to region and across time. Elites were motivated to be aware of their constituents' views, but the interaction between elites and voters does not have the mechanistic and predictable quality to it that Anthony Downs and others who take the electoral approach to policy would have us believe. In sum, the above discussion suggests that a *multiple-system approach to policy outcomes* is the most valid explanation of variation in the level of public expenditures. Moreover, the conceptual framework provided in chapter 1 and the discussion in the previous chapter of the policy process in the three Wisconsin cities are consistent with this view.

What are the implications of statistically oriented study after study which suggest that voting behavior has only a modest impact in shaping American public policy? Theodore Lowi, Walter Dean Burnham, Samuel P. Huntington, and many others have argued that the American party

40. For a discussion of the politics and economics of public health, see Edward Meeker, "The Economics of Improving Health, 1850-1915" (Ph.D. diss., University of Washington, 1970), and "The Improving Health of the United States, 1850-1915," *Explorations in Economic History* 9 (Summer 1972): 353-74; Mazyek Revenel, ed., *A Half Century of Public Health* (New York: American Public Health Association, 1921); State Board of Health of Massachusetts, *Twenty-eighth Annual Report* (Boston: Wright and Potter, 1817); U.S. Census, *Social Statistics of Cities, 1890* (Washington, D.C.: U.S. Government Printing Office, 1895); M. N. Baker, ed., *The Manual of American Water Works, 1897* (New York: The Engineering News Publishing Co., 1897); U.S. Department of Labor, *Bulletin*, no. 24 (September 1899).

and electoral systems are somewhat unique.[41] By categorizing the American as a "constituent" system, Lowi means that American parties have historically been primarily concerned with maximizing the number of their constituents, but elections, with the exception of a few crisis points, have seldom had a significant impact on public policy. According to Lowi, public policy has had more of an impact on electoral behavior than electoral behavior has had in shaping public policy.[42]

Because American parties have historically under-aggregated demands at the city, state, and national levels, voter identification has oscillated between long-term partisan stability and sudden outbursts for new policies at moments of crises which have generally been characterized by partisan realignments. But across time, the position of parties and candidates has tended to converge on policy matters, causing elections to be relatively unimportant in shaping policy.[43]

While scholars only recently have systematically attempted to assess the impact of elections on public policy in various European countries, the findings thus far suggest that the American experience is not unique, that electoral variables have not been much more important in shaping public policy in European systems than in the United States. For example, several studies of Italian cities demonstrate that the level of turnout and the general voting patterns of the Italian electorate have had little impact on the shaping of public policy.[44] In other West European countries the pattern is comparable. In English and Welsh county boroughs, the level of support for one party or the other apparently has had some modest influence in shaping housing and educational policies, but virtually no influence on other policies. Also at the borough level, the extent of party competition and the level of turnout have virtually no influence on public policy. Employing similar research styles, other scholarship reports that electoral behavior has little impact on public policy in the cities of West Germany, Austria, and Switzerland.[45]

41. Theodore Lowi, "Party, Policy, and Constitution in America," in *The American Party Systems*, ed. Chambers and Burnham , pp. 238-76; Walter Dean Burnham, "Party Systems and the Political Process," ibid., pp. 277-307; Samuel P. Huntington, "Political Modernization: America vs. Europe," *World Politics* 18 (April 1966): 378-414.

42. Lowi, "Party, Policy, and Constitution in America," p. 273.

43. This view is developed in Burnham's excellent *Critical Elections and the Mainsprings of American Politics*.

44. Fried, "Communism, Urban Budgets and the Two Italies," pp. 1009-51; Giorgio Galli and Alfonso Prandi, *Patterns of Participation in Italy* (New Haven, Conn.: Yale University Press, 1970), esp. chap. 6. A study by the research team of the Carlo Cattaneo Institute in Bologna is reported in the Galli and Prandi study. Also see Pietro Giarda, "Un analisi statistica sui determinanti delle spese cegli enti locali," in *Studi sulla finanza locale*, ed. Cesare Cosciani (Milan: Giuffre, 1967).

45. Noel T. Boaden, *Urban Policy-Making: Influence on County Boroughs in England and Wales* (Cambridge, Eng.: Cambridge University Press, 1971), pp. 49, 63, 70, 77, 112,

These findings are not simply artifacts of the methodologies employed, for historically oriented social scientists, using quite different methods to analyze recent history, have reached similar conclusions about the impact of electoral behavior on public policy. Jurg Steiner, for example, has reported in several studies that a consequence of the proportional representation system in Switzerland is to offer the electorate virtually no influence in shaping public policy.[46] For Norway, Sweden, the Netherlands, and West Germany, Stein Rokkan, Otto Kirchheimer, Lewis Edinger, Thomas Anton, and Hans Daalder, in separate studies, reach similar conclusions. Analyzing the highly organized and bureaucratized characteristics of these countries, these scholars stress the importance of bureaucracies and interest groups in shaping public policies. As Rokkan has suggested, voters decide parliamentary elections, but resources shape policy.[47]

---

and "Innovation and Change in English Local Government," *Political Studies* 19 (March 1971): 416-29; Noel T. Boaden and Robert R. Alford, "Sources of Diversity in English County Boroughs," *Public Administration* (London), 47 (Summer 1969): 203-23; R. R. Oliver and J. Stanyer, "Some Aspects of the Financial Behavior of County Boroughs," ibid., pp. 169-84; James A. Alt, "Some Social and Political Correlates of County Borough Expenditures," *British Journal of Political Science* 1 (January 1971): 48-62; Robert C. Fried, "Politics, Economics and Federalism: Aspects of Urban Government in Austria, Germany, and Switzerland," in *Comparative Community Politics*, ed. Terry N. Clark (New York: John Wiley and Sons, 1974), pp. 313-50.

46. Jurg Steiner, "The Principles of Majority and Proportionality," *British Journal of Political Science* 1 (January 1971): 63-70. Also see James A. Dunn, " 'Consociational Democracy' and Language Conflict: A Comparison of the Belgian and Swiss Experiences," *Comparative Political Studies* 5 (April 1972): 3-39. For a summary of the literature on the relationship between participation and public policy, see Alford and Friedland, "Political Participation and Public Policy," pp. 429-79.

47. Stein Rokkan, "Mass Suffrage, Secret Voting, and Political Participation," *European Journal of Sociology* 2 (1961): 2, and "Norway: Numerical Democracy and Corporate Pluralism," in *Political Oppositions in Western Democracies*, ed. Robert A. Dahl (New Haven, Conn.: Yale University Press, 1966), pp. 106-7; Hans Daalder, "The Netherlands: Opposition in a Segmented Society," ibid., pp. 235-36; Thomas Anton, "Policy Making and Political Culture in Sweden," *Scandinavian Political Studies* 4 (1969): 88-102; Hans Meijer, "Bureaucracy and Policy Formation in Sweden," ibid., pp. 102-16; F. G. Castles, "The Political Functions of Organized Groups, The Swedish Case," *Political Studies* 21 (March 1973): 26-34; Otto Kirchheimer, "Germany: The Vanishing Opposition," in *Political Oppositions in Western Democracies*, ed. Dahl, pp. 252-59; Lewis Edinger, *Germany* (Boston: Little, Brown, 1968), pp. 312-17.

For further support that electoral behavior and parties make little difference in shaping public policy in Great Britain, see Robert T. McKenzie, *British Political Parties* (New York: Praeger, 1964). For a general discussion of the problem in regard to British politics, see W. J. M. Mackenzie, "Mr. McKenzie on the British Parties," *Political Studies* 3 (June 1955): 157-59; Saul Rose, "Policy Decision in Opposition," *Political Studies* 4 (June 1956): 128-38; Robert T. McKenzie, "Policy Decision in Opposition: A Rejoinder," *Political Studies* 5 (June 1957): 176-82; Frank Bealey, Jean Blondel, and W. P. McCann, *Constituency Politics: A*

While common sense suggests that the electorate must play some role in shaping public policy, that influence, as suggested above, is very difficult to measure or detect in societies with universal suffrage and high levels of economic development. The more complex the society, the more difficult it is for public choices to be influenced and managed through elections. Once a society reaches a certain level of complexity, the range of problems confronting the electorate is simply too vast for elections to be systematically conducted on issues of public policy—except at moments of crisis. And it is then that the electorate most effectively influences public policy, for at moments of crisis, elections are often focused on only one or two issues and the policy positions of parties tend to diverge.

Of course, electoral behavior shapes policy outcomes in other circumstances, as we have already suggested. When a referendum is held on a special issue, the electorate obviously decides the outcome. And when the electorate either expands or contracts (as when blacks were disfranchised in the American South), policy outcomes are affected. But if we are to understand variations in policy outcomes—whether the unit of analysis be cities, states, or nation states—we should concentrate more attention on the way in which social, economic, and cultural variables influence public policy. There is an inner logic to the industrialization process which shapes the parameters and direction of public policy. Specific decisions about policy take place through the budgetary process, as Aaron Wildavsky and Charles Lindblom have observed. [48] Excepting moments of crisis, budget decision making operates to produce a process of incrementalism in public expenditures. Previous policy levels are rarely reopened

Study of Newcastle-under-Lyme (London: Faber and Faber, 1965); Allan Kornberg and Robert C. Frasure, "Policy Differences in British Parliamentary Parties," *American Political Science Review* 65 (September 1971): 694-703.

B. Guy Peters, "Economic and Political Effects of the Development of Social Expenditures in France, Sweden, and the United Kingdom" *Midwest Journal of Politics* 16 (May 1972): 225-38, lends qualified support to the views developed in our study, though Peters is unclear as to how he developed some of his indices.

48. Aaron Wildavsky, *The Politics of the Budgetary Process* (Boston: Little, Brown, 1964); Charles E. Lindblom, *The Policy-Making Process* (Englewood Cliffs, N.J.: Prentice-Hall, 1968). Also see Thomas Anton, "Rules and Symbols in the Determinants of State Expenditures," *Midwest Journal of Political Science* 11 (1967): 27-43; Gerald Sullivan, "Incremental Budget-Making in the American States: A Test of the Anton Model," *Journal of Politics* 34 (May 1972): 632-38. For a discussion of these problems within urban contexts, see J. P.Crecine, *Governmental Problem Solving: A Computer Simulation of Municipal Budgeting* (Chicago: Rand McNally, 1969); and A. J. Meltsner, *The Politics of City Revenue* (Berkeley: University of California Press, 1971). For the process of budget making in a variety of countries, see the "Papers and proceedings of the 27th Session of the International Institute of Public Finance at Nuremberg, September 14-17, 1971," published in *Public Finance* 27 (1972): 85-261.

and reexamined, but there are different amounts of change from one budget sector to another.

It is in relation to changes within budget areas that, at the elite level, struggle and conflict occur. Political elite variables will be more helpful to us than electoral variables if our goal is to understand the way that social and economic variables get translated into public policy. Thus, beyond the socioeconomic and cultural variables, we need to be sensitive to the processes internal to the black box of politics. That is one reason that it is important to move from large data sets to case studies, and back.

We should become increasingly sensitive to the theoretical implications of our research strategies. By focusing on popular voting behavior to explain public policy, we assume a micro-theoretical approach to the study of public policy, whereas as we have suggested in chapter 1, a macro or a structural approach is necessary to understand public policy. There, we suggested that the levels of spending and the allocation of resources are probably more responsive to the power of dominant interest groups than to popular electoral behavior. Even if there is widespread popular participation, voters cannot be expected to have much impact on policy when they are heterogeneously organized, fragmented ethnically and territorially, have limited specialized knowledge, and few intense interests. As we have argued in the two previous chapters, the dominant elites are by definition a minority of the electorate, and therefore have limited popular participation, but they have power resulting from homogeneous interests, less fragmented communication networks, and more intensely defined interests. Voters tend to respond symbolically to visible issues that have little to do with the way that a society is structured. Elites usually exercise power over issues that are often invisible to the electorate and which are often resolved at the level immune to the activity of the electorate. For the electorate, popular participation has often been a substitute for power, whereas dominant elites may forego popular participation because of the power which they possess.[49]

---

49. A full discussion of the literature supporting this view is Alford and Friedland, "Political Participation and Public Policy," pp. 427-79. Also see Roger Friedland, Frances Fox Piven, and Robert R. Alford, "Political Conflict, Urban Structure, and the Fiscal Crisis," in *Comparing Public Policy: New Approaches and Methods—Sage Yearbook in Politics and Public Policy*, ed. Douglas Ashford (Beverly Hills, Calif.: Sage Publications, 1977); and Roger Friedland, "Class Power and the Central City: The Contradictions of Urban Growth" (Ph.D. diss., University of Wisconsin, 1977).

4

Toward a Classification
of American Cities

NOT ONLY are there hundreds of cities in American society, but almost
every one has its own written history. For some cities there are indeed
numerous studies. Because in the United States there are dozens of state
and local historical societies and numerous historical journals, Americans
have long been encouraged to study the history of their communities, and
local historians have relatively little difficulty in publishing their materials.
Most local studies are narrative histories which highlight the chronology
of important events. Unfortunately, the overwhelming majority of local
histories are very weak conceptually, though a few are excellent. But
even the best local history is seldom informative about a larger society.
As a result, the reader seldom understands the significance of a local study
for American history.

Many authors justify their work by suggesting that the city under
investigation is typical of other cities. For example, Robert A. Dahl's *Who
Governs?*, which has almost become a classic in urban literature, states
that "New Haven is in many respects typical of other cities in the United
States."[1] But typical in what respects? After completing a history of a
particular city, the reader rarely knows if the city is similar to some other
cities, and, if so, which ones and in what ways.

Most studies of American cities are undertaken either because the
author has a strong sense of identity with a particular city, the sources
are readily available, the city has already been studied by others with
different perspectives, or, simply, the city has never been studied by anyone
else. In this connection Dahl has written "the community I chose to study

1. Robert A. Dahl, *Who Governs? Democracy and Power in an American City* (New
Haven, Conn.: Yale University Press, 1961), p. v. Also see Appendix A, p. 330.

was New Haven, Connecticut, and I chose it for the most part because it lay conveniently at hand."[2]

In short, the scholar's logic in choosing a particular city for study often is not well suited to reveal something of importance about a larger society. Historians could select cities for study by some randomized process if they had previously carefully defined a universe of particular types of cities and given each unit within that universe equal opportunity for chance selection. Obviously, there is no need to propose anything so radical, for historians would never choose their cities on such a basis. Our understanding of cities would be advanced, however, if they were classified in meaningful terms so that when a historian studies a particular city, he will have more insight as to which other cities are likely to be most similar as well as dissimilar on particular variables. Such a classification would offer the potential for building on the findings of extant studies. Moreover, a scheme which permitted us to classify cities at various points in time would help us to understand how and why cities change over time.

Obviously, cities can be classified in dozens of ways. They may be categorized as old or new, ugly or beautiful, wealthy or poor, cultured or uncouth. There is no correct way of classifying cities. Classifications are either useful or not useful, depending on the purposes to which they are put. And no matter what classification scheme we use, some scholars will find it useless. Nevertheless, we should aim for a classification of cities which introduces coherence into research and which promotes order in what would otherwise be chaotic data. And if we classify cities along several meaningful dimensions, we can gain insights concerning the relationship between some of our studies of individual cities and the larger society.

In recent decades a widely used scheme for classifying contemporary cities has been the one developed by economic geographers. They have attempted to classify cities according to their economic specialization or economic function. The assumption underlying this kind of classification is that the principal economic services of a city make a difference in the lives of most of its residents. Cities are usually placed in seven different functional categories: manufacturing, commercial, diversified, professional, resort, extractive or mining, or transportation.[3] Obviously, the list of categories can further be extended according to other social patterns.

With this type of classification the analyst arbitrarily designates a city as being manufacturing if it has a specified percentage of the labor force

2. Ibid., p. v.
3. See the discussion in Jeffrey K. Hadden and Edgar F. Borgatta, *American Cities: Their Social Characteristics* (Chicago: Rand McNally Company, 1965), pp. 2-29.

engaged in manufacturing. The same procedure is used with other occupational categories. Because the percentage of any city's labor force
engaged in either professional or transportation activities is relatively
small, some cities may be labeled as either professional or transportation
cities and still be given another classification as well.

This type of classification, while useful, does have serious deficiencies.
Because the categories are not mutually exclusive, a city may be placed
in more than one class. Moreover, there is no agreement as to when an
economic activity becomes important enough in a city to be of special
significance. For this reason, scholars frequently disagree as to how a
particular city should be classified. For example, during the 1950s Boston
was categorized by one analyst as a wholesale trade city, another classified
it as a nondurable manufacturing city, while a third identified it as a
center of finance, insurance, and real estate. And still another listed it as
a diversified city, with retail trade predominant in comparison with
manufacturing.[4] Thus, this kind of classification, while useful and better
than none, does not permit us to predict or to specify with very much
accuracy the consequences of a city's having one type of specialization
instead of another or the concomitants of particular specialization. Even
so, this kind of scholarship has enriched our understanding of cities in
relationship to one another.

Sensitive to the shortcomings of economic-function classification,
many recent scholars have attempted to develop a classification scheme
which is not based on any preconceived set of categories and which does
not rely on a single variable. To achieve such a goal, they have classified
cities by using a large number of social, economic, and political variables.
The technique employed is factor analysis, a procedure which seeks to
identify a few dimensions central to a large array of variables.[5] Given a
long list of variables, factor analysis determines which ones go, or cluster
together, and thus which ones might be considered as expressions of an
underlying phenomenon. A factor is named with consideration for the
variables which are mostly highly associated with it.[6]

4. Otis Dudley Duncan, W. Richard Scott, Stanley Lieberson, Beverly Duncan, and
Hal H. Winsborough, *Metropolis and Region* (Baltimore, Md.: The Johns Hopkins University
Press, 1960), p. 34.

5. For standard treatments of factor analysis, see Benjamin Fruchter, *Introduction to
Factor Analysis* (New York: Van Nostrand, 1954); and Harry H. Harmon, *Modern Factor
Analysis* (Chicago: University of Chicago Press, 1960).

6. For similar approaches to other cities, but for different eras, see C. A. Moser and Wolf
Scott, *British Towns* (Edinburgh: Oliver and Boyd, 1961); Daniel O. Price, "Factor Analysis
in the Study of Metropolitan Centers," *Social Forces* 20 (May 1942): 449-55; and Hadden
and Borgatta, *American Cities*, parts of which have been very helpful.

Each factor that one identifies thus becomes a potential basis for classification of cities, in that cities can be scored on each factor. Clearly, some factors are more useful than others as classification criteria. And it should be obvious that the nature of the factors that emerge is dependent on the variables employed.

By using factor analysis, scholars have sacrificed the simplicity of the economic specialization classification in order to gain a better understanding of the relationships among variables and of the major dimensions of cities. They do not sort cities into singular and distinct qualitative categories, or types. Rather, the cities are distributed along several dimensions, or factors. By scoring cities on the factors, scholars are able to perceive the differences which exist among them on a variety of dimensions. It then becomes possible to translate a factorial structure into a profile so that individual cities can be compared and analyzed on several factors. For example, a city might score high on a social-heterogeneity factor, low on economic stability, and so on.

There are serious inadequacies in the use of factor analysis for purposes of city classification, however. First, the variables which are selected for factor-analytic purposes are not chosen for any theoretical reasons. Rather, most scholars simply choose a large number of variables involving size, economic base, ethnic and religious composition, rate of growth, level of income, level of education, and rates of in-out migration. Indeed, one finds, after reviewing dozens of factor-analytic schemes in numerous studies involving many societies, that the most readily available social and economic data from published census materials are used as variables. In other words, it is the availability of data and not theoretical considerations which generally dictate the choice of variables. In one study Jeffrey K. Hadden and Edgar F. Borgatta chose sixty-five such variables; Brian Berry, the scholar who has made the most extensive use of this technique for city classification, chose ninety-seven variables for his study. Significantly, their variables were very similar, though in neither study were the variables chosen by theoretical considerations.[7]

Second, the factors which emerge are often difficult to identify. As an end product of factor analysis, the variables are loaded (or given weights) on each factor. The analyst must then label the factor with reference to the variables making up the factor, even though the variables with the highest loadings may not identify a factor that makes sense. In one recent study a factor labeled "stage in the life cycle of community residents"

7. Hadden and Borgatta, *American Cities*; and Brian Berry, ed., *City Classification Handbook* (New York: John Wiley and Sons, 1972), pp. 1-60.

emerged, but the fifth and sixth variables on the factor were population per household and persons per dwelling unit—variables not necessarily having much to do with the age of community residents.[8]

Third, the rankings of cities on the factors is often quite misleading or confusing. In one recent study Huntington Beach, California, ranked fourth on a factor labeled "foreign-born or foreign-stock population," when only 8 percent of its population was foreign-born—a percentage that should have given it a substantially lower ranking on this particular factor. In the same study, Urbana, Illinois, ranked third on a factor labeled "nonwhite population," when only 6 percent of its population was nonwhite, a percentage which should also have placed it much lower in the ranking. Because the labeling of factors may require awkward interpretations, the ranking of cities with factor-analytic schemes often has little utility.[9]

In the two above examples it would have been more appropriate to rank all cities by their percentage of foreign-born or nonwhite residents, rather than to rely on factor analysis. By using a single variable to rank cities, there is, of course, no problem in identifying the dimension with which one is working, and there is no uncertainty where cities should be placed in the ranking.

This is not to suggest that economic-functional and factor-analytic classifications of cities are useless. Rather, we wish to suggest that there is as yet no single appropriate method for classifying cities. Each of the methods has shortcomings, suggesting that an effort to classify cities might employ several methodologies, which could serve as checks on one another.[10]

This we attempt on a preliminary and modified basis in the section which follows. While we would like a classification of cities based on the typology developed in chapter 1, we must settle for something less, as we do not have systematic data on each variable for a large number of cities. For example, historical data on the political culture of cities would require an in-depth study of the political culture in each city in our universe of

8. Berry, *City Classification Handbook.*

9. Ibid.

10. For an interesting discussion of the shortcomings of a factor-analytic scheme of cities, see Robert Alford, "Critical Evaluation of the Principles of City Classification," in *City Classification Handbook*, ed. Brian Berry (New York: Wiley-Interscience, 1972), pp. 331-58. An interesting but very different type of strategy for classifying American cities is Edward M. Cook, *The Father of the Towns: Leadership and Community Structure in Eighteenth-Century New England* (Baltimore, Md.: The Johns Hopkins University Press, 1976).

cities. Unfortunately,we do not yet have this kind of systematic data on cities. The economic and political autonomy of cities are other variables for which systematic data on a large number of cities will be lacking until we have better measures resulting from in-depth studies of these variables based on a common conceptualization.

Lacking the data to develop a classification consistent with the typologies in chapter 1, we nevertheless will attempt in the section below to develop profiles along some of those dimensions. All 278 American cities with a population between 10,000 and 25,000 during the late nineteenth and early twentieth centuries are included. These profiles represent only a first step in classifying cities according to the typology in the first chapter. And as our information on these cities improves, we will ultimately be able to develop more complex profiles, and to move closer to using all the dimensions outlined in chapter 1.[11]

In the classification below we have relied on two broadly derived indicators of community life: an input indicator drawn from aspects of structural variation described in some detail in chapter 1, and an output indicator related to public policy. The input measure is the socioeconomic status of cities, which is a proxy for vertical differentiation in social structure. In chapter 1, some of the implications that variations in vertical differentiation have for other structural and cultural characteristics have

11. The following is a brief summary of the sources from which the data for this project were collected: U.S. Bureau of the Census, *Twelfth Census of the United States: 1900* (Washington, D.C.: U.S. Government Printing Office, 1901-2); U.S. Bureau of the Census, *Bulletin 20: Statistics of Cities Having a Population of Over 25,000, 1902-1903* (Washington, D.C.: U.S. Government Printing Office, 1907); U.S. Bureau of the Census, *Bulletin 45: Statistics of Cities with Population 8,000 to 25,000* (Washington, D.C.: U.S. Government Printing Office, 1907); U.S. Bureau of the Census, *Transportation by Water, 1906* (Washington, D.C.: U.S. Government Printing Office, 1908); U.S. Bureau of the Census, *Special Census Report on Benevolent Institutions, 1904* (Washington, D.C.: U.S. Government Printing Office, 1905); U.S. Bureau of Education, *Report of the U.S. Commissioner of Education for 1899-1900* (Washington, D.C.: U.S. Government Printing Office, 1901); U.S. Post Office Department, *Annual Report of the Postmaster-General, 1900* (Washington, D.C.: U.S. Government Printing Office, 1900); U.S. Bureau of the Census, *Statistical Atlas for 1900* (Washington, D.C.: U.S. Census Office, 1903); *Rand McNally Bankers Directory* (Chicago: Rand McNally, 1901); *Bankers Register, 1901* (Chicago: The Credit Company, 1901). Professional data on dentists and doctors were collected from *Polk's Medical and Surgical Register of the United States and Canada* (Detroit: R. L. Polk, 1900); *Polk's Dental Register and Directory of the United States and Canada* (Detroit: R. L. Polk, 1902); and *Directory of the American Homeopathic Association, 1900* (New York: American Homeopathic Association, 1900), while data on lawyers were collected from *Martindale's American Legal Directory, 1900-1901* (New York: Martindale Company, 1901). When data was missing, it was usually collected from the publication closest to 1900. We attempted to follow a policy of collecting no data which appeared prior to 1895 or after 1905. More detailed explanations of the sources for this project have been placed in the office of the Data Program and Library Service, University of Wisconsin.

been discussed. And elsewhere, the implications that social-economic variables carry for policy have been spelled out.[12]

The factor-analytic method has been used in previous studies to measure the socioeconomic status of communities, but, as indicated above, we consider this an inappropriate technique. Instead, we construct our socio-economic-status dimension by relying on the extent to which a city deviates from the average on several variables—a method which has rarely been used in the classification of cities, but one which may be more reliable than factor analysis in that the indicators are chosen on a conceptual basis. The indicators for socioeconomic status are, for each of the 278 cities, (1) per capita wealth; (2) percentage of children ages five to seventeen in school; (3) percentage of labor force not consisting of children ages five to seventeen; (4) percentage of population which is white; and (5) percentage of population consisting of professional people. On each variable, we gave each city a score, based on how many standard deviations its value is from the mean. The scores for the five indicators making up this dimension were summed and averaged for a final value for each city on the socioeconomic dimension. The cities were then divided in thirds and ranked as being high, medium, or low on the dimension.

The second dimension used to classify cities is that of governmental activity, a multifaceted measure that is a surrogate for governmental complexity or political differentiation. Complexity, which is another approach to political differentiation, is related to the number of functions undertaken by local governments. The more differentiated or complex political structures are, and the more functions they attempt, the greater their governmental activity. We use the same methodology to develop this dimension as that to construct the socioeconomic-status dimension— that is, we score cities as to the amount they differ from the mean on indicators of governmental activity in order to develop a composite score for each city on the dimension. The indicators are: (1) city government expenditures per capita; (2) city government debt per capita; (3) percentage of pupils in public schools; (4) value per capita of city government possessions which are income producing (for example, water works, electric utilities, etc.); (5) value per capita of city government possessions which are not income producing (for example, city hall, jail, fire houses, etc.); and (6) governmental outlay per capita (major capital expenditures). Here, also, cities were divided into thirds and ranked on the dimension as being high, medium, or low.

The classification resulting from the use of these two complex variables

12. J. Rogers Hollingsworth and Ellen Jane Hollingsworth, "Expenditures in American Cities," in *The Dimensions of Quantitative Research in History*, ed. William O. Aydelotte et al. (Princeton, N.J.: Princeton University Press, 1972), pp. 347-89.

is shown in table 4.1. The chart indicates graphically the previously described association between levels of socioeconomic status and levels of government activity. Cities which are high in socioeconomic status tend to be high in governmental activity, and the converse is true. Were the relationship invariant as this might suggest, cities would fall only into cells 1, 5, and 9. They do not fall into such neat patterns, although those three cells are all large. And the cells with the least likely combination—cells 3 and 7—are among the smallest. Still, there are twenty-one cities in cell 3 (high socioeconomic status and low governmental activity) which presumably could afford more government action. Janesville, Wisconsin, earlier described as being extremely conservative in fiscal matters, is one of the cities in that group. On the other hand, in cell 7 (low socioeconomic status and high governmental activity) there are fifteen cities which are overspending related to their resources. Southern cities are somewhat over represented in this group.

Because so many scholars have used economic-base identifications as classificatory devices, we have enriched table 4.1 by providing appropriate labels, using the seven functions commonly employed by economic geographers, appropriately modified. While systematic aggregate data on employment do not exist for cities of this size at the turn of the century, we can make judgments about the economic functions of all cities based on the data presented in chapter 3, a careful reading of the histories of these cities, and extensive examination of state and local gazetteers, city directories, and state and federal census materials. The percentage of the population employed in manufacturing assists in identifying manufacturing cities. Cities having between 14 and 43 percent of their population employed in manufacturing are designated as manufacturing cities. Those having between 9 and 13 percent employed in manufacturing are classified as diversified; and those cities having less than 9 percent in manufacturing are labeled as commercial. Lest one think that these decisions are arbitrary, we have read carefully in the sources and literature involving these cities, and our designations of manufacturing, diversified, or commercial appear to be consistent with that literature. In addition, we have, where possible, indicated in what kind of manufacturing the city specialized.

Many of these cities are designated as having several functions. It is useful to note that large cities generally provide more functions than small cities. Very small cities usually provide a very wide variety of functions when they are formed, after which they move into a phase with more specialization. The extent of specialization, obviously, varies according to a variety of other factors: the discovery of coal, the presence of pineries, the residential preferences of well-to-do commuters, the siting of a very large manufacturing facility. Because of the more specialized nature of

High socioeconomic status	Medium socioeconomic status	Low socioeconomic status
1 (N = 45)	4 (N = 32)	7 (N = 15)
Alameda CA 39 27 Port, Comm	Anderson IN 82 139 Man	Asheville NC 48 256 Resort
Auburn ME 83 60 Man (boots, shoes)	Attleboro MA 40 143 Man (machinery)	Athens GA 62 270 Comm, College town
Bangor ME 16 33 Div (lumber prod.)	Austin TX 69 106 Comm, State capital, College town	Braddock PA 90 209 Comm
Battle Creek MI 73 49 Div	Cranston RI 86 183 Res suburb	Clinton MA 67 185 Man (Textiles)
Berkeley CA 31 3 Res suburb, College town	Danbury CT 70 98 Man	Danville VA 71 268 Man (Textiles)
Beverly MA 6 54 Man (boots, shoes)	E Orange NJ 4 93 Res suburb	Great Falls MT 28 234 Div, Mining
Brookline MA 1 1 Res suburb	Flint MI 23 107 Man (Lumber prod.)	Greensboro NC 51 264 Comm
Charlestown WV 64 18 Comm, State capital	Gardner MA 7 156 Man	Henderson KY 50 262 Comm
Colorado Springs CO 2 11 Suburb, College town	Homestead PA 43 165 Suburb	Kearny NJ 57 237 Comm
Concord NH 25 87 Div, State capital	Ironton OH 80 155 Div, Port	Lynchburg VA 41 208 Comm
Evanston IL 52 4 Res suburb, College town	Jamestown NY 13 158 Man	Marquette MI 46 192 Port, Mining
Everett MA 22 55 Res suburb	Kingston NY 54 144 Div	Norwich CT 47 232 Man (Textiles)
Findlay, OH 45 58 Comm	Lansing MI 74 110 Comm, State capital, College town	Perth Amboy NJ 77 197 Port, Div
Framingham MA 78 76 Man (boots, shoes)	Leominster MA 32 164 Man (textiles)	Portsmouth VA 87 260 Port, Res suburb
Fresno CA 58 36 Comm	Lorain OH 59 174 Port, Man	Waco TX 36 200 Comm
Helena, MT 30 10 State capital	Marion IN 42 128 Man	
Lafayette IN 91 14 Comm, College town	Marlboro MA 27 137 Man (boots, shoes)	
Logansport IN 88 43 Comm	Middletown NY 65 119 Div	
Mansfield OH 81 26 Man	Moline IL 79 141 Man (agri. equip.)	
Marshalltown IA 83 53 Comm	New Brunswick NJ 68 153 Man	
Medford MA 3 39 Res Suburb, College town	Newburyport MA 56 150 Man (textiles)	
Melrose MA 5 14 Res suburb	Northampton MA 33 169 College town, Man (textiles)	
Montclair NJ 72 22 Res suburb	Ogden UT 53 126 Comm	
Mt. Vernon NY 12 34 Res suburb	Orange NJ 37 170 Res suburb	
Muskegon MI 44 85 Port, Man (lumber prod.)	Peabody MA 10 108 Man (boots, shoes)	
New London CT 8 69 Div, Port	Pittsfield MA 38 101 Man (textiles)	
Newport RI 55 15 Resort	Poughkeepsie NY 60 160 College town, Div	
New Rochelle NY 9 24 Res suburb	Sault Ste. Marie MI 18 100 Transport. center	
Niagara Falls NY 15 20 Resort, Man	Waltham MA 34 113 Man (textiles, machinery)	
Oklahoma City OK 14 91 Comm	Westfield MA 26 102 Man (Lumber prod)	
Parkersburg WV 75 8 Div	Woburn MA 35 95 Div (boots, shoes)	
Peekskill NY 76 92 Div	Zanesville OH 92 142 Man	
Port Huron MI 49 59 Port, Div (lumber, wheat prod.)		
Portsmouth NH 11 28 Div, Port		
Quincy MA 19 62 Res suburb		
Revere MA 17 47 Res suburb		
San Diego CA 20 5 Comm		
San Jose CA 61 6 Comm		
Saratoga Springs NY 24 12 Resort		
Sioux Falls SD 66 21 Comm		
Stockton CA 89 7 Suburb, Port		
Walla Walla WA 21 16 Div		

Medium
governmental
activity

2 (N = 26)

Watertown NY 85 44 Man (paper, flour)
Weymouth MA 29 77 Man (boots, shoes)
Wilkinsburg PA 84 41 Mining

Aurora IL 139 82 Man (metal prod)
Bath ME 114 32 Man (lumber prod)
Beloit WI 161 45 Man
Bloomington IL 104 70 Comm
Burlington VT 94 57 Div, College town
Butler PA 162 83 Comm
Cripple Creek CO 173 66 Comm
Decatur IL 125 40 Div
Ft. Scott KS 181 50 Comm
Galesburg IL 182 30 Comm, College town
Geneva NY 105 38 Div
Hornellsville NY 106 74 Div
Ithaca NY 165 2 Comm, College town
Kalamazoo MI 110 78 Man
Kokomo IN 156 51 Div
Lawrence KS 128 29 Comm, College town
Madison WI 142 19 Comm, College town, State capital
Marietta OH 93 48 Div
Meadville PA 98 37 Div
Muscatine IA 177 86 Man (lumber prod)
Ottawa IL 163 64 Div
Richmond IN 158 23 Man
Rock Island IL 149 52 Div (R.R. transport center)
Rutland VT 144 71 Div
Tiffin OH 151 25 Div
Waterloo IA 96 35 Comm

3 (N = 21)

Ann Arbor MI 201 9 Comm, College town
Appleton WI 242 89 Div (Lumber prod)
Ashland WI 244 84 Port (iron, steelworks)
Chillicothe OH 194 90 Comm
De... ... 202 75 Comm

5 (N = 35)

Adams MA 166 166 Man (Textiles)
Bradford PA 123 127 Comm
Burlington IA 183 145 Comm
Cumberland MD 124 182 Div
Dover NH 108 115 Man
Dunkirk NY 132 122 Man (lumber prod., machines)
E. Liverpool OH 115 114 Man
Eau Claire WI 171 125 Div (lumber prod.)
Elgin IL 113 118 Man
El Paso TX 174 132 Comm
Elwood IN 167 184 Man
Fond du Lac WI 148 134 Div (lumber prod.)
Gloversville NY 135 133 Man
Hamilton OH 112 131 Man
Hammond IN 137 120 Man
Huntington WV 126 99 Div
Jacksonville IL 130 148 Comm
Jeffersonville IN 172 220 Div (metal works)
Johnstown NY 102 109 Man
Keokuk IA 175 159 Div
Lewiston ME 120 172 Man (textiles, boots)
Lima OH 100 96 Div
Little Falls NY 111 176 Man (textiles)
Naugatuck Boro CT 133 149 Man
Newburg NY 119 136 Div
Oil City PA 150 116 Div, Oil
Oswego NY 138 97 Man (lumber prod.)
Piqua OH 141 151 Man
Pittsburg KS 121 138 Comm, Mining
Portsmouth OH 107 171 Man
Rome NY 109 167 Man
Sandusky OH 176 117 Port, Comm (Lumber prod.)
Sherman TX 147 152 Comm
Steubenville OH 146 146 Div, Mining
Wichita KS 95 124 Comm

6 (N = 26)

Alpena MI 275 157 Div (Lumber prod.)
Ansonia CT 202 163 Man
Augusta ME 185 104 State capital, Man (Lumber prod.)
Beaver Falls PA 220 177 Man

8 (N = 31)

Alexandria VA 164 250 Comm
Amsterdam NY 138 208 Man
Atchison KS 170 222 Comm, R.R., Transport, center
Bridgetown NJ 178 201 Man (glass, canning works)
Charlotte NC 103 271 Man
Cheyenne WY 117 261 State capital, Comm
Chicopee MA 131 218 Man (textiles)
Clinton IA 180 204 Div
Columbia SC 118 276 State capital, Div
Columbus GA 145 266 Man
Dunmore PA 155 229 Mining
E. Providence RI 122 186 Comm
Ft. Dodge IA 140 202 Comm, Mining
Guthrie OK 97 224 Territorial capital, Comm
Kenosha WI 152 193 Man (metal prod)
Leavenworth KS 136 226 Comm (military)
Lebanon PA 153 189 Man
Macon GA 143 195 Div
N. Adams MA 99 190 Man (textiles, boots, shoes)
Natchez MS 157 275 Comm
Owensboro KY 160 239 Comm, Mining
Paducah KY 169 263 Div
Petersburg VA 116 245 Man
Pine Bluff AR 179 238 Comm
Raleigh NC 154 255 State capital, Comm
Shreveport LA 127 233 Comm
Steelton PA 159 227 Man
Vicksburg MS 184 253 Comm
W. Bay City MI 101 207 Man (Lumber prod.)
Wilmington NC 168 240 Comm
Winston NC 129 272 Man

9 (N = 47)

Alton IL 261 242 Man
Ashtabula OH 197 216 Comm
Baton Rouge LA 277 264 Comm, State capital, College town
Belleville IL 267 199 Comm, Mining

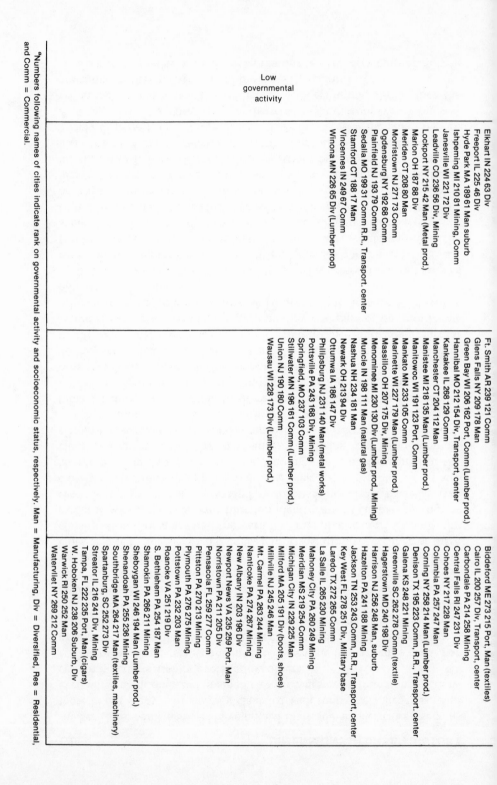

Low governmental activity	Elkhart IN 224 63 Div Freeport IL 225 46 Div Hyde Park MA 189 61 Man suburb Ishpeming MI 210 81 Mining, Comm Janesville WI 221 72 Div Leadville CO 236 56 Div, Mining Lockport NY 215 42 Man (Metal prod.) Marion OH 187 88 Div Meriden CT 208 80 Man Morristown NJ 271 73 Comm Ogdensburg NY 192 68 Comm Plainfield NJ 193 79 Comm Sedalia MO 199 31 Comm R.R., Transport. center Stamford CT 188 17 Man Vincennes IN 249 67 Comm Winona MN 226 65 Div (Lumber prod)	Ft. Smith AR 239 121 Comm Glens Falls NY 209 178 Man Green Bay WI 206 162 Port, Comm (Lumber prod.) Hannibal MO 212 154 Div, Transport, center Kankakee IL 268 129 Comm Manchester CT 204 112 Man Manistee MI 218 135 Man (Lumber prod.) Manitowoc WI 191 123 Port, Comm Mankato MN 233 105 Comm Marinette WI 227 179 Man (Lumber prod.) Massillon OH 207 175 Div, Mining Menominee MI 230 130 Div (Lumber prod., Mining) Muncie IN 198 111 Man (natural gas) Nashua NH 234 181 Man Newark OH 213 94 Div Ottumwa IA 186 147 Div Philipsburg NJ 231 140 Man (metal works) Pottsville PA 243 168 Div, Mining Springfield, MO 237 103 Comm Stillwater MN 196 161 Comm (Lumber prod.) Union NJ 190 180 Comm Wausau WI 228 173 Div (Lumber prod.)	Biddeford ME 273 215 Port, Man (textiles) Cairo IL 200 257 Div, Transport, center Carbondale PA 214 258 Mining Central Falls RI 247 231 Div Cohoes NY 217 228 Man Columbia PA 257 247 Man Corning NY 258 214 Man (Lumber prod.) Denison TX 195 223 Comm, R.R., Transport. center Galena KS 248 221 Mining Greenville SC 262 278 Comm (textile) Hagerstown MD 240 198 Div Harrison NJ 256 248 Man, suburb Hazelton PA 241 188 Mining Jackson TN 253 243 Comm, R.R., Transport, center Key West FL 278 251 Div, Military base Laredo TX 272 265 Comm La Salle IL 265 230 Mining Mahoney City PA 260 249 Mining Meridian MS 219 254 Comm Michigan City IN 229 225 Man Milford MA 205 191 Div (boots, shoes) Millville NJ 245 246 Man Mt. Carmel PA 263 244 Mining Nanticoke PA 274 267 Mining New Albany IN 203 196 Div Newport News VA 235 259 Port. Man Norristown PA 211 205 Div Pensacola FL 259 277 Comm Pittston PA 270 213 Mining Plymouth PA 276 275 Mining Pottstown PA 232 203 Man Roanoke VA 251 219 Div S. Bethlehem PA 254 187 Man Shamokin PA 266 211 Mining Sheboygan WI 246 194 Man (Lumber prod.) Shenandoah PA 255 236 Mining Southbridge MA 264 217 Man (textiles, machinery) Spartanburg, SC 252 273 Div Streator IL 216 241 Div, Mining Tampa, FL 222 235 Port, Man (cigars) W. Hoboken NJ 238 206 Suburb, Div Warwick RI 250 252 Man Watervliet NY 269 212 Comm

[a]Numbers following names of cities indicate rank on governmental activity and socioeconomic status, respectively. Man = Manufacturing, Div = Diversified, Res = Residential, and Comm = Commercial.

smaller cities, some analysts have argued that *only* smaller cities—such as those in this study—are usefully classified with functional categories. And even when a middle-sized or small city provides more than one function, certain functions usually overshadow others.

There are some correspondences between the two schemes used. For example, it is notable that, among the cities in cell 1 (high socioeconomic status and high government activity), there is strong representation of residential suburbs and college towns. Low socioeconomic status cells have only two college towns (both being in the South) and only one residential suburb. Cell 9 (low socioeconomic status and low government activity) has many mining cities and twice as high a percentage of manufacturing cities as cell 1. Yet there is no consistent association with either of these classification indicators and the variable "manufacturing." Overall, the extent to which the economic function identifications enable one to proceed more expeditiously to research problems is not clear. There are two closely related lines of inquiry that have their roots in table 4.1, or any counterpart similarly derived. First, one may take all (or some) of the cities in a given cell of the chart and, recognizing that socioeconomic circumstances and governmental complexity are in essence controlled, look at other similarities and dissimilarities. What processes not implied in table 4.1 do such cities seem to share? In what ways are such processes related to socioeconomic inputs and governmental complexity? On the other hand, what dissimilarities exist as to social processes in these cities: do they mean that certain kinds of variables and experiences are irrelevant to the nexus between socioeconomic circumstance and governmental activity? Or, as a second strategy, one may compare cities in different cells as to socioeconomic status and government activity to discover other types of variation.

Table 4.1 makes clearer, the utility of using conceptual frameworks rather than geography to compare cities. Whereas one might expect that cities in the same region, or at least the same state, would appear in the same cluster in the table, such is not the case. Of course, one would not expect to find in the same cluster suburbs from a major metropolitan area as well as semirural towns from the same state. The fifty-two cities of New England appear in all nine clusters, although they are mostly concentrated in cells 1 and 2. The cities of the Middle Atlantic states are disproportionately found in cell 9 (twenty of seventy-eight cities), but otherwise are widely dispersed. Even more dispersed are the cities of the Lakes region. And only two of the thirty-eight southern cities—both from West Virginia— are in cells containing cities with high socioeconomic status. (See the appendix for the arrangement of the cities by region.)

To put the matter more directly, regions tend to vary considerably in

the extent to which they are relatively cohesive and in the variables or constructs on which they are cohesive. A multilateral classification scheme such as the one developed in this study has the advantage of allowing the scholar to say, "City a is like city b on variables x or y or z," or to see along which dimensions regional communalities are expressed. Or, for carrying out comparative case studies, one can perhaps more appropriately choose communities with established similarities and proceed to focus analysis on the sources and aspects of differences as they may appear. For example, one might wish to study four Middle Atlantic cities. Using the approach in table 4.1, one would probably select cities from cell 9 (low socioeconomic status, low governmental activity) with confidence that, on major variables, variation was controlled. Or, from an opposite approach, one might wish to have controls on one variable and variation on a second. One might wish to study and compare communities with like manifestations of socioeconomic status, but different governmental activity patterns in order to see what other variables helped shape different policies in the cities. Using table 4.1, the reader also can make some refinement of economic classifications.

One of the most striking aspects of table 4.1 is the mixture of types of cities in most of the cells. For example, cities in cell 1 (high socioeconomic status and high government activity) are both old, well-established (Massachusetts cities) and new (California cities), residential suburbs and manufacturing (although to a lesser extent than in other cells). What is most striking is the large representation of state capitals and college towns, and the small representation of mining and southern cities. What this cell suggests, then, is that there are a variety of structural and cultural contexts within which high socioeconomic status is converted into government activity. And the distribution of cities into cells other than 1, 5, and 9 emphasizes the complexity of attributing causation for policy to certain structural regularities.

Cell 9 includes a very large number of mining cities as well as manufacturing cities and a disproportionate number of southern cities. Yet manufacturing cities occur in all cells, and southern cities are spread throughout cells 7, 8, and 9. Thus, there may be two or three main routes by which the nexus between socioeconomic status and governmental activity occurs, as shown in cell 9. Insofar as state capitals and college towns occur in cells 7-9, they are southern cities.

As suggested by the data and conceptualization in the earlier chapters of this book, most of these 278 cities were oligarchical in type around 1900. We believe the cities in the center cell (cell 5) of table 4.1 to be those which fit best the label of oligarchy. On a continuum the cities in cell 1 tend to verge more closely toward having characteristics resembling polyarchic

cities, and those in cell 9 tend to be somewhat closer to the autocratic type.

Table 4.1 explores how well some of the concepts discussed in chapter 1 go together, in a sense "testing" by using urban unit data. As suggested above, the "fit" between structural-input variables and policy-output variables is far from perfect, but it is moderately good. To extend our analysis, we have attempted to discern how well the political culture of cities follows the patterns suggested in chapter 1. That is, to what extent do patterns of political culture correlate with social, economic, and political structural variables as well as with policy outcomes? The measurement of political culture is a complex and intricate task requiring largely unavailable data. As an indicator of political culture, we have used voter turnout, a reflection of the extent to which eligible voters are participant-oriented. Survey data would be much preferable, although it is obviously inaccessible for the time-point at 1900. The turnout measure we use, as in chapter 3, is the percentage of the total population that voted in local elections from 1895 to 1903.

Cities with high socioeconomic status had 18 percent of their population vote in local elections. Cities with medium socioeconomic status had a turnout level of 17 percent, and those with low socioeconomic status had 12 percent. When turnout is measured as a percentage of males twenty-one years and older, turnout in cities tends to increase as the socioeconomic status of cities increases. In other words, our data suggest that the higher the level of socioeconomic status in the cities, the higher the level of turnout.

On the governmental activity dimension of table 4.1, however, there is no consistent association between turnout and increasing levels of governmental activity. Or to phrase it differently, political culture, as measured by turnout, does not systematically seem to relate to policy outcomes, to governmental activity.

These findings are interesting in that, first, they support the argument in chapter 1 that political culture is intricately linked with the social and economic structure of a city. Second, they further support the findings in chapter 3 that turnout and other participation variables have quite minor impact on policy outcomes, especially as contrasted with the influence of socioeconomic indicators.

Political culture, as measured by our proxy variable turnout, is already tapped by table 4.1, in view of its multi-colinearity with socioeconomic variables. This suggests that in that table we have, within certain limits, controlled for social, economic, and political-structural, as well as political-cultural, and policy dimensions. One may now use the table in order to select cities for more systematic and more refined investigations of structural, cultural, and policy dimensions. We hope this type of classification will provide a starting point for more careful selection of individual cities

for future investigations and for more complex and sophisticated classification systems.

While each reader may have some disagreement with this type of cluster analysis, we hope he will also find his imagination stimulated by our efforts. We do not contend that we have, once and for all, developed clusters of cities by their basic underlying social, economic, and political-structural characteristics.

Ideally, after critically assessing the analytical conceptualization in chapter 1, the scholar could proceed to isolate other variables with which to classify these cities. It should be possible not only to use this classification as a base for narrowing in on a set or subset of cities for in-depth analysis, but also to make it more complex with the addition of information. Obviously, there are losses of refinement and specificity as one moves from the particular city to large numbers of cities and aggregate data. What is suggested in this study is the desirability of using conceptualizations to order aggregate data sets, and thus of moving from general social process concerns to individual urban units. Studies of these units, whether concerned with single cities or small groups, can in turn enrich or modify the conceptualization and the interpretation of aggregate data.

We hope we have been successful in casting some light on a particular group of American cities and the extent to which cities with specified characteristics tend to cluster together. There are good reasons to think that the processes discussed for middle-sized cities are quantitatively and qualitatively different in urban units of larger sizes. There are impressionistic and scholarly studies to demonstrate the persistence of ethnic cultures in large urban milieus. With a large enough pool of Poles or Italians, for example, subcommunities with a relatively full set of institutions could persist. There might be schools, legal aid societies, hospitals, and large networks of voluntary organizations oriented toward the country of origin of immigrants. For smaller communities, aside from those peopled almost exclusively with immigrants from one country or small region, persistence of separate institutions was unlikely. Economic pressures militated against the continuation of schools using German, of "pure" ethnic neighborhoods, of industries or workshops employing only one nationality. The persistence of ethnic enclaves provided a different structural and cultural setting for policy. And policies, as measured by a series of quantitative variables, seem different for larger urban units (see table 4.2). Ideally, the same kinds of questions that have been raised in connection with small and middle-sized cities should be raised for urban units of larger sizes. As suggested above, there is some evidence that patterns may be different. But that is an empirical matter. Table 4.2 tells us, among

Table 4.2. Comparison of Cities by Size on Selected Variables in 1900

Variables (per capita)	City size		
	Over 300,000	100,000- 300,000	10,000- 25,000
Municipal expenditures	$17.76	$14.01	$11.31
Local governmental debt	81.55	54.50	30.18
Productive possessions	38.87	24.17	17.50
Unproductive possessions	72.27	37.68	26.53
Police spending	2.50	1.43	.72
Fire spending	1.42	1.34	.96
School spending	5.46	4.33	3.65
Wealth	$1247.58	$912.05	$797.10
N =	14	25	278

Sources: Sources for and definitions of these variables are given in chapter 3.

other things, that the per capita wealth figures in cities increase as city size increases, that city spending per person increases as does city size. Whether other socioeconomic structural variables and political variables have similar impact in units of different size at the turn of the century is still open to question. The above chapters suggest that a relatively parsimoniously chosen set of variables are important in explaining urban public policy and that these variables can be systematically woven together with policy variables to make useful typologies. Although these typologies are appropriate mainly for small and middle-sized cities, they may be strengthened, refined, and expanded as other sized cities are studied.

And yet, social science is still in a state of primitive beginning. While we may make progress in comprehending the variety of American urban landscapes, we are at best theoretically oriented, as we do not yet have a body of theory which will explain urban change. And for historians working with the tools of the social scientists, the data problems are so difficult as to be almost overwhelming. With sensitivity to conceptual problems and social change processes, however, the historian can begin to fit together small extant data sets as well as to elaborate large ones in quest of better understanding of the complexities of the urban process. That goal still seems very illusive.

Appendix

Index

Appendix

Cities in the United States with a Population of 10,000-25,000 in 1900 (n = 278)

NORTHEAST

Auburn, Maine*
Augusta, Maine*
Bangor, Maine*
Bath, Maine*
Biddeford, Maine*
Lewiston, Maine*
Concord, New Hampshire*
Dover, New Hampshire*
Nashua, New Hampshire*
Portsmouth, New Hampshire
Burlington, Vermont*
Rutland, Vermont*
Adams, Massachusetts
Attleboro, Massachusetts
Beverly, Massachusetts*
Brookline, Massachusetts
Chicopee, Massachusetts*
Clinton, Massachusetts
Everett, Massachusetts*
Framingham, Massachusetts*
Gardner, Massachusetts
Hyde Park, Massachusetts
Leominster, Massachusetts*
Marlboro, Massachusetts*

Medford, Massachusetts*
Melrose, Massachusetts*
Milford, Massachusetts
Newburyport, Massachusetts*
North Adams, Massachusetts*
Northampton, Massachusetts*
Peabody, Massachusetts
Pittsfield, Massachusetts*
Quincy, Massachusetts*
Revere, Massachusetts
Southbridge, Massachusetts*
Waltham, Massachusetts*
Westfield, Massachusetts*
Weymouth, Massachusetts
Woburn, Massachusetts*
Ansonia, Connecticut*
Danbury, Connecticut*
Manchester, Connecticut
Meriden, Connecticut*
Naugatuck Bor., Connecticut*
New London, Connecticut*
Norwich, Connecticut*
Stamford, Connecticut
Central Falls, Rhode Island

*Cities for which there are systematic political variables.

Cranston, Rhode Island   Newport, Rhode Island
East Providence, Rhode Island Warwick, Rhode Island

MIDDLE ATLANTIC

Amsterdam, New York   New Brunswick, New Jersey
Cohoes, New York*   Orange, New Jersey*
Corning, New York*   Perth Amboy, New Jersey
Dunkirk, New York*   Phillipsburg, New Jersey
Geneva, New York*   Plainfield, New Jersey*
Glens Falls, New York   Union, New Jersey
Gloversville, New York   West Hoboken, New Jersey
Hornellsville, New York   Beaver Falls, Pennsylvania*
Ithaca, New York   Braddock, Pennsylvania
Jamestown, New York   Bradford, Pennsylvania*
Johnstown, New York   Butler, Pennsylvania*
Kingston, New York   Carbondale, Pennsylvania
Little Falls, New York   Columbia, Pennsylvania*
Lockport, New York   Dunmore, Pennsylvania
Middletown, New York*   Hazelton, Pennsylvania*
Mt. Vernon, New York*   Homestead, Pennsylvania
Newburg, New York*   Lebanon, Pennsylvania*
New Rochelle, New York*   Mahanoy City, Pennsyvlania*
Niagara Falls, New York*   Meadville, Pennsylvania*
Ogdensburg, New York   Mt. Carmel, Pennsylvania
Oswego, New York   Nanticoke, Pennsylvania
Peekskill, New York   Norristown, Pennsylvania*
Poughkeepsie, New York   Oil City, Pennsylvania*
Rome, New York*   Pittston, Pennsylvania*
Saratoga Springs, New York   Plymouth, Pennsylvania
Watertown, New York   Pottstown, Pennsylvania*
Watervliet, New York   Pottsville, Pennsylvania*
Bridgeton, New Jersey   Shamokin, Pennsylvania
East Orange, New Jersey   Shenandoah, Pennsylvania*
Harrison, New Jersey   So. Bethlehem, Pennsylvania
Kearny, New Jersey   Steelton, Pennsylvania*
Millville, New Jersey   Wilkinsburg, Pennsylvania
Montclair, New Jersey*   Cumberland, Maryland
Morristown, New Jersey   Hagerstown, Maryland

LAKES

Ashtabula, Ohio   Findlay, Ohio
Chillicothe, Ohio*   Hamilton, Ohio
East Liverpool, Ohio*   Ironton, Ohio*

Lima, Ohio*
Lorain, Ohio
Mansfield, Ohio*
Marietta, Ohio*
Marion, Ohio*
Massillon, Ohio
Newark, Ohio*
Piqua, Ohio
Portsmouth, Ohio*
Sandusky, Ohio*
Steubenville, Ohio*
Tiffin, Ohio*
Zanesville, Ohio*
Anderson, Indiana
Elkhart, Indiana*
Elwood, Indiana
Hammond, Indiana
Jeffersonville, Indiana
Kokomo, Indiana
Lafayette, Indiana
Logansport, Indiana*
Marion, Indiana
Michigan City, Indiana*
Muncie, Indiana
New Albany, Indiana
Richmond, Indiana
Vincennes, Indiana
Alton, Illinois
Aurora, Illinois*
Belleville, Illinois
Bloomington, Illinois
Cairo, Illinois*
Danville, Illinois*
Decatur, Illinois*
Elgin, Illinois
Evanston, Illinois*

Freeport, Illinois
Galesburg, Illinois*
Jacksonville, Illinois*
Kankakee, Illinois*
Lasalle, Illinois
Moline, Illinois*
Ottawa, Illinois
Rock Island, Illinois*
Streator, Illinois
Alpena, Michigan*
Ann Arbor, Michigan*
Battle Creek, Michigan*
Flint, Michigan*
Ishpeming, Michigan
Kalamazoo, Michigan*
Lansing, Michigan*
Manistee, Michigan*
Marquette, Michigan
Menominee, Michigan
Muskegon, Michigan*
Port Huron, Michigan*
Sault Ste. Marie, Michigan*
West Bay City, Michigan
Appleton, Wisconsin*
Ashland, Wisconsin*
Beloit, Wisconsin*
Eau Claire, Wisconsin*
Fond du Lac, Wisconsin
Green Bay, Wisconsin*
Janesville, Wisconsin*
Kenosha, Wisconsin*
Madison, Wisconsin*
Manitowoc, Wisconsin*
Marinette, Wisconsin*
Sheboygan, Wisconsin*
Wausau, Wisconsin*

PLAINS

Mankato, Minnesota*
Stillwater, Minnesota
Winona, Minnesota*
Burlington, Iowa*
Clinton, Iowa
Fort Dodge, Iowa

Keokuk, Iowa
Marshalltown, Iowa
Muscatine, Iowa*
Ottumwa, Iowa
Waterloo, Iowa*
Sioux Falls, South Dakota*

Hannibal, Missouri
Sedalia, Missouri*
Springfield, Missouri*
Atchison, Kansas*
Fort Scott, Kansas*
Galena, Kansas
Lawrence, Kansas*
Leavenworth, Kansas*

Pittsburg, Kansas
Wichita, Kansas*
Guthrie, Oklahoma*
Oklahoma City, Oklahoma*
Denison, Texas*
El Paso, Texas*
Laredo, Texas
Sherman, Texas

SOUTH

Fort Smith, Arkansas
Pine Bluff, Arkansas
Baton Rouge, Louisiana*
Shreveport, Louisiana
Meridian, Mississippi
Natchez, Mississippi*
Vicksburg, Mississippi*
Key West, Florida
Pensacola, Florida
Tampa, Florida
Athens, Georgia
Columbus, Georgia*
Macon, Georgia
Asheville, North Carolina*
Charlotte, North Carolina*
Greensboro, North Carolina*
Raleigh, North Carolina*
Wilmington, North Carolina
Winston, North Carolina*

Columbia, South Carolina
Greenville, South Carolina
Spartanburg, South Carolina
Alexandria, Virginia*
Danville, Virginia
Lynchburg, Virginia*
Newport News, Virginia*
Petersburg, Virginia*
Portsmouth, Virginia*
Roanoke, Virginia*
Charleston, West Virginia
Huntington, West Virginia
Parkersburg, West Virginia*
Henderson, Kentucky
Owensboro, Kentucky
Paducah, Kentucky
Jackson, Tennessee
Austin, Texas*
Waco, Texas

WEST

Great Falls, Montana*
Helena, Montana*
Colorado Springs, Colorado*
Cripple Creek, Colorado
Leadville, Colorado*
Ogden, Utah*
Cheyenne, Wyoming*

Alameda, California*
Berkeley, California
Fresno, California*
San Diego, California*
San Jose, California*
Stockton, California*
Walla Walla, Washington

Index